D0929184

WITHDRAWN FROM
MACALESTER COLLEGE
LIBRARY

A BOOK OF JEWISH ETHICAL CONCEPTS

Biblical and Postbiblical

A BOOK OF JEWISH ETHICAL CONCEPTS

Biblical and Postbiblical

by
ABRAHAM P. BLOCH

KTAV PUBLISHING HOUSE, INC.
NEW YORK

COPYRIGHT © 1984
ABRAHAM P. BLOCH

Library of Congress Cataloging in Publication Data

Bloch, Abraham P.
  A book of Jewish ethical concepts.

  Bibliography: p.
  Includes index.
  1. Ethics, Jewish. 2. Ethics in the Bible. I. Title.
BJ1285.B55   1984   296.3'85   83-22267
ISBN 0-88125-039-2

MANUFACTURED IN THE UNITED STATES OF AMERICA

This book is lovingly dedicated to

BELLE

who patiently endured the travails of the wife
of an author at work.

Contents

Preface

THE TORAH is the primary source of ancient Jewish law, morality, and history. Its ethical dicta and legal principles have been fused into a religious code from which Jewish moral perceptions have been distilled. The recorded history of its heroes has served as a role model for posterity.

The post-Pentateuchal prophetic era was witness to a momentous struggle of monotheism against the inroads of paganism and its corruption. The prophet's academy was the marketplace and wherever else the masses gathered. His audience consisted of farmers and laborers, rather than students of law. The principal mission of the prophets and the authors of the Scriptures was the transmission of moral insights.

The end of prophecy ushered in the era of rabbinics, in which the intellectual leadership was assumed by teachers of law whose forum was the academy. The development of the law and its adaptation to ever-changing social and economic conditions became the prime function of the rabbis.

Their scholarly dissertations on the law brought a new impetus to the refinement of biblical ethical values. Most rabbinical legal discussions are interspersed with thought-provoking ethical aphorisms. Among the monumental tomes which comprise the Talmud there are volumes dedicated exclusively to the study of ethics.

The full scope of Jewish morality must be drawn from the Bible, Apocrypha, Talmud, and post-talmudic rabbinic works. All of these sources are amply quoted in this book. The English renditions of biblical and talmudic quotations are mainly those of the Soncino editions. Dates of ancient authors and literary works are provided for a better understanding of the develop-

1

ment of moral concepts within the context of an historical perspective.

This work supplements my two previously published books on the historical development of Jewish holidays and customs. The understanding of Judaism is incomplete without an appreciation of its major contribution to the universal ethical perceptions which form the basis of civilization.

Abraham P. Bloch

Introduction

IN THE IMAGE OF GOD

ETHICS IS defined as the science of proper human behavior. This definition presupposes a clear perception of propriety. That is a false assumption. There is no single standard of ethics by which the rectitude of human conduct can be measured. What we have come to label as civilized deportment reflects the moral values of a particular civilization in a particular era. All of man's values derive from religion and mores and are conditioned by economic necessities and geographic exigencies. Perfection is an abstract term subject to development and change. This precludes the establishment of a universal uniform standard of ethics.

Sociologists speak of a Judeo-Christian civilization. To the extent that major religions have accepted the Decalogue as the foundaton of morality there is a significant consensus among them. However, divergent developments have created many differences which are not insignificant. It is therefore proper to speak of Jewish ethics, Christian ethics, Islamic ethics, and other sets of ethics. They are all designed to serve the same purpose.

Jewish ethics are primarily based on the Bible, the whole range of rabbinic literature, and ancient traditions. Their structure and evolvement were predetermined by a single sentence in Genesis: "And God created man in his image" (1:27). The psalmist restated it as follows: "Thou hast made him but little lower than God and hast crowned him with glory and honor" (Ps. 8:6). The attribution of godliness to earthly man had a

3

dual effect. It heightened the degree of concern and respect that man must manifest in relations with his fellowman. It also imposed on man the duty to express his godliness through an emulation of the divine qualities attributed to God in the Scriptures.

The biblical assertion that God created man in his image marked a radical departure from pagan theology, which created its deities in the image of man. Like man, they warred, lusted, and committed murder. Paganism urged man to propitiate his deities but not to emulate them.

In the monotheistic tradition of the Hebrews, God is perfect. He is the source of excellence and light. In the words of the psalmist: "For with thee is the fountain of life; in your light do we see light" (Ps. 36:10).

The need for emulating God was stressed in the Talmud. "Abba Saul interpreted 'And I will be like him,' as he is gracious and compassionate, so be you gracious and compassionate" (*Shabbat* 133b). Abba Saul was a second-century Tanna who devoted much of his time to the instruction of ethics. He underlined the importance of ethical studies with his dictum: "Morality is greater than learning" (*Semachot* 11).

Abba Saul's injunction to emulate God did not originate with him. This idea is inherent in various statements in the Bible. It was clearly implied in the plea of Moses: "Show me now thy ways that I may know thee, to the end that I may find grace in thy sight" (Exod. 33:13). This was echoed by the psalmist: "Show me thy way, O Lord, teach me thy paths" (Ps. 25:4). The psalmist was searching for the way of righteousness, which he hoped to discover by finding the path of God. In his words: "All the paths of the Lord are mercy and truth" (ibid. 25:10). Although the path of God is obscure to many people, Moses urged them: "Thou shalt keep all this commandment to do it, which I command thee this day, to love the Lord thy God, and to walk ever in his ways" (Deut. 19:9).

God himself, we are told in the Bible, urged the people to adopt his divine attributes. Thus he said: "You shall be holy, for I the Lord your God am holy" (Lev. 19:2).

What are the attributes of God which man is enjoined to emulate? The Bible repeatedly refers to them.

"He shows mercy unto the thousandth generation" (Exod. 15:3).

"Lord God, merciful and gracious, long-suffering and abundant in goodness and truth" (Exod. 34:6).

"Know therefore that the Lord thy God, he is God, the faithful God, who keeps covenant and mercy with them that love him" (Deut. 7:9).

"He loves the stranger to give him food and clothes. Love ye, therefore, the stranger" (Deut. 10:18–19).

"He regardeth not persons, nor takes rewards. He executes justice for the fatherless and the widow" (Deut. 10:17–18).

God, we are told, is not lax in his insistence on virtue. He does not compromise with the forces of evil. He is "a God of zeal" (Exod. 20:5). He actively opposes iniquity and does not passively tolerate wickedness. "The Lord is a man of war" (Exod. 15:3). Similar descriptions of God's attitudes fill the pages of the Bible.

The major inspiration of the extensive Jewish ethical literature comes, of course, from the numerous biblical injunctions which are addressed to man. These, together with rabbinical interpretations and moral maxims, have provided the guidelines and framework for the continued growth of the Jewish moral code. The very abundance of this genre of literature is a sad reflection of the fact that man is in constant need of admonition to guide him along the way.

Despite the biblical assertion that man was created in the image of God, his free will leaves the choice of right or wrong entirely to him. Weakness and passion frequently tempt man to choose the course which has the greatest promise of satisfying his greed and many desires. The Bible attests to this weakness by stating that "man's inclinations are evil from his youth" (Gen. 8:21). Our ethical legacy is designed to tame him and to keep a proper balance between the earthly and heavenly aspects of human life, so that he may be worthy of the fact of having been created in God's image.

The faculty of free will and the capacity to distinguish right from wrong are truly divine attributes. Man, alone of all living creatures, was endowed with them. He must use them judiciously to make sure that this earth is a decent place to live in.

THE TWO FACETS OF ETHICS

All virtues have their counterparts. The opposite of love, humility, and generosity are hate, arrogance, and miserliness. These represent the two extremes of human behavior. It is the function of moral instruction to promote the former and to suppress the latter. The psalmist summed it up in a single sentence: "Abstain from evil and do good" (Ps. 34:15).

The biblical laws are divided into positive and negative injunctions. There are 248 positive injunctions and 365 negative injunctions. This division, though not in the same proportions, also appears in the Decalogue. The primary purpose of the negative injunctions is to protect society from the harmful acts of misguided individuals. Such behavior usually results from a normal response to bodily instincts. Cheating satisfies one's acquisitiveness. Overbearing conduct builds up one's ego. It is sad to reflect that many people are human but not necessarily humane.

The aim of the positive injunctions is to ennoble man's character and to reflect its godliness. Over and above the protection of society, they seek to enhance the quality of life and the distinctiveness of man. "Thou shalt not kill" guarantees human security. "Honor thy father and thy mother" is the basis of human progress. The psalmist wisely gives precedence to "abstain from evil." This is the initial step on the road toward excellence. Parental instructions to a young child are studded with more don'ts than do's. It is the latter, however, that have the potential for making man "a little lower than God."

One cannot "do good" unless he first learns to "abstain from evil." Yet the individual who refrains from evil without supplementing it with affirmative social action is not truly an ethical person. He may be a harmless member of society, but he contributes little to the ethical level of the community.

Biblical moral instructions address themselves to both extremes of human behavior. Thus man is admonished to "Love thy neighbor as thyself" (Lev. 19:19). This commandment is preceded by the injunction "Thou shalt not hate thy brother in thy heart" (Lev. 19:17). There is a need for addressing both of these human emotions. Love cannot be legislated nor conjured up with a magic wand. There are people who are incapable of love. The most they can do is to stop their predilection for hate. The same is true of many other moral precepts. In this book we will take note of the good and the evil and the comments they evoke in Hebrew ethical literature.

THE IMPACT OF LAW ON ETHICS

Judaic moral principles are based on biblical and talmudic ethical maxims, most of which have been enacted into law. The influence of ethics in the development of jurisprudence is an ongoing process common to all civilizations. In Judaism the reverse process is also evident. Its laws have shaped moral perceptions. A review of the evolution of ethics is essential to the understanding of this trend.

The earliest source of ethical concepts can be traced to the folkways and customs indigenous to primitive society. The term "ethics" is derived from the Greek *ethos,* the word for "customs." In time it took on the meaning of "character," reflecting the development of the idea that he who upholds customs is a person of character. The term "morals" is similarly derived from *mores,* the Latin expression for "customs" or "habits."

The tenacity of customs is attributable to their general usefulness to society. With their transmission from father to son, over the course of many generations, they have assumed the sanctity of tradition, hallowed by ancestral worship and an alleged divine origin. The transition of custom into law was the next step in an orderly evolutionary process.

The intrinsic weakness of ancient ethics lay in the criterion which determined moral values by the test of popular approval. Universal consensus, from time immemorial, assumed that God speaks through the voice of the multitudes. Opposing this view, the Bible cautioned: "Do not follow the majority which sanctions evil." To the ancient folk-mentality, such a statement was totally incomprehensible. Whatever society approves, by its very nature, cannot be deemed evil. If the suppression of a minority is advantageous to the majority, such an act is ipso facto consistent with society's moral standards. Ethical inhibitions apply only to individuals, never to the collective unit. Crime may not pay on an individual level, but it is always permissible on a national level. Isaiah's vision of the cessation of wars and the use of force must have been regarded by his contemporaries as an immoral and dangerous ideal.

The self-serving motif of folk-ethics is clearly projected in the exaltation of a sense of loyalty to the ruler. Unquestioning patriotism was considered the greatest of virtues, and disobedience, the most heinous of crimes. This concept is still invoked by modern national codes because it is dictated by the needs of national stability and survival. Religious codes and testaments, on the other hand, exalt patriotism only if it serves the ends of justice, and denounce disobedience only if it betrays the legitimate rights of the people.

Despite the parochialism of folk-ethics, ancient societies created some norms of high ethical substance which are still part of our heritage. Sumerian tablets, among the oldest written historical records in the world, attest to the fact that the Sumerians cherished goodness and truth, mercy, law and order. Urukagina, king of Lagash (24th cent. B.C.E.), proudly recorded that he had restored justice and freedom and that he had protected the widows and the orphans. However, neither the Sumerian codes nor other ancient codes reflect the positive aspects of these moral standards. The transformation of folk-ethics into law narrowed their scope and effectiveness.

Moralist preachers like the psalmists could exhort: "Remove thyself from evil and do good" (Ps. 34:15). Laws, however, must be confined to enforceable regulations and are generally concerned only with the "removal from evil." The maximal objective of ancient legal codes was the punishment of crime. The conversion of sociological ethics into legal injunctions produced a new concept—he who is not immoral is moral, he who is not guilty of a breach of ethics is ethical. This misconception still lingers in the technical terminology of our modern legislators. Thus the Senate's Subcommittee on Ethics is not a committee to enforce ethical conduct but a committee to censure and punish members guilty of a breach of ethics.

Religion eventually replaced folk-customs as the primary source of ethics. Divine approval was substituted for popular approval as the criterion of moral conduct. As religion progressively evolved from a narrow tribal cult to embrace the terminology of universalism, it projected a broad morality divorced from parochialism. The triumph of Judaic monotheism inevitably led to the introduction of universalist concepts. The Decalogue opened with a solemn declaration of monotheism, coupled with a declaration of the rights of man. Its universality was acknowledged by Luther, who considered it a summary of all Christian ethics.

The Age of Religion did not necessarily witness a rise of ethical societies. As a matter of practical expediency, religious leaders have accommodated themselves, at various stages in man's history, to slavery, feudalism, industrial baronism, military dictatorships, and paranoid nationalism. In that respect there was no clear break with primitive ethical standards. On a personal level, too, religious ethics were not adequately reflected in the daily conduct of individuals. An overemphasis on ritualism frequently led to the stifling of moralism.

Rituals are essential to the preservation of religion. They stimulate the exercise of self-discipline and safeguard the ethical principles with which they are associated. Yet the average religious individual finds it easier to express his piety through a zealous observance of rituals than to make the effort essential to the development of an ethical personality. Furthermore, moralism is a nondenominational concept, while ritualism is sectarian and has a greater appeal to a member of a particular creed. Ritualism has consequently come to be regarded as the primary objective of religion.

One may point to a number of statements in the Bible and Talmud which commend ethical conduct per se, regardless of one's zeal for ritual observance. Hillel considered the Golden Rule the very core and essence of Judaism. Rabbi Akiva upheld this rule as a "great principle of the Law." The injunction to love man was thus given greater prominence than the injunction to love God. The rabbinic priorities were reversed in Luke (10:27) in the establishment of the proper conduct which guarantees eternal life. Origen (3rd cent.), the outstanding Christian theologian of the early church, declared that a heretic whose moral life is good is to be condemned more than one whose moral life is unsatisfactory. This became the dominant view which appealed to pietists of many generations, undermining the moral force of religion. It was not until the seventeenth century that the lone voice of John Selden, an Anglican theologian, proclaimed that Jews who are morally correct are entitled to the same heavenly rewards as Christians, a prospect long held out by rabbinic sages for all righteous Gentiles. It was not until the nineteenth century that Tolstoy declared that "Love thy neighbor as thyself" is a summary of Christianity.

Religion has undoubtedly played a vital role in shaping man's ethical outlook. It is reasonable to expect that laws rooted in religion have also influenced moral insights. One is more likely to find this in Judaism and Islam, where law and morality flow from the same religious source. Judaism bases the relationship between man and God on a legal compact, the Covenant (Gen. 17:7). This helped Jews and Moslems to envision a link between law and ethics. The development of law in Judaism and Islam devolved on the legal scholar, who was also the exponent of religious ethics. Christendom, on the other hand, accepted Roman law as its own civil law. It adopted most of Rome's legal concepts and rejected only the Roman views of slavery and marriage.

The most momentous millennium in the history of law is the period between 450 B.C.E. and 550 C.E. Two great systems of law were developed in those years—the Roman law, from the Twelve Tables to the publication of the *Corpus Juris Civilis*, and rabbinic law, from Ezra to the final redaction of the Talmud. The latter, a religious code, created a vast literature of ethical concepts. The former, a civil code, failed to reflect Christian ethics, even though Christianity was the official state religion at the time of the publication of the Justinian Code. The emphasis given by the Romans to natural law legitimized and enhanced the authority of power and force. The husband, the father, and the master were given unlimited authority over the lives of those who had to look to them for protection. Such absolutism was contrary to Judaic and Christian ethics. The debasement of life and dignity, reflected in the rigorous treatment of insolvent debtors, is incompatible with any sense of ethics.

The profound impact of law on ethics in Judaism is illustrated by the law of bailment. This subject is of little interest today, except to the commercial community. In ancient times, however, it was a matter of deep concern to most individuals. In the absence of banks, vaults, safes, or even locked doors, it was common practice to leave valuables in the temporary care of a friend for safekeeping, or as a pledge with a creditor. Most ancient codes agree that the extent of care and degree of responsibility of a bailee depends on whether he renders his services free or for pay.

In rabbinic law a gratuitous bailee (*shomer chinam*) is liable only in the case of negligence. A bailee for pay (*shomer sachar*) is responsible in the event of theft or loss. The extent of liability was almost identical in rabbinic and Roman law. However, the connotation of the personal involvement of a bailee in the safety of the entrusted object was more pronounced in the Jewish tradition. To the Romans a bailment was a *depositum*, a descriptive term consistent with the passive role of the bailee. In the biblical law a bailment was a *pikadon*, which describes the active state of "watchfulness" that a bailee must maintain.

The personal involvement of a bailee was even more pronounced in the Hebrew term *shomer* ("watchman"). The original meaning of *shamor* was "to engrave" or "to preserve," projecting the duty of watchful vigilance against forgetfulness or loss. The connotation of an active commitment of guardianship had a far-reaching influence in the field of Hebrew philosophy and ethics, as a result of the varied and subtle nuances of the term *shamor*.

The expression *shomer mitzvot* meant not only an observer of God's commands but one who preserves them for posterity. God's role as a *shomer yisrael* was a promise of divine watchfulness and a commitment to Israel's preservation.

In the development of Judaic ethics the term *shomer* gradually took on the legal implications of this word. The extent of man's moral obligation to his fellowman was in direct proportion to the benefits accruing to him. The community was viewed as a mutual-aid society in which each member was responsible for the welfare of others. Cain's question "Am I my brother's keeper [shomer]?" was rebuffed by God. Man is his brother's keeper.

The fact that man is the recipient of the many benefits which society has to offer determined the extent of his responsibility to society and to each of its members. Ethically he is placed in the position of a shomer sachar (a bailee for pay). Consequently man does not fulfill his moral obligation to society by a passive restraint from harming his neighbor. He has an active duty to protect and "preserve" him.

From an ethical point of view, Judaism regards God, the Guardian of Israel, to have assumed the responsibility of a shomer sachar (a paid bailee) because man's moral conduct is pleasing and rewarding to him. The medieval liturgical poem Shomer Yisrael pleads for divine intervention to guard against the loss of Israel. To most people familiar with legal terminology, the justice of the plaintive litany was clearly understood. God's responsibilities are comparable to those of a shomer sachar, who is accountable for the loss of a bailment. This justifies the plea al yovad yisrael ("permit not the loss of Israel").

The legal distinction between custody and ownership also played a significant part in the development of ethical obligations in the field of social welfare. The biblical declaration that the land belongs to God (Lev. 25:23) limits man to the role of custodian of his wealth. Property was entrusted to man on condition that he use it for the good of all.

Modern states have enacted into law advanced social concepts to alleviate the plight of the needy. Yet no law has succeeded in transmitting a sense of ethics to its citizenry on a personal level. Secular education has failed to replace religion as a moral force. In the words of the late Chief Justice Earl Warren: "Without moral commitments of the people to obey, the law is quite helpless."

Admonition

Thou shalt not hate thy brother in thy heart; thou shalt surely rebuke thy neighbor, and not bear sin because of him.

—Leviticus 19:17

THERE ARE two types of admonitions. Parents and teachers admonish a child for the purpose of correcting him. People also admonish would-be offenders in defense of their bodies and property. Most individuals instinctively react when their rights are adversely affected. This instinct, however, is seldom in evidence when someone else's rights are threatened.

Let us imagine the following scenario. A gets in line at his bank to await his turn with the teller. B enters ten minutes later and squeezes himself into the line ahead of A. One may be sure that A will raise his voice in protest. Suppose, however, that B got into the line in back of A. Would A remonstrate with B that his unfair act deprives people of their rightful place? The probability is that he will keep his peace.

As a rule, people are reluctant to get involved in preventing a breach of ethics if their own interests are left untouched. Admonishing is a form of preaching, which one would rather leave to professional preachers. Furthermore, the popular adage "mind your own business" acts as a powerful brake. Another significant deterrent is the anticipation of a rebuff. No one accepts criticism with grace, and much less is one inclined to admit to a wrongful act. It is fair to assume that the person who is reprimanded will forcefully reject the admonition.

The Bible encourages decent people to correct offenders. At the same time it seeks to persuade offenders to accept admonition as a friendly act because it serves their interests.

13

"He that rebukes a man shall in the end find more favor than he that flatters with the tongue" (Prov. 28:23).

"Admonish a friend. It may be that he has not done it, and if he has done it, that he do it no more" (Ecclus. 19:13).

"He is in the way of life that heeds instruction; but he that forsakes reproof errs" (Prov. 10:17).

"The words of the wise gently spoken are more acceptable than the cry of a ruler among fools" (Eccles. 9:17).

Ezekiel's interpretation of the biblical injunction to "rebuke thy neighbor" introduced a new moral perception. A leader who refrains from admonishing the people is morally guilty of their crimes. "When I [God] say to the wicked 'Thou shalt surely die'; and thou [the prophet] givest him not warning, nor speakest to warn the wicked from his wicked way, to save his life; the same wicked man shall die in his iniquity, but his blood shall I require at thy hand" (3:18; 6th cent. B.C.E.).

About nine centuries later, Ezekiel's moral dictum was extended by the rabbis to apply to any head of a family who does not admonish his kin. "Whosoever can forbid his household [to do a wrong] but does not, will be punished" (*Shabbat* 54b). The phrase "his household" was deleted from another version of this maxim which was quoted in *Avodah Zarah* (18a). Apparently the amended version extends the moral responsibility expressed in the maxim to any individual, even a stranger, who has it in his power to correct an offender. If he fails to do so, he shares the offender's guilt. This warning was spelled out by Nachmanides (13th cent.) in his comment on Leviticus 19:17: "If you fail to rebuke him, you are at fault, and his sin is also your sin."

Some of the talmudic comments on admonition reflect a profound understanding of human nature. The failure of parents to correct their offspring is taken by the children as a sign of parental indifference. Reproach, on the other hand, is regarded as proof of concern and love.

"The greater the chastisement administered to one's son, the greater his love for his father" (*Shemot Rabbah* 1).

"Love which is totally free of reproof is not true love" (*Bereshit Rabbah* 54).

"Reproof leads to peace" (ibid.).

Rabbi Aaron Halevi of Barcelona (13th cent.) extolled the virtue of admonition. It offers an offender an opportunity for apologizing. Thus reconciliation is effected. On the other hand, when a person withholds admonition and continues to harbor hate in his heart, the cause of peace and harmony suffers (*Chinuch* 239).

The Talmud amplified the biblical injunction of admonition but also hedged it with several limitations.

1. The duty of admonishing is open-ended. If unsuccessful at first, one must try again and again (*Sifra*, Lev. 19:17).
2. A reproach must not be uttered in anger (*Shochar Tov* 6:2).
3. An erring person must not be intimidated if the reproof is to achieve its corrective goal (*Shabbat* 34a).
4. A reprimand should be given in private to avoid embarrassment to the offender (*Arachin* 16b). If he is humiliated he will reject the admonition.
5. One should not expose himself to ridicule and disrespect by admonishing an obstreperous person (*Yevamot* 65b). This restriction is based on a verse in Proverbs: "Reprove not a scorner, lest he hate thee; Reprove a wise man, and he will love thee" (9:8).
6. It is best to ignore minor infractions acceptable to a community. Such behavior is seldom amenable to correction. It is preferable that a community err in ignorance than in willful disregard of instructions (*Baba Batra* 60a).
7. It is proper, nay meritorious, to refrain from criticism, if the aggrieved person regards the offense as a minor and unintentional breach of ethics and it does not engender hate in his heart (*Mishneh Torah, Hilchot Deot* 6:9).
8. A person who reproves others must himself be beyond reproach. If his own record is tainted, he lays himself open to the retort: "Adorn yourself before you adorn others" (*Baba Metzia* 107b).

Admonitions may take the form of protest rallies, processions, and picketing. Such actions aimed at the prevention of a miscarriage of justice are legitimate and deserve the support of all decent citizens. However, when participants engage in unlawful acts, such as vandalism or interference with the flow of traffic, the demonstration loses its moral stance and its right to offer admonition.

The biblical injunction "Thou shalt rebuke thy neighbor" applies equally to religious and social offenses. However, in the context of this book, the definition of "ethics" is confined to breaches of proper social behavior. In modern societies, where conformity to religious practices is left to the individual's conscience, outside pressure constitutes improper interference which may be rebuffed. Under the guidelines previously listed, admonitions are not called for when a rebuff is to be anticipated.

The elimination of admonition in cases of religious violations is subject to a few exceptions. Religious leaders or laymen may warn against such infractions so long as their words are not directed against a particular individual. Religious parents may admonish their children because of their right to pass on their religious values to the succeeding generation.

There are instances when the dividing line between social and religious transgressions disappears. A person who enters the confines of a religious institution must conform to the standards of that institution. Any violation offensive to the sensitivities of the congregants constitutes a social offense. The same is true of a guest in a religious home or a visitor in a compact community where the vast majority follows a uniform religious code.

Advice

He is wise who hearkens to counsel.

—Proverbs 12:15

MOST PEOPLE have occasion to seek and give advice. A man not infrequently begins his day by soliciting his wife's advice on the selection of his outfit. His wife, in return, may ask for his advice regarding the dinner menu. If the couple plans to see a show or spend a weekend away from home, they may call an experienced friend and ask for a recommendation. All human beings face the necessity of seeking medical advice, legal advice, and advice on a host of other problems which they face in the course of a lifetime.

The wisdom of seeking advice has never been questioned, nor has any ethical consideration entered into it. Meiri, a thirteenth-century sage, aptly expressed it in his commentary on *Avot:* "Even the wisest of men needs advice" (1:8). Two heads are better than one. Furthermore, objective reasoning often eludes a person under emotional stress or the pressure of serious problems. The Book of Proverbs summed it up: "For want of counsel purposes are frustrated, but in the multitude of counsellors they are established" (15:22).

Advice-seekers should bear in mind some practical considerations. Paramount is the question of the competence of the counselor, his motivation and impartiality. The psalmist cautioned against accepting advice from corrupt people. "Happy is the person who has not followed the counsel of the wicked" (1:1).

The apocryphal Ben Sira discusses the qualification of counselors in greater detail. There might have been a historical reason for his interest in this subject. He was a contemporary

17

of the Hasmonean rebellion against Antiochus IV (168 B.C.E.). It was a time of tension and strife due to the king's proscription of the Jewish religion. Many Jews pondered their alternatives: to fight, to surrender, or to sell everything and run. There was a real need for good advice.

Here is what Ben Sira said: "Every counsellor praises counsel, but some counsels fit their own interests. . . . [Do not] consult with a woman touching her of whom she is jealous, neither with a coward in matters of war; nor with a buyer of selling . . . nor with an unmerciful man touching kindness, nor with the slothful for any work . . . and let the counsel of thy own heart stand" (Ecclus. 37:7–13).

The Talmud offers a few more observations. Rabbi Akiva (2nd cent.) admired the practice of the Medes, who offered advice in an open field to make sure that no outsider overheard their remarks (*Berachot* 8b). The maturity of a counselor is an important factor because "there is no reason in old men and no counsel in children" (Rabbi Jonathan [2nd cent.], *Shabbat* 89b). "A person in his fifties is best-qualified for counseling" (*Avot* 5:26). At that age a man has a wealth of experience, and his mind is still in full vigor. A man should consult his wife (*Baba Metzia* 59a). When a man loses his wife, his counsel is impaired (*Sanhedrin* 22a).

Giving advice entails a moral responsibility. It is a breach of ethics to offer advice despite one's awareness of one's own inadequacy. No advice is infallible. A counselor should preface his advice with a warning that a margin of error exists. All one can do is offer what appears to be the best advice in his judgment.

Sefer Chasidim (12th cent.) elaborates on the responsibilities of a counselor. He should always be aware of the possibility of misjudgment. If it turns out later that he was wrong and he is blamed by those who sought his advice, he should accept the criticism in silence and feel sorry for them. Some measure of blame must inevitably cling to him (108).

Josephus (1st cent.) denounced the offensive practice of some individuals who gave misleading directions to those who sought advice on how to proceed to their destination (*Antiq.*

bk. 4, chap. 8:31). Curiously, the same complaint is still valid today. It seems to serve some people's egos to demonstrate knowledge even when they lack it. Only the humble and the secure freely admit to ignorance.

Commercial and political ads are another form of advice. The merchant and the politician advise the public that their merchandise and political views are most desirable. The public is aware that such ads are self-serving and that their messages require critical scrutiny. Ads of this kind do not constitute a breach of ethics unless the sponsorship of the ads is concealed.

The admonition of Ben Sira to all would-be counselors still rings true today: "If thou hast understanding, answer thy neighbor; if not, lay thy hand upon thy mouth" (Ecclus. 5:12).

Anger

An angry man commits folly.

—Proverbs 14:17

THE THRESHOLD of human tolerance of provocation varies from person to person. Some are easily provoked into anger, others are seldom ruffled. Most people range somewhere in between. A similar variable characterizes the degree and intensity of the anger elicited by a provocation. Some become violent, others exhibit a mild annoyance. Most people react with an ire ranging between moderation and extreme.

Generally speaking, placid and contented individuals are slow in yielding to anger. Agitated and frustrated people react instantaneously. However, regardless of the volatility of one's temper, no one is totally resistant to anger. It may burst forth precipitately or climax a long period of brooding and resentment.

Man is possessed of some potentially harmful emotions. Of all of them, anger and arrogance seem to have been singled out in the Bible and Talmud for harsh criticism. The following few quotations illustrate these strictures.

"An angry man exalts folly" (Prov. 14:29).

"An angry man stirs up discord" (Prov. 15:18).

"He who becomes angry, if he is a scholar, his wisdom departs from him" (Resh Lakish [3rd cent.], *Pesachim* 66b); "the divine presence is of no importance to him" (Rabbah son of Rav Huna [3rd cent.], *Nedarim* 22b); "he forgets his learning and becomes more stupid" (Rabbi Jeremiah of Difti [4th cent.], ibid.); "he may be compared to an idol worshipper" (*Mishneh Torah, Hilchot Deot* 2:3 [12th cent.]).

Rabbi Akiva (2nd cent.) took note of people who in a fit of

20

rage tear their clothes and break their furniture. Such individuals, he commented, will in the end give in to the most despicable insolence, not excluding idolatry (*Avot deRabbi Natan* 3:8).

There was ample reason for regarding anger with such gravity. It converts the passive energy of hate into an active and destructive force. It is the trigger which releases violent emotional explosions. It deprives man of his power of self-control and warps his sense of reality.

The Talmud recommends some antidotes to the deadly stranglehold of anger. "Rabbi Eliezer [2nd cent.] said: 'Be not easily moved to anger,' " (*Avot* 2:15). In other words, one must nip it in the bud, while he is still in control of his emotions. Maimonides interpreted Rabbi Eliezer's dictum as a warning against planning ahead to use anger as a weapon against an adversary. Rabbi Jonah Gerondi (13th cent.) interpreted the dictum somewhat differently. Anger, he said, is at times unavoidable, but one must not develop a desire for using it, nor cultivate it as a habit.

The Qumran sect (1st cent. B.C.E.) imposed similar restraints upon its membership. "When anyone has a charge against his neighbor, he is to prosecute it truthfully, humbly, and humanely. He is not to speak to him angrily" (*Manual of Discipline* 5).

To encourage self-discipline, the Talmud declared any individual who restrains his anger to be greatly beloved by God (*Pesachim* 113b).

The Bible, Apocrypha, and Talmud suggest other precautionary measures against anger: (1) do not associate with people given to anger (Prov. 22:24); (2) avoid arguing with an angry person (Ecclus. 8:16); (3) mollify anger by a soft answer (Prov. 15:1); (4) if you bear a grudge, reveal it to the one who offended you, for if he apologizes there will be no reason to feel angry (Rashi, Num. 12:9); (5) do not attempt to calm an angry person until his anger has cooled off (*Avot* 4:23).

Severe condemnation of anger influenced the rise of a small school of thought which advocated the total elimination of the emotion of anger. Philo the Alexandrian (1st cent.) was an early exponent of this view: "It is necessary completely to extirpate and eradicate anger from the soul" (*Treatise on the Allegories of the Sacred Laws* 3:65). A moralist society founded in Vilna, Russia, in the nineteenth century, proclaimed a similar aim of eradicating all traces of anger, regardless of the nature of the provocation.

Such a noble goal does not serve the ends of society. Occasionally one must give vent to some anger for the preservation of his health. Additionally, anger is commendable in the face of crime, injustice, and poverty. Justifiable anger has prompted the enactment of remedial legislation and the building of institutions which help the underprivileged. Compassion alone, without the catalyst of anger, would achieve very little.

Maimonides summed up the normative view of Judaism: "Man should not cultivate a temper which lends itself easily to anger, nor should one be as insensitive as a corpse, but rather should he adopt a middle course. He should be angry only in important matters, when such anger will prevent the repetition of an offense" (*Hilchot Deot* 1:4). In other words, anger should not be used as a self-serving tool to ease one's hurt but rather as a corrective agent to improve the quality of life.

Appearance and Attire

Thou shalt make a laver of brass . . . and Aaron and his sons
shall wash their hands and their feet thereat.
—Exodus 30:18–19

ONE OF the hygienic practices that young children resist most
is the washing of hands and face. The temporary discomfort
caused by soapy water in the eyes outweighs the advantages of
a scrubbed appearance. Most mature adults quickly outgrow
such childish aberrations. Cleanliness is essential to self-
esteem and the approval of our fellowman.

The custom of washing one's feet prior to entering another
man's home was common among ancient Eastern nations.
Abraham's invitation to the three strangers to enjoy his hospitality was preceded by the suggestion that "a little water be
fetched and wash your feet" (Gen. 18:4). Washing one's feet
before retiring to bed was another commendable practice. The
heroine of Solomon's Song of Songs was reluctant to leave her
bed to answer a knock on the door. "I have washed my feet,
how shall I defile them?" (Song of Songs 5:3).

Despite the chronic shortage of water in the subtropical
climate of Israel, the use of water for keeping the body clean
was gradually increased in Judaism. The Bible prescribes
purification by immersion for people who had been contaminated by bodily discharges, leprosy, or contact with dead
bodies. King Solomon (10th cent. B.C.E.) was said to have
instituted the custom of washing of hands prior to eating the
flesh of sacrificial animals (*Shabbat* 14b). Ezra (5th cent.
B.C.E.) decreed immersion for men defiled by seminal ejacula-
tions (Jer. *Berachot* 3:4).

The custom of washing the hands before a meal most likely

dates from the first century C.E. (*Chulin* 106a). The washing of
one's fingers after a meal was instituted in the third century
(*Chulin* 105a). One must also wash his hands upon rising in
the morning (*Berachot* 15a, 3rd cent.). Occasions for washing
were added in the Middle Ages. These include, among others,
the rinsing of one's mouth in the morning, the washing of one's
hands after the use of a lavatory, upon leaving a bathhouse,
after the trimming of one's nails, the removal of shoes, the
touching of one's feet or the private parts of the body, etc.
(*Orach Chaim* 4:17–18).

Hygienic considerations no doubt were an important factor
in the establishment of these sanitary laws. However, the
Judaic concept of man as a creature made in the image of God
added a socioreligious mystique to the subject of cleanliness. A
dirty body is in contempt of the divine image. This view is
reflected in a talmudic statement: "One must wash his face,
hands, and feet daily in his maker's honor" (*Shabbat* 50b). A
clean body, according to Rashi, is a testimonial of honor to
God, who made it in his image (ibid.).

Nachmanides offers the same rationale for the religious
custom of washing the hands before a meal. Handling food
with clean hands is a gesture of respect for God, of whose
bounty we are partaking (Nachm. Exod. 30:19).

The practice of honoring the Sabbath by bathing on the eve of
the holy day dates back to the second century (*Shabbat* 25b).
The rabbis intimated that this practice had already been in
vogue in the era of the Solomonic Temple. Thus Jeremiah's
lamentation on his loss of "good fortune," following the destruction of the Temple, was allegorically interpreted as a
reference to the deprivation of the luxury of a bath before the
Sabbath (*Shabbat* 25b).

A clean body must be complemented by proper clothes to
give it presentability. The rationale is once again the respect
due to man's divine image. The value of a gift is enhanced by an
attractive package. A dirty wrapper denigrates the gift and
insults the recipient of the present. The human body, likewise,
requires a fitting wrapper.

The rabbis censured the wearing of patched sandals. "Six

things are unbecoming for a scholar . . . he should not go out in patched sandals" (*Berachot* 43b). Although this passage mentions "scholars," it includes all people whose position and status entitles them to public respect. A person lacking in self-respect is not worthy of other people's respect. The wearing of soiled garments was similarly banned in the third century (*Shabbat* 114a).

In addition to the aesthetic test, proper garments have to meet standards of modesty. Indecent exposure, in men as in women, was strongly condemned in the Bible (Deut. 23:15). A man who exposes his nudity was branded in the Talmud "an abominable person" (*Yevamot* 63b).

In addition to the broad guidelines based on considerations of modesty, religious motivations demanded that man cover his head. Due to an awareness of God's omnipresence, one should not expose the nakedness of the head to him. This practice, dating from the second century, was originally confined to worshippers. *Masechet Soferim,* a work compiled in the eighth century, provides as follows. "A person who wears tattered clothes, revealing his legs or body, or one whose head is uncovered, is not permitted to mention God's name" (chap. 14).

There is no objection to bareheadedness on purely ethical grounds. The religious objection remains in force, leaving each individual to follow his own conscience. However, if a bareheaded person joins a congregational service where worshippers normally cover their heads, he is guilty of a breach of ethics because his behavior is offensive to the congregants.

The modern saying that clothes make the man has its ancient parallel in the maxim "clothes honor the man" (*Shemot Rabbah* 18). Garments worn on weekdays, even if clean, should not be worn on the Sabbath (*Shabbat* 113a). Thus the "Sunday suit" has its parallel in the talmudic "Sabbath suit."

Due to the great importance attached to proper garments, man was cautioned to treat them respectfully (*Berachot* 62b). Those who remove their jackets and throw them on a chair or on the floor are guilty of unethical conduct.

Man's appreciation of his clothes was heightened by a reminder of the long and arduous process which culminates in the manufacture of garments. "How many labors Adam had to carry out before he obtained a garment to wear. He had to shear [the wool], wash, comb, and spin and weave it, and then at last he obtained a garment to wear: whereas I [any individual] get up and find all these things done for me" (*Berachot* 58a).

Fashions of women's garments were strictly regulated to avoid infringements of standards of morality. Traditional Judaism requires women to cover their bodies from neck to knees. Sleeves must cover the arms to the elbow. Ancient custom also required women to cover their heads (*Ketubot* 72a). Female hair, the crown of woman's beauty, was considered to be potentially seductive (*Berachot* 24a).

The rigid regulations concerning female attire were frequently ignored in countries where the social climate was more permissive. Those who follow styles which are accepted in the community at large may not be charged with unethical conduct. Compliance with religious standards must be left to the individual's conscience. However, it is important to add a word of caution. Social permissiveness may be tolerated only if it is kept within the bounds of propriety. No society has a right to disregard man's instinctive aversion to a public demonstration of pruriency.

Tradition has encouraged the use of cosmetics by women to enhance their beauty and to preserve their allure in the eyes of their husbands. Jewelry, too, is considered a desirable adjunct of a woman's appearance (Jer. *Nedarim*, chap. 9). Men, however, were forbidden to use cosmetics or feminine jewelry. Such practices come under the biblical ban of "Let no man wear female attire" (Deut. 22:5). A similar reason motivated the biblical prohibition of shaving off one's beard and thereby diminishing the natural hallmark of masculinity. This subject is discussed in greater detail in a subsequent essay, "Respect for Nature."

Maimonides summed up the Judaic concept of proper appearance and attire in his usual concise and lucid style. "A scholar's garment should be unsoiled and presentable, free of stains and spots. . . . He should not don garments worn by beggars because they degrade. . . . He should not wear transparent garments which reveal his body. His cloak should not be exceedingly long and be dragged on the ground. Sleeves should not protrude beyond the fingers. Patched shoes are not becoming. Man may not use perfume nor wear perfumed clothes" (*Mishneh Torah, Hilchot Deot* 5:9).

There were periods in ancient history when arid conditions forced religious hermits, isolated in the desert, to make a virtue out of necessity. They came to regard the giving up of bathing facilities and proper garments as an act of extreme piety. In a parallel development in modern times, a youthful generation of hippies denounced proper appearance and conventional attire as the hallmarks of a decadent society. Aberrations of this kind come and go without affecting the mainstream of human ethical conduct. Good appearance and attire are still essential to human dignity.

Appreciation and Gratitude

Give thanks unto him and bless his name, for the Lord is good. His mercy endureth for ever.

—Psalm 100:4–5

THE VALUE of a friendly word or deed is enhanced by proper appreciation. An ethical individual acknowledges a favor by an expression of thanks which reflects a moral indebtedness to the benefactor. Failure to show recognition constitutes an undeserved rebuff and brands one as an ingrate.

There are several reasons why some individuals neglect to show gratitude. Absent-mindedness and egocentricity are prime factors. The following are a few examples: A opens a door and is about to enter the store when he spies B behind him. Thoughtfully, he holds the door open to let B enter ahead of him. B, scanning his shopping list, walks into the store without a nod of appreciation. D, driving his car on a busy thoroughfare, spies E, whose car is parked at the curb, desperately trying to enter the lane of traffic. D stops his car and permits E to pull out ahead of him. E, delighted by this opportunity, zooms ahead without a wave of recognition. L rises early on a frosty morning to sweep away the fresh snow before it hardens into ice. Moved by a generous impulse, he does the same for his next-door neighbor, M. Later that morning M emerges to go to work. He notices the cleared path but does not give it a second thought.

One can cite such examples by the dozen. Many people have experienced similar situations. A, D, and L will readily admit that the offenders did not consciously seek to denigrate the generosity of the benefactors and that there was no malicious intent on their part. Yet they cannot but feel discouraged and rebuffed. Will they continue to act in their accustomed gentlemanly manner? Some will, but some will not.

In addition to the absent-minded category of thoughtless people, there are also willful offenders whose lack of gratitude is deliberate and reprehensible. There are some misguided individuals who labor under the illusion that whatever assistance they receive is coming to them and that those who help them are not entitled to any gratitude. A hardened beggar will occasionally let loose a stream of invectives against those whose beneficence falls short of his expectations. Administrators of private and public welfare agencies are often treated to abuse rather than thankfulness.

The worst offenders are those who stifle their sense of appreciation due to a lack of humility. People who have an exaggerated perception of their own superiority, based on wealth, power, or fame, will not deign to acknowledge a service rendered by a person whom they consider beneath their lofty status. Whatever is done for them is viewed as an act of obeisance to which their position entitles them.

Biblical accounts of exemplary behavior are intended to be viewed as models of ethical conduct. The virtue of appreciation has not been overlooked. The scenario of Abraham's purchase of a burial plot is one example. Ephron the Hittite offered to make a gift of the desired plot. Abraham was aware that the offer was a hollow display of showmanship. Nevertheless, he indicated proper appreciation and "bowed down before the people of the land" (Gen. 23:12).

King David's deathbed instructions to Solomon included a lesson in appreciation. "Show kindness unto the sons of Barzillai the Gileadite, and let them be of those that eat at thy table; for so they drew nigh unto me when I fled from Absalom thy brother" (I Kings 2:7).

The ritual of the sacrificial thanks offering (*korban todah*) was a constant reminder to ancient Israel of the need to express one's appreciation and gratitude. The psalmist exalted this ritual because "those who offer a sacrifice of thanksgiving honor me [God]" (Ps. 50:23). The Midrash noted that God does not derive any honor from the rituals of sin and guilt offerings (*Vayikra Rabbah* 9:1). The thanks offering was further extolled in a rabbinic prediction of the messianic age. "Even when the sin and guilt offerings cease [due to the absence of crime], thanks offerings will never cease" (*Shochar Tov, Tehilim* 56).

The rabbis utilized prescribed benedictions, prayers, and homiletic passages to emphasize the importance of appreciation. Rabbi Samuel the son of Nachman (3rd cent.) composed a short prayer which was to be recited upon rising in the morning: "I thank thee God, my Lord, for having taken me out from darkness into light" (*Bereshit Rabbah* 68). This version inspired the composition of a later prayer which has become the first prayer in the traditional prayer book: "I thank thee, O living and abiding king, for having mercifully restored my soul to me. Great is thy trust."

The abundance of benedictions which Jews recite in the course of the day attests to the significance attached to expressions of appreciation. Their formulation was in accord with a basic talmudic principle: "It is forbidden to enjoy anything in this world without the recitation of a benediction" (*Berachot* 35a).

Man must be appreciative of the enjoyments which he derives, even when he has no direct contact with the persons who have provided those enjoyments. Thus Ben Zoma (2nd cent.) urged people who break bread to ponder: "What labors Adam had to carry out before he obtained bread to eat! He plowed, he sowed, he reaped, he bound, he threshed and winnowed and selected the ears, he ground and sifted, he kneaded and baked, and then at last he ate; whereas I get up and find all these things done for me" (*Berachot* 58a).

The farmer and the baker are compensated for their work. That, however, does not relieve one of an ethical duty to feel grateful to them. Similar obligations come into play in other fields of human endeavor. It is the common practice of people who enjoy an opera or a theatrical performance to express their satisfaction and gratitude through applause. This is both proper and ethical.

All employees, regardless of the nature of their work, are entitled to an expression of appreciation by their superiors, if their performance merits it. Some employers selfishly withhold commendation for fear of inviting demands for an increase in salary. Such practice is short-sighted and unethical.

Public servants, even more than employees in the private sector, fail to get proper recognition. Ecclesiastes decried the short memory and ingratitude of some communities and nations. "There was a little city, and few men within it, and there came a great king against it. . . . Now there was found in it a man poor and wise, and he by his wisdom delivered the city; yet no man remembered that same poor man" (9:14–15)

Arrogance and Pride

I will cause the arrogance of the proud to cease, and I will lay low the haughtiness of the tyrants.

—Isaiah 13:11

THERE IS a substantial difference between the qualities of arrogance and pride. *Funk & Wagnalls Standard Dictionary* defines arrogance as a state of mind which claims much for itself and concedes little to others. Pride, on the other hand, is defined as an absorbing sense of one's own greatness. We will adopt these definitions for the purposes of this essay.

Arrogance is a two-edged sword. One edge is an exaggerated subjective assessment of one's capabilities and achievements. The other edge is a reckless disparagement of other people's competence. The two are interdependent. It is the denigration of others that feeds the growth of self-deceit, and vice versa.

Pride is not necessarily an antisocial quality. A proud person does not measure his own merit on a comparative scale in relation to other people. It is only excessive pride that assumes an offensive posture.

Moderate pride is potentially a positive trait which can contribute much to the quality of life. It can also serve as an incentive to self-improvement. A laborer who takes pride in his work will strive for perfection. A teacher who prides himself on the results of his instruction will entertain an absorbing interest in the progress of his students. Pride and modesty are not necessarily self-excluding. They become mutually antagonistic only when pride turns obsessive and ceases to be a constructive instrument.

The line separating arrogance from pride is admittedly hard to perceive in some instances. The Talmud occasionally lumps

32

the two together in its denunciations. Yet Rav (3rd cent.) is quoted to the effect that a scholar should possess "one-eighth of one-eighth" of pride" (*Sotah* 5a). He was obviously mindful of the need for maintaining a proper degree of dignity, without which neither scholar nor learning would command the necessary respect. A modicum of pride is an essential ingredient of dignity.

Arrogance supported by power can pose a serious threat to the welfare of mankind. An ordinary arrogant individual can be isolated by society and thus neutralized. Such treatment is ineffective in the case of arrogant kings and tyrants. The Bible enjoined the kings of Israel to place a copy of the Pentateuch in their libraries. It was hoped that its precepts would exercise a moderating influence upon them. The king was to study the Bible to the end "that he may learn to fear the Lord his God, to keep all the words of this law . . . that his heart may not be moved by arrogrance to lift him up above his brethern" (Deut. 17:19–20).

When arrogance makes an alliance with wickedness, they use their combined resources to prey upon the helpless elements of society. In the words of the psalmist: "Through the arrogance of the wicked the poor are hotly pursued" (Ps. 10:2). Rabbah the son of Huna (3rd–4th cent.) labeled all people possessed of arrogance as "wicked" (*rasha, Taanit* 7b). Rabbi Nachman the son of Isaac (3rd–4th cent.) ruled that it is permissible to hate an arrogant individual (*Taanit* 7b). This rule was particularly significant in view of the explicit biblical injunction: "Thou shalt not hate thy brother in thy heart" (Lev. 19:17). Apparently he placed the arrogant beyond the pale of brotherhood.

Rabbi Hamnuna, a contemporary of the previously mentioned two rabbis, expressed the strongest condemnation of the arrogant by asserting that the Almighty punishes the world for tolerating arrogance by withholding rain from the land (*Taanit* 7b). The strictures of the three Babylonian sages seem to allude to a serious public-relations problem with people considered arrogant due to their disregard of established communal policy. At that time in history, the strife between the

Romans and the Parthians in Babylonia flared into warfare. The Jewish community sided with the Parthians as the lesser of two evils, a decision which must have met with some opposition.

An arrogant person is unfit for leadership because of his inability to establish a proper rapport with the people. "The Almighty," according to the Talmud, "weeps at the sight of arrogant leaders" (*Chagigah* 5b). Rabbi Simon son of Yochai (2nd cent.) equated arrogance with idolatry (*Sotah* 4b). Mar Ukva (3rd cent.) declared that the Almighty and the arrogant cannot coexist in the same world (*Sotah* 5a).

Arrogance occasionally parades behind a mask of judicious prudence. The scholar who regards with disdain the elementary questions of ignorant students is betraying raw arrogance. The head of a department who declines to answer public inquiries and refers them to subordinates is afflicted with arrogance. The physician who is too busy to explain his diagnosis to the patient or his family is guilty of arrogance. The rich brother who finds no time to invite his poor brother for a social visit is a victim of arrogance. All racial and religious prejudices are based on arrogance.

The quality of arrogance is not endemic to human nature, nor is it hereditary. It is mainly shaped by environmental factors and by imitation. Those who are not trained to exercise self-discipline may easily succumb to this fault.

With this in mind, Rabbi Judah HaNasi (2nd cent.) composed a short and meaningful prayer which he recited on concluding the morning service. It was a warning against unexpected pitfalls which one is likely to encounter in the course of the day. "May it be thy will, O Lord our God, and the God of our fathers, to deliver us from the arrogant and arrogance, from an evil man . . . whether he be Jew or Gentile" (*Berachot* 6b). This prayer was incorporated into the traditional prayer book as an introduction to the morning service.

Asceticism

Wherefore I perceived that there is nothing better than that a man should rejoice in his works.

—Ecclesiastes 3:22

THE BELIEF that asceticism constitutes a most virtuous mode of life has been endorsed by theologians of different faiths. Self-denial of physical pleasures has been equated with saintliness and extolled as a model of moral and ethical conduct. Not all theologians agree with this view. Many regard asceticism as an antisocial philosophy and a slur on the majority of mankind who consider the legitimate enjoyment of pleasure consistent with morality and ethics.

Religions which stress the hereafter, in the belief that true life begins beyond the grave, instinctively downgrade all the earthly joys of man's existence. They may grudgingly concede the need for satisfying some bodily cravings in the interests of survival and the perpetuation of the species. Such concessions notwithstanding, the postulate that pleasure is intrinsically evil has been repeatedly reaffirmed. Indeed, they prefer celibacy because it eliminates the pleasure of sexual intercourse. Some ascetics are said to have swallowed their food whole to avoid enjoying the pleasure of eating.

Judaism is a this-worldly faith, primarily concerned with the quality of life on earth. It does not recommend the suppression of natural human urges and regards the enjoyment of permissible pleasures as salutary and wholesome. It decries asceticism but at the same time condemns inordinate pursuit of self-gratification.

Most Judaic rituals and precepts have a socioreligious base. The incentive of heavenly reward in the hereafter was muted in

35

the Bible. It was stressed in postbiblical literature as a disciplinary tool for keeping man's conduct within the bounds of morality. Extraordinary acts of piety are not required to assure man of a niche in heaven. Self-affliction is deemed an offense against religion, ethics, and society.

Judaism considers life on earth the most prized God-given gift. The biblical command to perserve one's life takes precedence over nearly all other religious precepts. The same holds true for the preservation of other people's lives.

Rabbi Akiva boldly pointed to the command "And thou shalt love thy neighbor as thyself" (Lev. 19:18) as a major biblical principle (Jer. *Nedarim* 9:4). Had he stressed the hereafter he undoubtedly would have chosen the parallel commandment, "And thou shalt love the Lord thy God" (Deut. 6:5), as the major biblical principle.

Even the injunction to love God was interpreted by the rabbis to have a social significance. One's love for God must be demonstrated by a proper regard for his fellowman. "If an individual studies Bible and Mishnah . . . and thereby learns to be honest in business and to speak pleasantly to people, what do they say concerning him? 'This man has studied the Torah, look how fine his ways are, how righteous his deeds' " (*Yoma* 86a).

Despite the opposition of the Bible and the Talmud to asceticism, there was an interval of several centuries, immediately preceding the talmudic era, which witnessed the emergence of a nonrabbinical Judaic school that evinced ascetic trends. This tendency is reflected in the practices of some Essenic sects and in the writings of Philo the Alexandrian and several apocryphal authors.

Rabbinical opposition to asceticism also gave rise to a controversy regarding the need for imposing some curbs on the normal pursuits of pleasure, as a precaution against breaches of morality. These differences produced strict and liberal schools of thought whose views will be discussed later.

An analysis of the Jewish attitude to asceticism must begin with the Bible. Does the Bible favor excessive fasting? Does it consider celibacy a virtuous state?

The Pentateuch enjoined only a single annual day of fast, Yom Kippur. The phrase "You shall afflict your souls" (Lev. 16:29), a synonym for deprivation of nourishment, might conceivably have given substance to the notion that self-affliction is a meritorious practice. Such an assumption is erroneous, as is evidenced by the twin commandment relating to Yom Kippur: "and you shall do no manner of work in the same day" (Lev. 23:28). Surely there is no merit to abstention from work except in the context of a formally established religious observance. The same is true of the abstention from food.

Fasting was regarded by people as an expression of intense contrition, as a symbolic ritual of self-sacrifice, or as fervent prayer for divine mercy and forgiveness. Due to the physical severity of fasting, it was instituted only on the most solemn day of the year. Eventually, it was resorted to on occasions of major emergencies. Although there was no dearth of emergencies in the days of Moses, there is no mention in the Pentateuch of any public voluntary fast aside from Yom Kippur.

The earliest biblical account of public fasts dates from the post-Pentateuchal period, several centuries after Moses. The war of the tribes against the tribe of Benjamin (ca. 11th cent. B.C.E.) produced a sense of deep distress which was expressed through fasting (Jud. 20:26). Another public fast was observed in the days of Samuel (ca. 10th cent. B.C.E., I Sam. 7:6). Shortly thereafter another fast was observed as a sign of mourning (I Sam. 31:13). When the custom of fasting assumed greater frequency, the practice lost some of its profound significance and sincerity. Such fasts were considered a mockery by Isaiah (8th cent. B.C.E., 58:3) and Jeremiah (6th cent. B.C.E., 14:12). In the same century the practice of establishing memorial fasts in commemoration of anniversaries of national tragedies came into being (Zech. 7:5).

Biblical approval of fasting is clearly limited to special occasions. "Affliction of the soul" on a regular basis is contrary to the "preservation of life." At no time does the Bible allude to fasting as a recommended virtuous practice for people of piety and zeal.

Does the Bible oppose the drinking of wine as a hedonistic

pursuit of pleasure? It opposes drunkenness for obvious reasons (Prov. 23:20), but drinking in moderation is considered salutary (Ps. 104:15). The fact that wine was used in the sacrificial rite of wine-offering (Lev. 23:13) is a clear indication that the fruit of the vine was considered a worthy agricultural product.

There were several exceptions to this rule for individuals whose sensitive duties demanded total sobriety. Stringent restrictions were prescribed for priests entering the sanctuary to perform religious services (Lev. 10:9) and for the judge who is sitting in judgment (Prov. 31:4).

Another major exception was the Nazirite, who had taken a vow of abstinence from wine. A Nazirite was generally motivated by a religious impulse "to consecrate himself unto the Lord" (Num. 6:2).

Does the Bible consider the Nazirite a saint or a sinner? Nowhere does it praise naziritic restraints as a virtuous practice. The only exception is in the account of Samson, whose parents were ordered to raise him as a Nazirite (Jud. 13:5). The rabbis attributed this command to the fact that Samson, possessed of unbridled passions, was in need of naziritic restrictions (*Bereshit Rabbah* 63).

The prescribed guilt-offering which a Nazirite was required to bring upon the expiration of his naziritic term has an ambivalent implication (Num. 6:14). Rabbis of the strict school attributed the Nazirite's guilt to the termination of his abstinence. The liberals, on the other hand, regarded the guilt-offering as proof of the Bible's displeasure with naziritic vows. The phrase "and after that [the bringing of the offering] the Nazirite may drink wine" (Num. 6:20) clearly reflects no moral objection to the drinking of wine and appears to support the view of the liberal school.

Does the Bible approve of, or even condone, celibacy? Emphatically no. Celibacy is contrary to the marital obligation of procreation (Gen. 1:25). Furthermore, sex is a conjugal right and duty inherent in the marital status. This duty is independent of procreative obligations and must be discharged even if the latter have already been fulfilled (Exod. 21:10).

The foregoing discussion leads us to the inescapable conclusion that asceticism is contrary to the letter and spirit of the Bible.

NONRABBINICAL ASCETICISM

The ascetic sympathies of the pretalmudic school mentioned earlier are highlighted in several works.

According to the author of the Book of Jubilees (2nd cent. B.C.E.), no sexual intercourse is permitted on the Sabbath. This prohibition reflects the view that coitus is a contaminating, impure act which is inconsistent with the sacredness of the Sabbath.

The Wisdom of Solomon (1st cent. B.C.E.) was a popular book among the early Christian fathers, who found its extremist sentiments to their liking. Its author dismissed the whole subject of sex with a single concise sentence: "Better to have no children and to have virtue." As for those who like pleasures and savor the taste of wine, the author excludes them from the community of believers. " 'Let us enjoy the good things that are present. . . . Let us fill ourselves with costly wine and ointments.' . . . these are the words of the ungodly."

Philo the Alexandrian (1st cent. C.E.) was a contemporary of the first generation of the rabbis whose work created the gigantic Talmud. However, he was not familiar with them, nor does his philosophy reveal any rabbinical influence. Drawing his inspiration from Hellenic culture, he strongly condemned pleasurable experiences as a source of evil. "The desire [of sex] causes pleasure in their bodies which is the beginning of iniquities and transgressions" (*Treatise on the Creation of the World* 24).

The following are some of his illuminating statements:

Man must resist "every passion and especially pleasure. . . . The life of the wicked is governed by pleasure as by a master" (*Treatise on the Allegories of the Sacred Law* II, 24).

"God hates pleasure" (ibid. III, 24).

"If one learns to be indifferent to meat and drink . . . what can there be of things superfluous that he would find difficulty in disregarding?" *(On the Ten Festivals, The Ninth Festival).* So much for Philo the Alexandrian.

Regarding the Essenes we quote from Josephus' description of Essenic doctrines: "The Essenes reject pleasure as an evil, but esteem continence and the conquest over our passions to be a virtue. They neglect marriage" (*Wars*, bk. II, 8:2).

To the Essenes, "Oil is a defilement . . . to be sweaty is a good thing, nor do they allow a change of garments or of shoes [a display of vanity], till they first be entirely torn to pieces" (ibid. 4).

"As for death, they esteem it better than living always" (ibid. 10).

"No sexual intercourse is permitted with pregnant wives. In this manner they [the Essenes] demonstrate that they did not marry out of regard to pleasure but for the sake of posterity" (ibid. 10).

"A settled measure of milk and meat is allotted" (ibid. 5).

Unlike the above-mentioned apocryphal authors and Philo, the Essenes, an indigenous Palestinian sect, were not influenced by Hellenic culture. They were an outgrowth of social and political conditions which had threatened the viability of Judaism. Some factions, such as the Qumran sect, were at odds with the high priests, whom they regarded as usurpers who desecrated the true faith.

The Palestinian Jewish community in the last two centuries before the common era had become the hapless victim of dynastic rivalries between the heirs of Alexander the Great. Ancient religious standards were undermined by an invasion of paganism and epicureanism. Despairing of changing the course of events, groups of pious individuals chose to withdraw from society and to strengthen their defenses by adopting strict and extremist policies which segregated them from a hostile environment. Their mode of living reflected and reinforced a siege mentality.

It is not surprising that some of these pious people developed a death-wish as a solution to their agonizing problems. Celibacy was a shortcut to the achievement of this goal. Under similar conditions, the prophet Elijah, many centuries earlier, ran off into the wilderness and prayed for death to relieve him from his misery (I Kings 19:4). Jeremiah, too, acknowledging his impotence to save his people, looked to a withdrawal from society as the only recourse left to him. "Oh that I were in the wilderness, in a lodging place of wayfaring men, that I might leave my people and go from them." (9:1).

Rabbinical Judaism, temporarily forsaking nationalist aspirations in the wake of Rome's decisive victory, embarked upon the building of a new community united by bonds of faith and culture. The new order held out a promise of hope, internal harmony, and inner joy. Piety no longer lived under siege, and asceticism lost its allure. Whatever curbs were to be imposed on human behavior would be dictated by a sense of morality rather than despair.

THE STRICT RABBINICAL SCHOOL

The strict school favored the exercise of self-control in the pursuit of pleasure, even when such pleasures were not contrary to the moral code. Like the liberal school, it condemned asceticism but favored moderate restrictions as a precautionary measure.

Rabbi Judah HaNasi (2nd cent.), head of the Palestinian Patriarchate, commanded great wealth and enjoyed princely prerogatives. Yet he lived a life of austerity. His routine was no doubt intended as a precaution against overindulgence in the luxuries that were available at his court (*Ketubot* 104a).

Rabbi Eliezer Hakappar (2nd–3rd cent.) declared that "excessive desires and overreaching ambitions take a man from the world" (*Avot* 4:28). Rabbi Jonah Gerondi (13th cent.), a medieval follower of the strict school, considered Rabbi Eliezer's statement applicable even to such desires as are legitimate. It is their "excessive" nature that makes them potentially dangerous. Gerondi's opinion was in keeping with the maxim of the famous Babylonian sage Rava (4th cent.): "Sanctify thyself by abstaining from the permissible" (*Yevamot* 20a).

The following is a statement typical of the strict school: "He who abstains from wine in order to guard against sin is worthy of receiving all the blessings contained in the Priestly Benediction" (*Bamidbar Rabbah* 11:1).

One talmudic member of the strict school adopted the extremist view that he who engages in a fast is considered holy (*Taanit* 9a). This met with the response of Samuel (3rd cent.), who labeled an abstainer from food a sinner (ibid.).

On the subject of marital sex both schools adopted the talmudic moral dictum: "Scholars should not always be with their wives like roosters" (*Berachot* 22a). A detailed, flexible schedule of marital sex, deemed moderate and proper, was spelled out in a Mishnah (*Ketubot* 61b). The strict school favored greater restraint than what was indicated by the author of the Mishnah. The additional restrictions were considered necessary as a precaution against sexual overindulgence. However, it was stipulated that self-imposed limitations must not conflict with procreational obligations or a wife's conjugal rights.

Rabbi Jacob b. Asher (13th–14th cent.), a follower of the strict school, described in his authoritative code the three factors which enter into the rationale for marital sex: fulfillment of procreational obligations; satisfaction of the wife's conjugal rights; safeguarding against illicit sexual relations with other women (*Tur, Orach Chaim* 240).

THE LIBERAL RABBINICAL SCHOOL

The liberal school opposed the imposition of curbs on legitimate bodily functions unless such restrictions were demanded by compelling reasons. Simon the Just (ca. 3rd cent. B.C.E.) was opposed to naziritic vows. In one instance, however, he expressed effusive praise for a young Nazirite. The handsome lad's agreeable looks were enhanced by beautiful curly hair. The hair would have to be cut upon the expiration of the naziritic term. Disturbed by the impending waste of the boy's good looks, Simon inquired about his motives. The boy responded as follows: "I am a shepherd . . . . While drawing water from a well, I chanced to notice my reflection in the water. Overwhelmed by my good looks, evil desires rushed upon me." To curb his sudden lust, he took a naziritic vow. Simon kissed him on his head and said: "May there be many Nazirites like you in Israel" (*Nedarim* 9b).

Rabbi Isaac expressed the liberal point of view in his reprimand of a Nazirite: "Are not the things prohibited in the law enough for you that you want to prohibit other things?" (Jer. *Nedarim* 9:1).

The liberal philosophy was further elucidated by Rav (3rd cent.): "Man is accountable to heaven for refusing to enjoy the delicacies which are available to him" (Jer. *Kiddushin* 4:3).

The liberal point of view contributed to the shaping of legal development. If a man marries a woman on condition that she be free of restrictive vows, and it is later discovered that she had taken a vow of abstinence from meat, wine, and colorful apparel, the marriage is void. Enjoyment is of the essence of congenial life. It is proper to derive pleasure from food, sex, and all other enjoyable activities, so long as they are kept within the framework of moral propriety.

The influential medieval moralist Bachya Ibn Pekuda (11th cent.) criticized those who concentrate solely on worldly pleasures but was equally critical of those who seek to suppress their bodily desires (*Chovat HaLevavot, Shaar HaPerishut*).

Judah Halevi's (12th cent.) support of the liberal school was expressed in a forceful sentence: "Our submission to the Almighty on fast-days does not bring us closer to God than our joys on Sabbaths and festivals" (*Al Chazari* 2:50).

Maimonides (12th cent.) decried the "practice of some pious people to tend to extremes by indulging in fasts, rising at night for prayers, abstaining from meat, wine, and sex . . . . Their motives are misunderstood by the common people, who attribute merit to such conduct. As a result they resort to self-affliction under the misconception that such behavior will improve their character and bring them closer to God. It is as if the Almighty hates the human body and seeks its destruction" (*Shemonah Perakim* 4).

Despite the rational approach of Judaism to the subject of abstinence, asceticism has continued to have a powerful hold on the hearts and minds of sundry zealots and mystics throughout the ages. Practical kabbalists, who believed that supernatural powers could be attained by indulging in fasts and prayers, were particularly vulnerable to asceticism. The advent of modern Chasidism, with its stress on serving God through joy, led to a decline in the vestiges of the cult of self-denial.

Beauty

The beauty of a woman cheers the countenance, and a man loves nothing better.

—Ecclesiasticus 36:22

Judaism holds beauty in high regard. A harmonious blend of grace and symmetry bears the imprint of divine perfection and is a tribute to the marvels of God's creation. One should therefore address to God his thankfulness for all the beautiful sights he is privileged to behold. An ancient talmudic custom called for the recitation of a benediction of thanksgiving whenever one comes across majestic views of nature or lovely creatures, including beautiful women (*Berachot* 58b).

Theologians considered man's esthetic appreciation an incentive to greater faith in God. By the same token, the destruction of the beauty of nature was deplored as a diminution of the image of God. People were therefore urged to spare and preserve the beauty of the environment (*Yalkut Shimoni, Pekudei* 422).

The Judaic definition of beauty is not limited to visual physical charms. It also includes refined human traits, such as dignity, deportment, and character, which are pleasing to people's minds. This comprehensive view of beauty is projected by the author of Proverbs: "The glory of young men is their strength, and the beauty of old men is the hoary head" (20:29). The old man who acts with the dignity of his age and does not compete in areas which belong to youth is a beautiful person.

Beauty is an adjunct of religious acts. The Pentateuchal verse "This is my God and I will beautify him" (Exod. 15:2) was interpreted by the rabbis as an injunction to give an attractive appearance to religious articles (*Shabbat* 133b).

45

Thus one should build a beautiful sukkah, affix an attractive mezuzah, and write a distinctive Torah (*Masechet Soferim* 3:11).

Priests, the living symbols of a functioning religion, were also under orders to present a handsome appearance. The high priest is described in the Bible as "the priest who is superior among his brethren" (Lev. 21:10). His superiority must be manifested, according to the Talmud, in his "strength, comeliness, and wisdom" (*Yoma* 18a). In reality, wisdom is the most essential ingredient of good leadership. Yet men in the public eye quickly discover that strength and comeliness, qualities visible to all, are central to early impressions and evaluation of a leader.

Rabbi Aaron of Barcelona (13th cent.), author of the *Chinuch,* points out that the effectiveness of a leader must be measured by his impact on the people he leads. A leader who suffers from a deformity will inevitably attract attention to his condition rather than to his message. His effectiveness is accordingly diminished (275).

The Bible bars deformed priests from officiating at Temple services (Lev. 21:17). This prohibition was carried over into the post-Temple era. Kohanim who are deformed are not permitted to pronounce the Priestly Benediction at congregational services. Sacrificial animals similarly had to be free of blemishes, in consideration of aesthetic tastefulness (Lev. 20:22).

Exclusion of deformed priests from the Temple service attached no stigma to the individual so afflicted. He did not forfeit his priestly privileges and was permitted to enter the Temple to perform some tasks in privacy (*Eruvin* 105a).

In the opinion of one talmudic authority, judges, too, should be disqualified by physical defects. His opinion was not accepted. Wisdom, integrity, and a sense of compassion have always been the qualifications which determine the fitness of individuals for judicial office.

Despite its admiration of beauty, Judaism never developed a beauty cult similar to that of the Greeks and Romans. The struggle waged against paganism and its statuary motivated the strict biblical prohibition of some forms of plastic art (Exod. 20:4).

The Judaic attitude to feminine beauty is somewhat ambivalent. On the one hand, there was an instinctive impulse to sing its praises in poetic phraseology. The biblical Song of Songs attests to that inspiration. Yet the Song of Songs is atypical among the ancient sacred and secular Jewish literary works. Indeed, had it not been for the rabbinical allegorical interpretation of the Song of Songs as depicting a romance between God and his people, the book would have never been included in the canon.

Feminine beauty was greatly admired, but its role in provoking lust, a cardinal sin, imposed a moral restraint upon the free expression of poets and singers. The biblical law regarding a pretty heathen captive of war (Deut. 21:11) warned of the potential power of beautiful women to defeat religious scruples.

The eminent talmudic sage, Rav (3rd cent.) ruled that "one is forbidden to say, 'How beautiful is that idolatress' " (*Avodah Zarah* 20a). He was obvioulsy fearful that even an innocuous expression of admiration might lead to an intimate relationship. Rav's strict opinion was consistent with some of his other legal dicta pertaining to morality (*Sotah* 7a). However, his view did not represent the rabbinical consensus.

Rabbi Simon b. Gamliel (2nd cent.), head of the Palestinian Patriarchate, expressed a more liberal opinion. It was reported that he had encountered a pretty heathen woman on the Temple Mount. Struck by her exceptional beauty, he instinctively repeated the phrase of the psalmist, "How great are thy works, O Lord" (104:24; *Avodah Zarah* 20a). It is conceivable that Rav's strictness was a response to conditions in third-century Babylonia, under which free social intercourse between Jews and pagans prevailed. Even Rav raised no objection to an expression of admiration for the beauty of a nonpagan woman.

We noted earlier that religions which stress the hereafter tend to downgrade the importance of physical appearance and beauty. Creeds which regard celibacy as a condition of noble virtue have an even more cogent reason for a negative attitude to feminine charm.

A similar attitude seems to be reflected in the thirty-first chapter of the Book of Proverbs, which lists the attributes of a "woman of valor" (31:30). It omits beauty as one of the ingredients. The phrase "grace is deceitful and beauty is vain" is almost ascetic in tone, a sentiment alien to mainstream Judaism. It is likely, however, that in his analysis of a woman of character, the author regards physical beauty as an irrelevant element. His final sentence, couched in that vein, concludes that "a woman who fears the Lord is the one to be praised."

Despite their moral misgivings, the rabbis had a compelling reason for stressing the importance of feminine beauty. To diasporic Jewry, besieged by hostile and destructive forces, the maintenance of a high rate of childbirth was essential to physical survival. The natural beauty of young girls is the most valuable asset in promoting matrimony. Any effort to keep that asset under wraps would prove counterproductive.

Beauty is also important to married women as a means of strengthening the bonds of matrimony. However, for the sake of morality, the rabbis insisted that the married woman direct the force of her charms exclusively toward her husband.

Whatever ambivalence is detected in the rabbis' treatment of the subject of feminine pulchritude is due to their awareness of a causal relationship between excessive beauty and moral infractions. A strong exercise of self-control was the best advice they could offer. "If you are handsome, do not be ensnared by lewdness, but honor your creator, and fear him, and praise him with the beauty with which God has endowed you" (Pesikta Rabbati 127a).

Due to the importance of matrimony, the religious leadership of the Temple era permitted the holding of annual coming-out parties by the girls of Jerusalem (Taanit 31a). Even though self-praise is normally frowned upon (Prov. 27:2), pretty girls were encouraged on that occasion to boast of their beauty. Public concern for the proper appearance of young girls was enacted into law. Thus a girl of marriageable age was prohibited

from neglecting her looks even in the week of mourning for a
parent (*Taanit* 13b).

A woman's skill in enhancing her beauty was highly prized
and encouraged. A betrothed bride was generally allowed a
period of twelve months, prior to her marriage, to learn the art
of the proper application of cosmetics (*Ketubot* 57a).

The great reformer Ezra (5th cent. B.C.E.), who tried to
repair the ravages of intermarriage with heathen women, ordained that merchants deliver jewelry and cosmetics to Jewish
women in the countryside (*Baba Kama* 82b).

Wedding guests were urged to praise the bride's beauty so as
to endear her to the groom (*Ketubot* 16b). This practice gave
rise to a controversy between the strait-laced members of the
School of Shammai and the genial members of the School of
Hillel (2nd cent.). How does one praise an ugly bride? Is it
permissible to bend the truth for the sake of matrimonial
endearment? The former insisted that lies are abominable.
Under the circumstances it is best not to bring up the subject of
beauty. The latter, with tongue in cheek, recommended that
the ugly bride be praised for her beauty. We cannot but whole-
heartedly agree with them. After all, love is blind, and beauty is
in the eyes of the beholder.

Women's license to self-beautification did not grant them a
right to create the kind of beauty which is calculated to provoke
lust. The distinction between demure and vulgar beauty is the
dividing line between the ethical and the immoral.

The pursuit of beauty, open to women, was barred to men. A
male's use of cosmetics or jewelry normally worn by women is
considered an act of effemination, banned by biblical proscription (Deut. 22:5).

Charity

For the poor shall never cease out of the land, therefore I command thee, saying: "Thou shalt surely open thy hand unto thy poor and needy brother, in thy land."

—Deuteronomy 15:11

The biblical prediction that poverty will never be wholly eradicated has been fully substantiated by history. Even the wealthiest of nations has its share of needy and deprived people.

A stroll along the crowded streets of any modern metropolis brings into sight nondescript beggars asking for a handout. Tourists, making the rounds of places of interest, are repeatedly assailed by droves of mendicants. The outstretched hand of poverty reaches into the home as well. The mail delivers heart-rending requests for charity, appealing to one's conscience and pocket.

To give or not to give is a question no one is permitted to dodge. The answer depends upon the individual and his innate disposition. Some give indiscriminately, others are selective, and still others dismiss all requests on the grounds that "they are all phony" or that "charity begins at home." In all honesty, one must admit that not all appeals are a fraud and that charity does not begin at home but in the home.

Occasional disclosures by government agencies of mismanagement in the distribution of charity funds, even by some of the reputable private welfare organizations, lends support to those who view the pressure tactics of professional fundraisers with skepticism. Yet such disclosures should not foreclose the claims of the poor upon the conscience of the affluent. However, they do impose an investigative duty on all contributors to charity to make sure that their largess is channeled to institutions and individuals where it will do the most good.

The social approach to charity has gone through three stages of development. In its initial stage all charity was dispensed on an individual level, involving a person-to-person relationship. In the second stage, communal welfare agencies came into being, as a supplement to individual initiative, in order to keep pace with a growing need for assistance. A developing awareness of a national obligation to care for the indigent introduced a third stage in which the needs of the poor have become a governmental responsibility. The three stages, supplementing each other, round out the picture of modern philanthropy.

The biblical precepts pertaining to charity date from the first stage. They address themselves to assistance rendered on an individual level. These encompass voluntary and compulsory contributions. Maimonides lists seven biblical commandments enjoining the giving of charity (*Sefer HaMitzvot* 120–124, 130, 197). These multiple laws attest to the great importance attached to charity in Judaism and also to the need for overcoming a well-entrenched natural reluctance to part with one's hard-earned money.

Of the seven commandments, six are obligatory levies raised from the produce of the soil. Interestingly, the single voluntary charity specified in the Bible is not an outright gift of money but a loan (Exod. 22:24). Judaism regards help extended to the poor with a view toward enabling them to become self-supporting as the most laudable form of charity (*Mishneh Torah, Hilchot Matanot Aniyim* 10:7). The Book of Psalms brackets making an interest-free loan with giving alms as an act whose merit shall endure forever (112:5,9).

Charitableness is motivated by compassion (*Baba Batra* 10) and a sense of responsibility for the welfare of one's fellowman (Lev. 25:35). The significance of charity as a religious rite conducive to salvation and divine forgiveness is another important factor (*Rosh HaShanah* 16b). The underlying rationale, which denies the individual the choice of whether to give or withhold charity, is the premise that all wealth belongs to God (Haggai 2:8) and that the possessor of property is merely a custodian who is permitted to manage it for the benefit of all. Hence, the rabbis said, he who gives no charity will in the end come to lose his property and have to depend on charity for his subsistence (*Bamidbar Rabbah* 18). On the other hand, if one is a generous contributor to charity, and as a result runs out of funds, the Almighty will provide him with additional money so that he may continue his philanthropy (*Baba Batra* 9b).

The rationale of charity, based on God's ownership of all wealth, is implicit in the phraseology of several biblical injunctions. Thus the command to help the needy "within any of the gates in thy land, which the Lord thy God gives you" (Deut. 15:7) stresses the point that it was God who gave the land and who lays down the rules for its disposition.

The law of the sabbatical year similarly restricts the ownership rights of the farmer. In "the seventh year thou shalt leave it [*unetashtah*] that the poor of thy people may eat, and what they leave the beasts of the field shall eat" (Exod. 23:11). The Hebrw verb *netosh* is occasionally used in the Bible in juxtaposition to the verb *azov*, which means "to leave" or "to forsake" (I Kings 8:57; Ps. 27:9, 9:14). The farmer was told in effect that he loses control over the produce of his farm in the sabbatical year. When Nehemiah (5th cent. B.C.E.) reimposed the law of the sabbatical year in the era of the second Temple, he used the same verb, *venitosh* ("we shall leave the land"), in describing the observance of the sabbatical year (10:32). In a theological sense, the concept of an absolute vested right of ownership does not exist.

Rabbinical Judaism, drawing upon the rich biblical background, gave added emphasis to the importance of charity. With the shift from an agricultural society to a largely landless community, the problem of Jewish poverty and starvation assumed a more acute character. The situation became particularly grave in the diaspora, where exile and confiscation of property were frequent occurrences. It was in the talmudic era that individual charity had to be supplemented by communal assistance to the poor.

The merit of charity, said Rav Assi (3rd cent.), is as weighty as that of all the biblical precepts combined (*Baba Batra* 9a).

Judaism regarded paganism as a heartless creed, devoid of compassion. Hence the comparison of a person who gives no charity, thus demonstrating a lack of a sense of compassion, to an idol worshipper.

With the rabbinical transformation of alms-giving into a rite essential to salvation, a new and powerful impetus was given to the practice of charity. The link of charity to divine forgiveness was first expressed in the apocryphal Tobit (2nd cent. B.C.E., 4:10). It was later popularized by the Talmud with the slogan: "Prayer, charity, and penitence annul a harsh decree" (*Rosh HaShanah* 16b). The new motivation made the practice of charity a national habit. Every Jew was henceforth required to give alms. Even paupers who depend upon charity were not exempt from this obligation (*Gittin* 7b).

The following are some ancient guidelines pertaining to charity.

1. Charity should be given with a cheerful countenance and an expression of sympathy.

"He that oppresses the poor blasphemes his maker, but he that is gracious unto the needy honors him" (Prov. 14:31). "Let it not grieve thee to bow down thine ear to the poor, and give him a friendly answer with meekness" (Ecclus. 4:8). "In all thy gifts show a cheerful countenance, and dedicate thy tithes with gladness" (ibid. 35:9).

2. An alms-giver must avoid embarrassing the recipient of his gift.

There was a room in the Temple known as the "Chamber of anonymous givers." Ethical people used to leave their contributions in that chamber to be given in secrecy to needy people who were reluctant to accept charity in public (*Shekalim* 5:6). A poor person who is ashamed of accepting charity from a close friend should be given help through an intermediary (Jer. *Peah* 8). If a person who is in need declines to accept charity, help should be extended to him in the guise of a loan (*Ketubot* 67b). It is best to dispense one's charity through an official in charge of the distribution of alms in order to avoid an embarrassing confrontation (*Chinuch* 479).

3. The needs of the poor are not properly served by those

who wait for an appeal for help. One should give before he is approached by the poor (*Shabbat* 104a).

4. One should not publicize his philanthropy for the sake of deriving admiration and honor.

The ancient sages clearly perceived that philanthropy does not always glitter with pure altruism. Thus they listed four categories of people representing four different attitudes to charity. There are some who are liberal in their giving but dislike anyone who matches their generosity (they seek exclusive credit and honor). There are those who persuade others to give but offer nothing of their own (they have empathy for the poor but are too stingy). There are people who contribute and get others to do likewise (a praiseworthy disposition). There are those who do not contribute and hope that no one else will contribute (they would feel embarrassed; *Avot* 5:16).

Anonymous charity reflects true nobility of the soul. "He who gives money anonymously is greater than Moses" (*Baba Batra* 9b). Despite such admonitions, the practice of honoring large donors through paid advertisements in the press and at public dinners is pervasive. Organizations which pander to the weakness of patrons by showering them with praise in exaggerated and flattering terms are guilty of unethical conduct. Such practices are justified by some on the ground that they produce needed funds and stimulate potential givers to come forward with sizable contributions. One cannot lightly dismiss the practical weight of this position. Yet unsolicited honor, given with discretion and good taste, is much more rewarding to a generous contributor and at the same time meets the dictates of proper ethics.

5. A pledge of charity made in public must be speedily redeemed.

According to Rabbi Yochanan b. Zakkai (1st cent.), the failure to redeem public pledges of charity was one of the causes of the downfall of Jerusalem (*Avot deRabbi Natan* 31).

6. One who lacks funds for charity should not dismiss a person who asks for help in an abrupt manner.

A cordial reception and kind words of sympathy may do more for an indigent than a monetary contribution (*Avot deRabbi Natan* 13).

7. A rich man who gives less than his means warrant is as morally guilty as he would be if he had robbed the poor (*Sefer Chasidim* 415).

8. No beggar should be turned away emptyhanded (*Yoreh Deah* 241).

An exception would have to be made in case of people who deliberately refuse employment or are known to spend their money on liquor or drugs.

9. A person who begs for food should be promptly helped, regardless of his integrity or credibility (ibid. 251:4).

10. One must not give his money away to charity at the expense of creditors to whom he is indebted (*Sefer Chasidim* 454).

11. One should not give to charity a sum greater than a fifth of the value of his estate (*Ketubot* 50a).

This guideline was decreed by the Sanhedrin of Usha (2nd cent.) for fear that one who squanders his money may become a public burden. The fact that there was a need for such an enactment attests to the presence of a considerable number of people who were extremely generous.

12. A request for help to buy luxuries need not be honored (*Ketubot* 67a).

The Talmud recommends that poor people be helped to maintain the same standard of living they enjoyed prior to their improverishment (ibid.). Such idealism is adaptable only to individual or voluntary charity. Strict equality must be observed in the disbursement of public funds.

13. People who pretend poverty to qualify for charity rob the poor.

In the end such deceivers will be impoverished and come to depend on charity (*Ketubot* 68a).

14. The most menial work is preferable to charity (*Baba Kama* 110a).

15. Officials in charge of the distribution of charity must not favor their poor kin (*Yoreh Deah* 257:10).

Maimonides lists eight degrees of charity in a descending scale of their relative merits (*Mishneh Torah, Hilchot Matanot Aniyim* 10:7–14):

1. A loan or an offer of employment.
2. A donation of charity which leaves the identity of the recipient secret from the donor, and vice versa.
3. A donation which reveals the identity of the recipient but not of the donor.
4. A donation that reveals the identity of the donor but not of the recipient.
5. A contribution given without solicitation.
6. A contribution given in response to a solicitation.
7. A contribution smaller than what is warranted by the donor's wealth.
8. A contribution given grudgingly.

Compassion and Justice

Let thy tender mercies come unto me, that I may live.
—Psalm 119:77

COMPASSION IS a most appealing human trait. Without it, the hungry would be left to starve, the invalid to languish, and the sick to die.

The quality of mercy appears at an early age. The little girl who cries when she imagines her doll to be in pain sheds tears of compassion. The little boy who brings a crippled bird into his home for convalescence is moved by compassion. The soft-hearted teenager who turns over his week's allowance to the first pitiful beggar in the street has compassion flowing in his veins.

Youthful compassion is sentimental, unaffected by a sense of reality. The doll experienced no pain, the crippled bird might have been better off had it been left to its own devices, the beggar might have been the wrong person on whom to lavish one's allowance. Yet these reactions of merciful exuberance must never be ridiculed or stifled by parental admonitions. All these youngsters need is a mature appreciation of reality to mold their innate empathy into the constructive force which is the mainstay of civilized society. That will come with time.

The cultivation of the quality of mercy is a prime goal of Judaism. The Pentateuchal description of God's divine traits was revealed to Moses in the following words: "The Lord, the Lord God, merciful and gracious, long-suffering and abundant in goodness and truth; keeping mercy unto the thousandth generation, forgiving iniquity and transgression and sin" (Exod. 34:6–7). The phrase "merciful and gracious God" is repeated nine times in the Bible.

57

Most biblical social laws are motivated by compassion. Sympathy for the poor inspired thirteen distinct commandments which are broadly grouped under the heading of charity (*Mishneh Torah, Hilchot Matanot Aniyim*). The same motivation shaped the law of the sabbatical year, at which time the poor were given free access to the produce of the soil (Exod. 23:11). Consideration for the plight of the indigent enjoined the nightly restoration of a garment taken from a poor borrower in pledge for a loan. "For that is his covering, it is his garment for his skin; wherein shall he sleep? And it shall come to pass when he cries unto me, that I will hear, for I am gracious" (Exod. 22:26).

The widow and the orphan are repeatedly singled out in the Bible as a class deserving special consideration and sympathy (Exod. 23:21, Deut. 14:29). The alien, frequently the target of xenophobic prejudice, is protected by several laws based on mercy. "And a stranger shalt thou not wrong, neither shalt thou oppress him, for you were strangers in the land of Egypt" (Exod. 22:20). "The stranger that sojourns with you shall be unto you as the native among you, and thou shalt love him as thyself" (Lev. 20:34).

Handicapped people were treated as the rejects of society in the past, and their special needs were neglected. Their very helplessness invites criminals to perpetrate their mischief. The elderly are the most common victims of muggers. The same is true of the lame, the blind, and the slow-witted. Compassion for the incapacitated is the basis for the biblical injunction: "Thou shalt not curse the deaf, nor put a stumbling-block before the blind" (Lev. 19:14).

The apocryphal II Esdras summed up man's social obligations which are motivated by compassion: "Do right to the widow, judge for the fatherless, give to the poor, defend the orphan, clothe the naked, heal the broken and the weak, laugh not a lame man to scorn, defend the maimed, and let the blind man come into the sight of my clearness" (2:20–21).

The Bible mercifully extended its protection to the most lowly human being in ancient society, the slave. He must not be mistreated. He is entitled to a weekly day of rest (Exod.

20:10). A master's abuse of a slave, resulting in the loss of an eye or tooth, sets him free from bondage (Exod. 21:7).

Regard for animals is stressed in numerous biblical injunctions. This subject is discussed in detail in the essay entitled "Consideration for Animals."

The Prophets and the Hagiographa frequently refer to the theme of compassion and foreshadow ethical perceptions developed in talmudic literature a thousand years later. God is merciful to those who show mercy to others (II Sam. 22:26). God is merciful even to those who are undeserving of it (II Sam. 24:14, *Pesachim* 87b). However, the prophet Isaiah (8th cent. D.C.E.) warned that the incorrigibly wicked cannot appeal to God's mercies. "Therefore the Lord shall have no joy in their young men, neither shall he have compassion on their fatherless and widows; for everyone is ungodly and an evildoer" (10:16). Thus he echoed the warning of Moses of the dire consequences of a rebellion against God (Deut. 28:15–68). The prophet Habakkuk (ca. 7th cent. B.C.E.) appealed to God that compassion dominate his judgment even in time of anger and reproach (3:2).

The plea of Habakkuk is supported on a philosophical level in a psalmist's eloquent passage. Justice and mercy stem from the same source. Mercy must precede justice if the end of righteousness is to be properly served. God has the strength to inflict any punishment he desires, but strength may be used only to promote the cause of justice. "Thine is an arm with might; strong is thy hand and exalted is thy right hand. Righteousness and justice are the foundation of thy throne; righteousness and truth go before thee" (Ps. 89:14–15).

In another passage, the psalmist extols the broad sweep of God's mercy, which embraces all living creatures. "The Lord is good to all, and his tender mercies are over all his works" (Ps. 145:9).

The primacy of compassion in Judaism was elaborated in the Talmud. It is man's duty to be merciful because he is under an injunction to emulate the ways of God. "Just as he [God] is gracious and merciful, so you [man] must be gracious and merciful" (*Shabbat* 133b). Victims of assailants were urged to pray to God that he extend his mercy to the wrongdoers, even if the latter fail to beg foregiveness (*Tosefta, Baba Kama* 8). God is merciful even to those who are unworthy of it (*Berachot* 7a). Even when the Almighty is angry, he is moved by mercy (*Pesachim* 87b). The prophet Habakkuk's prayer that God's anger be tempered by mercy is reversed in a rabbinical allegory in which it is God who prays that mercy transcend his anger (*Berachot* 7a). It was the quality of mercy, which Moses demonstrated when he tended the flock of Jethro, that determined his fitness to become the shepherd of God's flock, the Children of Israel (*Shemot Rabbah* 2:2).

The talmudic amplification of biblical social laws reflected a progressive development of perceptions of compassion. A few examples will suffice to illustrate the whole range of its humanitarian legislation. The Bible enjoined the giving of charity. The Talmud ruled that the entrance to a home must remain unlocked so that beggars who come for help may gain easy admittance (*Baba Batra* 7b). The Bible enjoined fair treatment of a servant. The Talmud enhanced his privileges to the point where it had to admit that "he who acquires a Hebrew servant acquires a master over himself" (*Kiddushin* 22a).

The emphasis on compassion in everyday life, stressed at home, in the academy, and in the synagogal liturgy, had as its educational goal the building of human character. As a result, the quality of mercy became deeply rooted in the Jewish psyche. King David is alleged to have said: "This nation [Israel] is distinguished by three characteristics: They are merciful, bashful, and benevolent" (*Yevamot* 79a).

There are two grades of compassion, sentimental and rational. The former is motivated by pity, the latter by justice. It is the latter that is focal in Judaic ethical literature.

Sentimental compassion, excited by sensory perception, emerges in early life. The sight of pain, suffering, and tears inevitably stimulates a reaction of pity. The underdog syndrome is sure to evoke popular sympathy for the person who is outnumbered in a trial of strength. Kinship is another factor in assuring man's sentimental compassion for those who are close to him by bonds of blood and love.

Sentimental compassion is frequently misplaced and at best only transitory. An underdog deserves no sympathy if he was a bully when he had the upper hand. Compassion based on the sight of pain vanishes when the sufferer is no longer within range of vision. Mercy based on love for an individual is self-serving and lasts only so long as the love persists.

Rational compassion, on the other hand, stems from a conscious realization of the existence of a need or a wrong and a consequent commitment to offer help. In common parlance, it is a compassion that flows from the mind rather than the heart. Such commitments are noble and lasting.

People capable of sentimental compassion are not necessarily kind individuals. We have already noted that young children are prone to demonstrate a quality of mercy. Yet it is common knowledge that compassionate juveniles are also capable of indescribable cruelty. Ganging up on a young friend is a passionate pursuit of youngsters. Torture of animals is widespread among the young. Teasing and taunting is part of their daily routine. The Bible and the Talmud regard cruelty as the antonym of compassion (Jer. 6:23, *Sukkah* 14a). Yet, like good and evil, compassion and cruelty coexist in the human breast.

It is axiomatic that every human impulse can be made to serve a good purpose (*Berachot* 54a), not excluding hatred and harshness. Hate of crime is salutary. The withholding of pity from murderers is commendable. Indiscriminate compassion unwittingly rewards the criminal and punishes his victim. The biblical injunction "thine eye shall not pity him" (Deut. 13:9) is repeated many times to stress the necessity of acting mercilessly against criminals whose offenses are of major gravity.

An analysis of the concept of compassion in Judaism is incomplete without a discussion of the areas in which the Bible calls for stern justice. We must also explore such biblical injunctions as the expulsion of the indigenous Canaanites from Palestine and the eradication of the Amalekites, which appear unduly harsh by the standards of enlightened civilized behavior. Why does the Bible tolerate capital punishment and war? How does one explain the law of the blood-avenger (Num. 35:21) or the so-called lex talionis (Exod. 21:24)?

The answer to these questions rests on two assumptions. (1) Some biblical moral perceptions were not intended to establish a permanent norm of ethical behavior. They were merely responses to the temporary exigencies of a particular moment. (2) Biblical ethical values are expressed in terms comprehensible to primitive man, who was heir to long-established, ancient concepts of morality.

New ethical concepts, designed to raise the moral level of human behavior, can be effective only if they do no violence to the generally accepted values of society at any given stage of man's development. New stndards must be endowed with elasticity that permits them to keep pace with the growth and progress of civilization. This view is correlated to the talmudic maxim: "The Torah adopted language which is understandable to human beings" (Berachot 31b). In its broader connotation, the teaching of ethics was linked to man's capacity of understanding and acceptance. Each stage of human advancement permits an upgrading of moral perceptions by an evolutionary process.

The principle of the evolution of moral values is not inconsistent with the traditional tenet of the immutability of the Bible. A distinction must be drawn between biblical laws and biblical ethical perceptions. The former cannot be amended or abrogated to fit changing conditions. The only concession to a process of adaptation of legal provisions is the right of judicial review of the law, within the framework of prescribed rules of interpretation.

The principle of immutability precludes the use of allegorization, which divests a law of its literal meaning, or the use of rationalization, which declares a law inoperative under changed circumstances. Thus, for instance, one may not allegorize the prohibition of pork as a euphemistic admonition against being a swine at heart. Nor may one rationalize the prohibition as a precautionary health measure which has lost its force under modern sanitary conditions.

It is quite clear, however, that the tenet of immutability does not apply to moral perceptions. Thus the doctrine of the punishment of children for the sins of their fathers (Exod.

20:5), a practice common in ancient societies on the assumption that punishment of a child strikes at the father, was upgraded by the prophet Ezekiel, who stated: "Behold, all souls are mine; as the soul of the father, so also the soul of the son; the soul that sins, it shall die" (18:4). In the words of the Talmud: "Ezekiel came and annulled it" (the punishment of children; *Makkot* 24a).

There was no compelling need or reason for this talmudic statement. Ezekiel's doctrine could have been reconciled with the Pentateuchal pronouncement relating to the punishment of children by attributing to the prophet the talmudic opinion that limits the transfer of parental guilt only to children who persist in the sin of their ancestor (*Yoma* 68a). Furthermore, it is widely assumed that the Pentateuchal transfer of guilt is exclusive to the sin of idolatry. By the time of Ezekiel (6th cent. B.C.E.) idolatry was no longer a threat to monotheism (*Shir HaShirim Rabbah* 7:13). The prophet would therefore have been justified in reverting to the normal biblical standard of compassion and justice. The Talmud ignored these explanations and instead chose to establish the principle of an evolutionary process of moral precepts which gave the prophet the right to "annul" a Pentateuchal perception.

We may now proceed to examine the areas in which a biblically prescribed harsh treatment appears to be contrary to established principles of compassion. A survey reveals two distinct concerns of early Judaism. One was the survival of monotheism in an ocean of paganism. The other was the eradication of bloodshed in a primitive society where feuds were normally resolved by murder. In both of these areas the Bible demands strict justice untempered by mercy.

The promise of the Land of Canaan to the Children of Israel was contingent upon their acceptance of monotheism. Moses warned that the Canaanites must be expelled and their idols destroyed (Num. 33:52). Coexistence with the Canaanites, a morally corrupt people, would have aborted the growth of monotheism at its very inception. The harsh decree of expulsion was an emergency measure which did not establish an ethical norm. It was never applied to the pagans of other countries, for their practices posed no danger to the viability of monotheism in Palestine. Thus when the prophet Jonah rued God's willingness to forgive the Ninevites (4:2), God retorted: "Shall I not have compassion for Nineveh, that great city, wherein are more than sixscore thousand persons?" (4:11).

In every situation where idolatry threatened to weaken the will of the people to uphold monotheism, the Bible warned against permitting compassion to undermine the determination to uproot idolatry. This admonition was couched in the oft-repeated classical phrase: "Thine eyes shall not pity them" (Deut. 7:16). It applied equally to pagans and to backsliding Jews guilty of inciting the people to revert to idolatry (Deut. 13:9).

The same admonitory phrase was also used in the second area of concern, the protection of human life (Deut. 19:13, 21). The sanction of the death penalty as a deterrent against murder and other crimes did not violate biblical standards of morality. Indeed, no nation prior to the twentieth century expressed any misgivings about the propriety of capital punishment. Yet as far back as the sixth century B.C.E. the prophet Ezekiel alleged that God is averse to the death penalty. "Have I any pleasure at all that the wicked should die?, says the Lord God, and not rather that he should return from his ways and live?" (18:23).

Jurisdiction over capital punishment was taken away from the Jewish court by the Roman authorities in about the year 30. Yet, a century later, the rabbis continued to discuss the morality of the death penalty. Some of its opponents were undoubtedly influenced by the potential for judicial error. Others considered the taking of a life, even that of a convict, legal murder. Thus it was said that a Sanhedrin that sentenced a man to death once in seven years was called a "destructive" court. Rabbi Elazar b. Azariah (2nd cent.) said that the same was true of a court which issued a death sentence only once in seventy years. Rabbis Tarfon and Akiva (2nd cent.) said: "If we had been in the Sanhedrin no death sentence would ever have been passed" (*Makkot* 7a). Ostensibly, they would have accomplished this end by a thorough cross-examination of witnesses. They were obviously opposed to capital punishment on moral grounds. A dissenting opinion was offered by Rabban Simon b. Gamaliel, the religious and administrative head of the autonomous Jewish community. He was conscious of the need for a strong deterrent against crime, particularly that of murder. "If so, they [Tarfon and Akiva] would have multiplied murders in Israel" (ibid.).

The order to eradicate the ancient nation of Amalek (Exod. 17:14) was a unique and exceptional measure which did not establish a precedent. Its severity is justified in the Bible by an historical encounter in which the Amalekites were guilty of an unprovoked attack on the Hebrews, with the intent of committing genocide. There was no other explanation for the attack. Surely they were not motivated by considerations of self-defense or even by a desire to rob a neighboring nation of its land. There was to be no compassion for a people possessed of such irrational and pathological hatred.

Amalek was the ancient prototype of the modern Nazis, killers without any redeeming features. The ancient law of the eradication of the entire nation would surely be unacceptable under modern progressive standards. Yet the biblical admonition against mercy for Amalek is surely binding with regard to Nazis whose guilt has been proven. A rising demand for leniency toward criminals and forgiveness of their crimes does an injustice to the future of mankind. In a statement of profound insight, the rabbis alleged that a person who is moved to express pity for cruel people will in the end adopt some of their cruel traits.

The desire to eradicate bloodshed was paradoxically responsible for the biblical tolerance of the institution of the blood-avenger. A blood-avenger was an heir of a victim of murder who considered it his duty to avenge the death of his kin by killing the murderer (Num. 35:19). This practice most likely originated in the distant past prior to the establishment of competent criminal courts. Avenging a kin's death was a debt of honor. There were also some who believed that the victim's soul would find no rest unless the killer was destroyed.

Moved by such emotional considerations, a blood-avenger

would neither understand nor comply with any law which attempted to suppress his right to avenge his kin's death. The Bible intimates that God took into consideration the "heat of anger" of an avenger (Deut. 19:6). The practice was therefore left undisturbed by the Pentateuch, in the words of Maimonides, "in its great zeal to eradicate bloodshed" (*Mishneh Torah, Hilchot Rotzeach* 1:4). However, the Bible imposed limitations on the avenger's right to take the law into his own hands. Thus, while tolerating the practice, it practically eliminated it. The avenger was permitted to catch the killer, but he could not execute him until such time as the suspect was convicted by a court (Num. 35:12). In the event that the homicide was unintentional, the killer was granted sanctuary in cities of refuge (Num. 35:11). In time, the law of the avenger became obsolete.

The lex talionis ("eye for an eye") has been singled out as a classical example of biblical harshness. The criticism of this law that appears in the New Testament (Matt. 5:38–42) has given it a wide prominence which no anti-Pentateuchal polemicist has dared ignore.

It is incontrovertible that the mutilation of a human body is repugnant to modern minds. Yet, even while rejecting the practice of an eye for an eye, the law of a life for a life was never put in question by critics of the lex talionis. Is the taking of a life less cruel than the taking of an eye? Is capital punishment more acceptable because the executed criminal is buried and forgotten, while a maimed criminal survives as a visible monument to society's barbarism?

Was the lex talionis ever practiced in ancient Israel? The answer is no. Ancient Middle Eastern nations supported the lex talionis as a punishment which fits the crime. The Babylonian and Assyrian codes approved of it. The inclusion of this law in the Pentateuch (Exod. 21:24) did not shock the ancient Hebrew. On the contrary, its omission would have puzzled him. However, while the law was left intact, it was, to all intents and purposes, voided by an alternative option, the payment of damages, which was the case in all tort actions.

The provision for the payment of damages was attached to the law prescribing the punishment of the owner of a goring ox which killed a human being. The owner's negligence carried the death penalty (Exod. 21:29). However, he was permitted to redeem his life by the payment of damages (Exod. 21:30). That the alternative of payment of damages applied to all cases of tort is made clear in Numbers (35:31), which singles out murder as a crime that cannot be expiated by the payment of damages.

The sequence of the sentences in Exodus pertaining to the punishment of the owner of a goring ox sheds light on the ancient procedure of criminal courts in such cases. First there was a pronouncement of the sentence of death. The sentence was then commuted upon payment of damages. This procedure served to emphasize society's moral outrage at the negligence of the owner.

A similar procedure was undoubtedly followed in an action against an assailant who caused the loss of a victim's eye. At first he was sentenced to lose his own eye, reflecting the enormity of the crime. The penalty was then remitted upon payment of damages. In time the first part of the procedure was eliminated because that penalty was never enforced.

There is no record in the Bible, Talmud, or other sources that the lex talionis was ever implemented even once. The talmudic rabbis cited many arguments in support of their view that the lex talionis was never intended to be taken literally (*Baba Kama* 83b). Divested of its literal meaning, the rabbis took the law as a moral condemnation of a cruel crime which deserves severe punishment. Ironically, the rule of conduct suggested in the New Testament in place of the lex talionis "Whosoever smites you on the right cheek, turn to him the other also," similarly cannot be taken literally but only as an expression of a moral perception. Judaism disagrees with this perception. As for those who take this maxim literally, few are known to have practiced it.

What is the biblical attitude to war? War brutalizes mankind. It inflicts suffering upon innocent people. Military rules brook no compassion. Whatever justification warrants self-defensive wars does not apply to aggresssive wars. The biblical attitude to such wars must once again be judged within the framework of mankind's attitude to war in the time of Moses.

To ancient man war was as natural as farming, hunting, and fishing. The prohibition of murder, in itself a radical departure from the law of the jungle, was never logically extended to racial or tribal wars, which have enjoyed a legitimacy of their own. The annihilation of vanquished nations, the enslavement of their women and children, and the appropriation of their property were always considered the undisputed right of the victor. A biblical prohibition of war would have appeared as incomprehensible and unacceptable as a prohibition of hunting and fishing. Yet the Bible intimated an intrinsic opposition to war by means of various regulations and ethical maxims.

The maxim "Love thy neighbor as thyself" (Lev. 19:19) is a moral goal which can be applied on a universal scale only when international peace prevails. The biblical exemptions from military service (Deut. 20: 5–8) are so comprehensive that full compliance with these regulations would render the raising of a large army a practical impossibility. The purpose of these exemptions was to limit the army to a small number of men whose confidence in combat would depend upon the benevolence of God rather than their physical might. Such men would be more likely to avoid cruelties which are offensive to God. Furthermore, small armies do not readily rush into aggressive wars.

"Fearful and faint-hearted" men were among those who were exempted from serving in the army. In the opinion of one rabbi, the "fearfulness" was not based on cowardice but rather on an awareness of one's sinful life. (Deut., Sifre 112). This insightful comment reflects a true appreciation of the real intent of the Pentateuch, the exclusion of the rowdy element which is likely to lower the moral standard of an army. This aim was clearly spelled out in the Deuteronomic verse: "Justice, justice you should pursue, in order that you may keep alive and take possession of the land which God, your Lord, is giving you" (16:20).

The Bible placed limitations upon the scope of war and its destructiveness. "When thou drawest nigh unto a city to fight against it, then proclaim peace unto it" (Deut. 20:10). Even under conditions of war, care must be taken not to destroy natural resources essential to life (Deut. 20:19).

A moral condemnation of war was inherent in the prohibition of the use of metal tools in the construction of the sanctuary's altar (Exod. 20:25). The use of a chisel, an implement of war, would profane the altar, a symbol of peace and reconciliation. King David was not authorized to build a temple in Jerusalem because "thou hast shed blood abundantly and hast waged great wars" (I Chron. 22:8).

An idealized picture of an era of lasting peace, millennia ahead of its time, was drawn by prophets of the eighth century B.C.E. in poetic terminology which has not lost its force with the passage of time. "And he [God] shall judge between nations and shall decide for many peoples; and they shall beat their swords into plowshares and their spears into pruning forks; nation shall not lift up sword against nation, neither shall they learn war any more" (Isaiah 2:4).

The cessation of war will come when the discordant elements of mankind learn to live in unity and peace. This vision was expressed by Isaiah in the following allegory: "And the wolf shall dwell with the lamb, and the leopard shall lie down with the kid; and the calf and the young lion and the fatling together, and a little child shall lead them" (11:6). Isaiah's prophecy was echoed in almost identical words by his younger contemporary, the prophet Micah (4:3–4).

The dream of a messianic age emerged in the sixth century B.C.E. The prophet Zechariah envisioned it as an era of disarmament and peace when nations will be governed by law and not by the sword. "Not by might, nor by power, but by my spirit, says the Lord of hosts" (4:6). "And I will cut off the chariot from Ephraim, and the horse from Jerusalem, and the battle-bow shall be cut off, and he shall speak peace unto the nations" (9:10). In the view of Maimonides (12th cent.) the messianic era will not usher in a change in the order of nature, except that there will be neither famine nor war, neither rivalry nor contention (*Mishneh Torah, Hilchot Melachim* 12:5).

Needless to say, even in the messianic era there will be a great need for the quality of compassion. Its value, then as now, will depend on whether it is used to promote justice or to defeat it.

Compromise and Conciliation

Sweet language will multiply friends, and a fair-speaking tongue will increase greetings.

—Ecclesiasticus 6:5

THE CHOICE between conciliation and confrontation is open to every person embroiled in conflict. Those who truly seek conciliation must be ready to accept a compromise.

Conflicts are endemic to human life. Indeed, they are desirable in the early years of a child's growth. A ripening sense of ownership brings a child into conflict with his peers who attempt to divest him of favorite toys. In a subsequent stage of development, when a child begins to assert his rights, he will be in conflict with his parents. He may reject the diet offered by his mother or he may demand the privilege of a late bedtime granted to his older siblings. He will increasingly chafe at the regimen imposed by parental discipline.

Most early conflicts are transitory. They are useful indices of a child's mental growth and teach him the need for adjusting to situations which are not entirely to his liking.

Conflicts which arise in adult life are frequently intractable, enduring, and highly damaging. National and racial conflicts run deep and endanger the peace. Domestic conflicts undermine the family structure. Business transactions are rife with dissensions which fill the air with vituperation and clog judicial dockets. Disparaging remarks whispered in social circles lead to enmity and fisticuffs. Most destructive of all are conflicts born of prejudice. Lacking a rational basis, they are not amenable to rational resolutions.

70

Even reasonable and restrained individuals cannot avoid conflicts. Each party to a controversy is convinced of the justice of his case, a conviction which blinds him to the merit of his opponent's arguments. Few controversies fall within the category of a clearcut right versus an unquestioned wrong. In some instances, strife is the result of the collision of two well-established rights. In such cases, not even a King Solomon could come up with a fair solution.

When demands go unanswered, nations may resort to war and individuals may seek justice in the courts. Resolutions imposed by wars and courts inevitably aggravate the hostility between the parties. A test of strength proves who is stronger but not who is right. Defeated nations never concede that their cause has been unjust, and losing litigants continue to protest a miscarriage of justice.

Judaism, with all its reverence for the law, is nevertheless aware of its shortcomings. A second-century rabbi, wrestling with this problem, came to the conclusion that compromise by consensus is by far more preferable to imposed decisions dictated by the law, which grants all to the winner and nothing to the loser.

What appears to be the earliest recorded compromise is reflected in the biblical account of the shift from God's strict judgment prior to the Flood to a more yielding stance after the Flood. Initially, God was reported as saying, "The end of all flesh is come before me, for the earth is filled with violence through them, and behold I will destroy them with the earth" (Gen. 6:13). After the Flood, however, God said: "I will not again curse the ground on account of man, for the impulse of man's heart is evil from his youth" (Gen. 18:22). The Midrash reads into this verse a compromise which softened the original condemnation of mankind. God conceded that man was not entirely at fault. "If I had not created him with an evil impulse, he would not have rebelled against me" (*Bereshit Rabbah* 27).

It was in the second century that the merit of arbitration in preference to the law was hotly debated. Does a judge, before whom an action has been brought for legal adjudication, have the right to suggest that the dispute be arbitrated? Judaic laws are based on the Bible and hence are a part of the religion. To relegate the law to a secondary position might reflect on the fairness and wisdom of the divine judgment. Rabbi Eliezer insisted that the law must take its course, regardless of the consequences (*Sanhedrin* 6a).

Rabbi Joshua b. Kochba took the opposite view. He based his opinion on a verse in Zechariah: "Execute the judgment of truth and peace in your gate" (8:16). Commenting on the objective of truth and peace, he said: "When there is strict justice there is no peace, and where there is peace there is no strict justice. What is that kind of justice with which peace abides? We must say arbitration" (*Sanhedrin* 6b).

Conciliation is most successful in the early stages of a disagreement. What is needed is a willingness to engage in dialogue and an open mind. A person who refuses to discuss differences acts unethically.

When a next-door neighbor comes to your door to complain that your son's drum practice drives him up a wall, don't tell him to mind his own business and slam the door in his face. Invite him in and hear him out. You may discover that he has a just grievance and tell your son to tone down the percussion. In this manner your good-neighborly relations will not suffer. One moment of conciliation outweighs years of confrontation.

Confidence and Insecurity

I will fear no evil, for thou art with me.

—Psalm 23:4

CONFIDENCE, LIKE all human qualities, ranges from the maximal to the minimal. An overconfident person gives an appearance of bravery, but it is more appropriate to call it recklessness. An overcautious person gives an appearance of conservatism, but it is more appropriate to call it insecurity.

Religion inspires a confidence which stems from trust in God. Such trust may strengthen man's resolve to work harder in his endeavors, in the hope that God will bless his efforts. However, such confidence must not be used as a substitute for hard work or as a pretext for laziness. In the words of a talmudic epigram: "If a person fails to prepare his Sabbath meal before the Sabbath, what will he eat on the Sabbath?" (*Avodah Zarah* 3a).

Does a person who is given to worry about his future betray a lack of faith? Rabbi Elazar HaModai (2nd cent.) said: "He who has what to eat today and cries out, 'What will I eat tomorrow?', betrays a lack of faith" (*Mechilta, Beshalach* 2). Excessive worry will not provide the next day's meal, but it will make it impossible to enjoy today's meal.

The daily hazards facing ancient man normally produced a sense of deep concern for the future. Irresponsible people used the chaotic conditions as a pretext for merrymaking. "Let us eat and drink, for tomorrow we shall die" (Isa. 24:13). The rabbis, on the other hand, felt that the uncertainties of life and the high incidence of death should be used as a moral incentive against both excessive worry and its opposite extreme, overbearing confidence. "He who rejoices today may not be in a position to rejoice tomorrow, and he who is distressed today may no longer be distressed tomorrow" (*Tanchuma, Shemini* 2).

Bachya Ibn Pekuda, an eleventh-century moralist, elaborated on this theme. "He who has confidence in God and has his day's needs provided should not be overly concerned about his needs for the next day, for he does not know when his life's span will end. He should have faith that God will prolong his years and provide him with an adequate livelihood. The thought of death will also sharpen his concern for the moral standard of his conduct" (*Chovat HaLevavot, Shaar HaBitachon* 4).

A presumption of life is basic in talmudic law. Thus a man who was seen alive last year is presumed to be still alive this year. Morally, however, the rabbis stressed the possibility of death as an incentive to ethical conduct. Their objective was to promote self-reliance and bolster it with faith in divine assistance.

Modern man, enjoying unprecedented longevity, may find a consciousness of impending death morbid and depressing. The inculcation of morals by repeated reminders of man's mortality would prove counterproductive. It is not fear of death but respect for life that dictates the imperative of moral conduct. Religion, however, remains a vital factor in strengthening one's sense of security and confidence in the future.

A misconception of the true implication of trust in God may lead to unwarranted conclusions. Does confidence in God's protection justify the throwing of caution to the winds and the taking of unnecessary risks? The number of people who subscribe to such a belief is startling. The gullible foolishly repeat a stale slogan: "If my number is not up, nothing will happen to me." Exposing oneself to unnecessary danger is the surest way of hastening the moment when one's number will be called up.

Rabbi Moses Luzzatto, an eighteenth-century moralist, made the following succinct comment: "Man is warned against taking chances. There is confidence and there is folly. The Almighty endowed man with sense and logic to guide his conduct, to avoid harmful situations. . . . He who is reckless in facing danger does not demonstrate confidence but folly" (*Mesilat Yesharim* 9).

The degree of man's confidence or insecurity will depend upon previous experiences. A man who has never suffered privation will entertain a positive attitude of confidence. One who has experienced hardship will view his future with much anxiety. The Talmud illustrated this reaction with the following anecdote: A teacher walks into a classroom carrying a rod. The students take immedite note of what is in the teacher's hand. Which one of the students reacts with instant fear? The one who has been lashed in the past (*Sukkah* 29a).

Confidence is a quality which is to be commended, but overconfidence is to be deplored because it smacks of arrogance. There are people who are positive of their ability to accomplish everything they undertake, regardless of a record of previous failures. Such vanity is self-destructive. There are also people who have unlimited confidence in the perfection of their character and boast of a total immunity to evil influences. To them the rabbis addressed a strict warning: "Trust not in thyself til the day of thy death" (*Avot* 2:5); "Even for the righteous there can be no self-confidence, so long as he lives on earth" (*Bereshit Rabbah, Vayishlach* 76).

Rabbi Judah HeChasid (12th cent.) commented: "Do not be overconfident and claim that a minor transgression will not affect your character. In the end you will discover that minor transgressions invite major transgressions" (*Sefer Chasidim* 78).

Confidentiality

If thou hast opened thy mouth against thy friend, fear not, for there may be a reconciliation; except for upbraiding, or pride, or disclosing of secrets. . . . for these things every friend will depart.

—Ecclesiasticus 22:22

INDIVIDUALS PRIVY to a spicy bit of gossip, which is given confidentially to them, will seldom honor their promise to keep the news secret. Indeed, their breach of confidence is frequently committed with frivolous mischief. It is not that these talebearers are devoid of a sense of honor. It is only that they and their sources of information regard the request for confidentiality as a pro forma ritual which need not be taken seriously.

An addicted spreader of gossip may not be guilty of a breach of confidence; nonetheless his conduct is highly unethical. Judaism is critical of talebearing, even if the tale is common knowledge, and such practice is severely condemned in the Bible (Lev. 19:16).

In areas other than idle gossip, a breach of confidence is a major offense, potentially injurious to life and fortune. One who discloses the secret itinerary of an important official may expose him to the risk of an attack. Revelation of trade secrets may ruin a business. The same is true of many other situations in every walk of life.

Modern law recognizes the principle of confidentiality in relationships between clergymen and parishioners and attorneys and their clients. The law occasionally imposes secrecy on individuals who have access to sensitive information. Secrecy may also be self-imposed by contractual commitment.

However, in most instances a breach of confidence constitutes an ethical rather than a legal violation.

Judaism condemns breaches of confidence on several grounds. A person who agrees to a request for secrecy but never intends to honor his agreement brands himself a liar as soon as he proceeds to make a disclosure. According to the Bible: "Lying lips are an abomination of the Lord" (Prov. 12:22).

A person who was originally sincere in his acceptance of a pledge of secrecy but later changes his mind may not be a liar in the strict sense of the word, but he is guilty of unethical conduct. A breach of promise is a violation of the spirit of the biblical injunction: "That which is gone out of thy lips thou shalt observe and do" (Deut. 23:24). The Talmud holds that a breach of promise is as serious an offense as idolatry (Sanhedrin 92a).

As we mentioned before, a breach of confidence may lead to very serious consequences. A person who fails to take such an eventuality into account is surely acting contrary to the biblical injunction: "Love thy neighbor as thyself" (Lev. 19:18).

Lastly, an individual who fails to honor a pledge of secrecy is guilty of being a dissimulator and a deceiver. He masks his hostile actions with a pretense of friendship. The apocryphal Ecclesiasticus warns against glib acceptance of an individual's assurances unless he is known to be trustworthy. "If thou wouldst get a friend, prove him first, and be not hasty to credit him" (6:7).

The preservation of confidentiality took on a new dimension under a ruling of Rabbah (3rd–4th cent.). In his opinion, information received from a second party, even when not labeled confidential, may not be repeated to other parties without explicit instruction or permission of the informant (Yoma 4b). Rabbi Judah HeChasid (12th cent.) urged people to refuse to receive confidential information as a precaution against involvement in unlawful or unethical conduct.

Some promises are expressly or by implication contingent upon the maintenance of secrecy. Individuals who assume personal or financial obligations for the benefit of another party may occasionally insist, for reasons of their own, that the beneficiary refrain from making the arrangement public. In the event that the beneficiary disregards the pledge of secrecy, the benefactor is freed from any moral obligation to fulfill his promise. This is the clear implication of the biblical account of Joshua's scouts. The scouts, on a spying mission in Jericho, found shelter in the home of Rahab. As her reward, the lady demanded that the scouts take an oath that in the event of hostilities her life and that of her family would be spared. The scouts took the oath but insisted on secrecy and added the following warning: "If you disclose our words we will be released from the oath which you made us swear" (Josh. 2:20).

Despite the rigidity of the prohibition of breaches of confidence, common sense dictates the allowance of discretion if the benefit of disclosure clearly outweighs the moral imperative of preserving secrecy. A person who receives confidential information of a potential danger due to the faulty construction of a building is duty bound to breach the confidence. The same is true if an informant demands secrecy because he is trying to hide a criminal intent or act.

Consideration for Animals

Should I not have pity on Nineveh, that great city, wherein are more than sixscore thousand persons . . . and also much cattle?

—Jonah 4:11

JUDAISM HAS always manifested a humane attitude to animals. This attitude is inherent in the biblical account of the creation of living creatures: "God saw that it [the emergence of animals] was good. And God blessed them" (Gen. 1:21–22). The act of blessing is an expression of care, concern, and love.

Animals were placed in "subjection" to man (Gen. 1:26). Their subordinate position granted man the right to domesticate them, to use them as beasts of burden, and to derive whatever benefits are beneficial to him. However, man's sovereign power did not give him a license to mistreat or torment helpless creatures. Indeed, according to the Talmud, man was initially barred from using animals as a source of food, a right granted only after the Flood (*Sanhedrin* 59b).

The significance of God's "blessing" of animals was lost upon primitive man. Living creatures were subjected to torture in superstitious rites designed to propitiate evil spirits. Cruelty to animals did not provoke any objection or protest.

Biblical intimations of a loving relationship between God and all living creatures had a profound influence upon the universalist poetic creativity of the psalmists. God's promise to provide food for all creatures (Gen. 1:30) inspired the psalmists' depiction of beasts looking to heaven for their subsistence. "The maned young lions are roaring for prey and seek their food

79

from God" (Ps. 104:21). "Living creatures, small as well as great, . . . all of them wait for you to give them their food in due season." (Ps. 104:24, 27). The psalmists lauded God for his kindness to animals by providing their food. "He is making green grass sprout forth for the beasts" (Ps. 104:14). "He gives to the beast his food, and to the young ravens which cry" (Ps. 147:9). "He extends help to man and beast" (Ps. 36:7). In the psalmists' rich poetic imagery, the earth and all creatures are inspired by God's munificence and utter paeans of praise to him (Ps. 148).

Ecclesiastes took note of an unorthodox view current in his time, placing man and animal on the same level. "Man has no preeminence above a beast. . . . Who knows the spirit of man, whether it goes upward, and the spirit of the beast, whether it goes downward to the earth?" (Eccles. 3:19, 21). Such speculation, even if unorthodox, demonstrated a prevailing tendency to find a common denominator between all living beings. Such a trend could not but generate a feeling that man's concern for the welfare of man must also be extended to animals. Hence the assertion in the Book of Proverbs: "A righteous man is considerate of the life of his beasts" (12:10).

The rabbis pointed to God's kindness to animals as a model for man to follow. "Just as the Almighty is merciful to man, so is he merciful to animals" (*Tanchuma, Noah* 5). "He who shows mercy to animals will receive mercy from God" (*Shabbat* 151b).

Kindness to animals was considered the ultimate test of a noble character. Rebecca's fitness to be the wife of Isaac was proven by her offer to fetch water for Abraham's emissary, Eliezer, and for his thirsty camels (Gen. 24:20). Moses proved himself qualified to lead the Jewish people by demonstrating his tender care for the sheep in his herd (*Shemot Rabbah* 2).

Rabbi Judah HaNasi (2nd cent.), the eminent editor of the Mishnah, was once afflicted with a painful illness. After a prolonged period of distress, the sickness finally disappeared. A talmudic anecdote seeks to shed light on the background of this painful episode. It seems that a calf, which was being led by a butcher to an abattoir, tore loose and ran to Rabbi Judah

HaNasi, who had witnessed this scene, as if to plead for his protection. The rabbi looked at the calf and commented: "Go, my little creature. This is what you were created for." Heaven was displeased with his callousness and inflicted a punishment upon him. Years later, the rabbi stopped his maid from sweeping out some young weasels which she had discovered in his study. "We must be mindful," he said, "of the biblical verse 'and his [God's] mercies are over all his works' [Ps. 145:9]." Heaven took note of his concern for the weasels and decreed an end to his illness (*Baba Metzia* 85a).

Biblical consideration for animals was the basis for the following laws:

1. A passer-by who comes across a fallen beast of burden, which is unable to rise due to its heavy load, must stop to help unload the burden (Exod. 23:5).

The Talmud bases this injunction on the broad principle of prevention of pain to animals (*tzaar baalei chaim; Baba Metzia* 32b). Medical research on animals was exempted by the medieval rabbis from the restrictions of this principle (Rema, *Even HoEzer* 5:14). Hunting as a sport, not for the purpose of procurement of food, is considered cruel and sinful (*Avodah Zarah* 18b).

2. Animals must be permitted to forage for food in fields and farms which lie fallow in a sabbatical year (Exod. 23:11).

3. Beasts of burden, like human beings, must be permitted to rest on the Sabbath (Exod. 23:12).

4. A mother animal and its young may not be slaughtered on the same day (Lev. 22:28). Rabbi Aaron of Barcelona (13th cent.) explained this restriction as follows: "The purpose of this injunction is to instill in our character the quality of mercy and to remove ourselves from cruelty" (*Sefer HaChinuch* 294). To permit an animal to witness the killing of its young is an act of gross cruelty.

5. It is forbidden to remove a mother bird simultaneously with its fledglings or eggs from a nest. The mother bird must be sent away to spare it the sight of the taking of its young (Deut. 22:6).

6. Animal meat processed for food may be eaten only when

the animal was slaughtered in accordance with the law of ritual slaughtering, known as *shechitah* (traditional interpretation of *vezovachto,* Deut. 12:21).

Proper *shechitah* requires the cutting of the windpipe and gullet. The knife must be honed sharp and be free of any notches and indentations to prevent ripping of the throat. These precautions are essential to the minimizing of pain.

7. Animals of different species may not be harnessed together to form a team for the performance of labor (Deut. 22:10).

Rabbi Aaron of Barcelona (13th cent.) asserts that the teaming up of animals of different species, which do not normally mingle and are possessed of disparate traits, is an unnatural act highly distressful to them (*Sefer HaChinuch* 550). He bases this injunction on a broad-based principle which is equally applicable to human associations. Incompatible partners cannot conduct a successful business. For the same reason, committees composed of incompatible members will not function properly. He cautions against associating men of education, integrity, and reasonableness with individuals who lack these qualities.

8. An animal which works in an operation that exposes it to food which is eaten by animals must not be muzzled (Deut. 25:4). In such circumstances, the prevention of the animal from eating is an act of cruelty. Josephus (1st cent.) places this injunction on a moral plane of equity and fairness. "It is not just to restrain our fellow-laboring animals . . . of the fruit of their labor" (*Antiq.* 4:8).

The required degree of animal care reached a noble dimension in rabbinic literature. It is forbidden to buy animals or fowl unless preparation of food for their sustenance has been made in advance. (Jer. *Yevamot* 15:3). Rav (3rd cent.) is the author of a rule which stipulates that owners must feed their animals first before sitting down to enjoy their own meals (*Berachot* 40a). It is important to bear in mind that Rav's rule applies exclusively to owners, since they bear a responsibility for the feeding of their cattle. No such preference is proper when one has to satisfy the needs of a hungry guest and his hungry animal. The interest of man must precede that of an animal.

The major concern for the welfare of man has led the rabbis to discourage the raising of dogs. A dog which attacks or frightens strangers will inevitably deter the poor from entering a home for the purpose of soliciting charity or help (*Shabbat* 63a). For the same reason the rabbis urged that all dogs be kept on a leash (*Baba Kama* 79b).

Contentiousness

A fool's lips enter into contention.

—Proverbs 18:6

ENCOUNTERS WITH contentious individuals are highly irritating experiences which one is best advised to avoid. Of course, that is more easily said than done. One meets them in the street, at one's place of work, at lecture halls, at organizational meetings, and at social gatherings.

A contentious person is a highly opinionated human being who takes joy in forcing his views on everyone else. He tolerates no dissent. The hardy and the brave who insist on their right to independence of judgment are belittled, humiliated, and shouted down.

It is futile and foolish to attempt to debate an issue with a contentious person. He will compulsively take the opposite stand, not out of a conviction of the merit of his opinion but solely to proclaim his opponent wrong. His method of persuasion is based on physical forcefulness and intimidation which compensate for a lack of information and common sense.

Weaklings, who dread the onslaught of the contentious, meekly surrender to their aggressiveness for fear of becoming targets of attacks. Thus they become followers and accomplices, creating a clique manipulated by the ringleader. As a result of such submission, a disruptive and divisive element, harmful to social harmony, is foisted upon the community.

What motivates the contentious who thrive on strife and relish a feud? The author of Proverbs addresses himself to this question and lists three distinct motivations.

The first anlaysis attributes the instigation of controversy to the trait of arrogance. "By pride comes only contention" (Prov.

13:10). According to this view, the arrogant feed their egos by seizing opportunities for demonstrating their superiority. To this end they employ scorn and contempt to demolish their opponents. The author of Proverbs offers some practical advice for those who prefer to steer clear of contention. When an argumentative person, bent on strife, joins an organization, expel him so that the ethical stance of the group may be maintained. To quote his concise text: "Cast out the scorner and contention will go out" (Prov. 22:10).

The second analysis attributes contentiousness to an angry disposition. People filled with rage release their fury in heated discussions. They welcome controversy for its opportunity to vent their anger. In the words of the biblical text: "A wrathful man stirs up discord; but he that is slow to anger appeases strife" (Prov. 15:18).

The third analysis attributes contentiousness to folly. "It is an honor for a man to keep aloof from strife, but every fool will be snarling" (Prov. 20:3). A fool assumes that verbosity reflects wisdom. For such fools the author of Proverbs has the following advice: "Go not forth hastily to strive, lest you know not what to do in the end thereof, when thy neighbor has put thee to shame" (Prov. 25:8).

When contentiousness enters the halls of an academy, scholarship suffers. Selfish ambitions warp one's judgment and generate debates colored by self-interest, jealousy, and vindictiveness. In reflecting upon the two rival rabbinical schools of Shammai and Hillel (1st cent.), the Talmud welcomed their initial emergence as a contribution to the understanding of the Torah. However, "when the disciples of Shammai and Hillel multiplied and were infiltrated by students who were not adequately versed in knowledge, Israel and the Torah became like two distinct Torahs" (*Sotah* 47b). In a similar vein of criticism, Rabbi Judah (2nd cent.) barred his academy to disciples of Rabbi Meir "because they are disputatious and do not come to learn Torah" (*Nazir* 49b).

Contentment and Discontent

A contented heart makes a cheerful countenance.
—Proverbs 15:13

CONTENTMENT IS craved by all but attained by few. Causes of discontent, dormant at times, are easily activated by circumstances over which man has little control.

Is it possible to ignore disturbing factors and to retain one's peace of mind in spite of them? Theologians and philosophers have maintained that happiness is a state of mind which responds to man's control through self-discipline. Unfortunately, most people find that oppressive problems cannot be wished away by verbal command or mental resolve.

To meet the craving for contentment, chemical tranquilizers fill our medicine chests. They temporarily anesthetize man's sensitivities but in the end destroy his will and ability to solve his problems. Our bookshelves also display popular literary tranquilizers which promise to palliate human anxieties by means of inspirational thoughts and soothing words. "Laugh your way to good health" is a popular recipe recommended by many humorists. Regretfully, depressions powdered over with flakes of humor will emerge with greater force before the last chuckle has vanished.

"Count your blessings" is a course greatly urged by solicitous preachers and authors. It is noble to count one's blessings because it teaches man the virtue of gratitude. As for inducing perpetual contentment, it is an impotent psychological placebo. People who have occasion to visit hospital wards filled with moribund patients frequently emerge with a renewed sense of appreciation of their own state of health. Many react with a resolve to feel contented ever after. Such a resolve, however, generally evanesces before one reaches the portals of his home. All the "blessings" in the world are incapable of canceling out a single "curse" which troubles one's mind. A localized toothache cannot be dismissed by the knowledge that the rest of the body is in fine shape.

A failure to attain full contentment, however, does not hamper one's ability to allay discontent. Whenever the causes of distress are identifiable, one must do his utmost to remove them in toto or in part. One may also ease his stress by learning to accept conditions which cannot be remedied but with which one can live.

There are major categories of causes which rob man of his contentment. Among these are poor health, grief, deprivation, displeasure with one's failure to have fully developed one's potential for success, and discord. Even fortunate individuals who are free from the above-listed distressing conditions do not necessarily generate a positive feeling of contentment. There is a tendency to become inured to one's happy state and to take it all for granted. The state of contentment is based on a constant awareness of one's good fortune. This is where the advice to count one's blessings is most effective.

The realities of life rarely follow the pattern of fairy tales, wherein the good people live happily ever after. Aggravations of one kind or another are endemic to human existence in the course of a lifetime. The success of one's quest for relief will depend on the strength of one's character and the nature of the sources responsible for the distress.

Physical pain and invalidity are primary causes of discontent. Pious people of most creeds find comfort in the belief that suffering atones for sins. This view is also prevalent in Judaism (*Yoma* 86a, *Avodah Zarah* 4a). Some individuals of exceptional zeal have even cherished their pain and rejoiced in it (*Sanhedrin* 101a). The Dead Sea Scriptures boldly proclaim: "I accept thy judgment and am content with my affliction" (Book of Hymns, chap. 9). Yet most people, even among the pious, rarely feel that their belief is an adequate compensation for suffering and pain. So eminent a sage as Rabbi Yochanan (3rd cent.) was frank to admit that he would rather forgo pain and its celestial rewards (*Berachot* 5b). People who suffer pain have an ethical right to express their discontent.

Minor pain, which man learns to live with, is effectively allayed by mental distraction. An absorbing hobby, an interesting book, or a good artistic performance will allow one to forget his discontent and produce a sense of contentment. People engaged in creative work derive an enjoyment which makes them immune to some irritants. Rabbi Joshua b. Levy (3rd cent.) listed various categories of pain which are eased by engaging in the study of Torah (*Eruvin* 54a).

Grief is a serious cause of discontent. The loss of a dear one leaves a scar which is never wholly healed. Pious people take refuge behind Job's classical exclamation: "The Lord gave and the Lord has taken away; blessed be the name of the Lord" (Job 1:21). Yet such submission to a superior power is of little comfort to the average religious person. The distressing question "Why me?" usually goes unanswered. Even Job in his agony articulated his doubts with the question: "Wherefore do the wicked live, become old, yea wax mighty in power?" (Job 21:7).

Most people learn to accept a loss after time has had an opportunity to heal the wound. Judaism considers mourning a legitimate expression of one's discontent and a mark of honor for the dead. However, it sets limitations to the period of mourning and regards excessive grief beyond that time as improper and sinful (*Moed Katan* 27b).

Deprivation is another cause of discontent. An inability to provide the higher standard of living enjoyed by many other people results in great unhappiness. This is particularly true of individuals who stress material values. In contrast, those who deliberately choose fulfillment in public service or a religious calling are contented despite their sacrifice of a higher standard of living.

Similarly, people who dedicate their lives to creative scholarship feel amply compensated for their loss of many comforts. Thus the ancient rabbis said: "This is the way that is becoming for the study of Torah; a morsel of bread thou shalt eat, and water by measure thou must drink. . . . If you live thus, happy shalt thou be" (*Avot* 6:4). In a similar vein they redefined wealth: "Who is rich? He who rejoices in his portion" (*Avot* 4:1).

Even those whose modest earnings are derived from work which does not serve ideological ends find contentment in the pride they take in earning a livelihood by hard labor and uncompromised integrity. This consideration is emphasized in the Book of Proverbs: "Better little with the fear of the Lord, than great treasure and turmoil therewith" (Prov. 15:16).

A feeling of guilt for having failed to develop one's full potential is a common source of discontent. Those who blame others for their own shortcomings are indeed doomed to a lifetime of discontent. Those who blame themselves may find ultimate contentment after a reassessment of their potential. An individual whose career falls short of his original expectation need not reproach himself if the disappointment is not due to his own neglect. All that we may expect of any individual is that he do his best, no more and no less.

Discord, domestic or otherwise, is an irritant as grievous as pain. Fortunately one can do much to remove this cause of discontent. If his manner and character are at fault, he must make amends and change. If another party is at fault and his remonstrances are not heeded, he can physically remove himself from the source of discord. The Bible describes in great detail the discord sowed by Korah due to his jealousy of Moses. When all attempts at reconciliation failed, an order was issued to the people: "Depart from the tents of these wicked men" (Num. 16:26). A physical departure may restore contentment.

Curiosity

Be not curious in unnecessary matters.

—Ecclesiasticus 3:23

NO ONE is free from curiosity, but everyone is capable of controlling it. Rumor has it that women are more prone than men to be inquisitive. This is not a scientifically established fact. Curiosity is mainly aroused when one's interests may be affected by the desired information. Women, to a greater extent than men, are sensitive to changing life-styles, and have a greater reason to be curious about new fashions, new decorating ideas, and new recipes. It was with a bit of amusement that an ancient rabbi noted that "a woman will lift the cover of her neighbor's pot to see what she is cooking" (Tosefta, *Taharot* 8).

It is not unethical to experience curiosity when one's interests are involved. An applicant for a job is justly curious when his interviewer whispers something to his secretary. Hosts at a party, whose guests whisper to one another when the main course is served, have cause to be curious. A woman who admires a friend's dress, which was moderately priced, has a right to be curious where the dress was bought.

There are curiosities which should be suppressed because the individual who seeks to ferret out the information has no personal interest in it. "I wonder whether Joe and Jane are as affectionate at home as they appear to be in public?" "I wonder whether X and Y are having an affair?" "I wonder whether Joe is telling the truth about his health?" The answer to all these questions is: "Mind your own business."

Generally, people should not be faulted for expressing curiosity. Indeed, there are occasions when curiosity is desirable. It is essential to the learning process of young children. Par-

90

ents, likewise, should be curious to know what their children are doing. Teachers should be curious about the progress of their students. The police should be curious about the whereabouts of criminals, and so on. It is the manner in which one proceeds to obtain secret information, to which he is not entitled in the first place, that should be faulted. One who tries to pry secret information from a young child, a naive relative, or a gossipy neighbor is reprehensible.

Private conversations and family secrets are private property which belong exclusively to their owners. If they wanted to share their secrets with other people, they would have made them public. Any use of devious methods to violate an individual's privacy is the moral equivalent of trespass and burglary.

According to Rabbi Judah HeChasid, the twelfth-century moralist, one should refrain from questioning people about matters which they prefer to keep secret. Although such an approach is open and aboveboard, he objects to it for the following reason. "If you notice people whispering to one another, and you are curious to know what they are whispering about, do not ask them directly. If they are determined to keep their conversation secret, you will force them to tell a lie" (*Sefer Chasidim* 1062). The inquisitive person thus compounds his wrong by forcing other people to commit another wrong.

Disclosure of Source of Information

And she [Esther] reported in the name of Mordecai.
—Esther 3:22

AUTHORS, INVENTORS, and scientists, people in government, the professions, and the business world, owe much of their success to the ideas of predecessors in their fields. This is what education is all about. If each generation were to start from scratch, civilization would still be in its primitive stage. True wisdom, said Ben Zoma (2nd cent.), "is the ability to learn from all men" (*Avot* 4:1). How does one who possesses such wisdom acknowledge his indebtedness to all the men from whom he has learned? Ben Zoma does not discuss this question in his maxim.

Men of wisdom do not always have a forum for acknowledging their indebtedness. Authors, however, have little excuse for withholding acknowledgments. The preface is an appropriate place for such disclosures. The same is true of speakers, who can easily give recognition in their introductory remarks.

Audiences and the reading public are not overly concerned about originality. Speakers who are widely known to make use of ghost writers receive unstinting adulation. A popular book appears on the market and gains instantaneous acclaim. The author gets effusive praise and acquires fame and fortune. This is his just desert. Any speculation about the sources of information from which an author draws his inspiration is left to literary critics. They are the ones who are aware that literature is not created in an intellectual vacuum.

Is an author morally obligated to trace in his preface the

numerous influences which have shaped his perceptions? This is hardly a reasonable demand. Subtle and indirect factors constantly affect the subconscious human mind and remain forever hidden in obscurity.

There are, however, intellectual communications which are open and obvious. A scientist who bases his results on principles enunciated by others, a novelist who consciously patterns his plot along lines developed by others, a composer who knowingly adopts themes of great musicians—have an obligation to give credit where credit is due. Needless to say, one who lifts other people's statements without framing them in quotation marks is guilty of fraud. It is to prevent such deception that laws against plagiarism have been enacted in all civilized countries.

The failure to give proper acknowledgment was regarded by the talmudic rabbis as a more serious offense than a mere breach of ethics. They branded such dishonesty as moral theft. In modern times there is a common realization that intellectual creativity is a highly prized financial asset. Appropriation of someone else's words and thoughts is easily recognized as an act of theft. In ancient times there were no copyrights, and literary production brought no financial rewards. Authors often preferred anonymity and not infrequently attributed their own works to better-known writers. Yet even under those conditions the rabbis had the insight to regard the absence of proper accreditation as the equivalent of moral theft.

Their perception of intellectual thievery was based on a verse in Proverbs: "Rob not the poor because he is poor" (22:22). The text would have made more sense had it admonished against robbing the rich because he is rich. What possession does a poor man own to tempt a robber to commit his crime? The rabbis accordingly interpreted the "rob" and the "poor" in Proverbs as a reference to the robbing of the intellect of a wise man. Biblical moralist literature identifies the wise man as a poor man (Eccles. 14:15).

In addition to the condemnation of the robbing of wisdom as theft, the rabbis also pointed out the practical benefits which the public may derive from the disclosure of sources. This lesson is germane to the story of the Book of Esther. Mordecai saved the life of King Ahasuerus. Esther reported the incident to the king and gave Mordecai his due credit. This information was eventually responsible for the king's show of gratitude to Mordecai, and the ultimate downfall of Haman. Hence, said the rabbis: "He who quotes a source and gives credit to the author brings redemption to the world" (*Megillah* 15a).

The corroborating events in ancient history, proving the value of the disclosure of sources, are duplicated in modern history. High public officials are occasionally appointed on the basis of the views they have expressed in various articles. It is critically important to know whether such articles reflect creative originality or merely a parroting of other people's ingenuity.

The ethical imperative of assigning credit to those who deserve it is not confined to people in artistic and academic circles alone. It comes into play every time an individual is complimented for a deed or choice for which someone else should get the credit. An ethical person should decline the compliment and address it to the one who deserves it. The same is true of a person who repeats in public a story or an opinion heard from a friend. The friend should be identified if he is known to the audience.

Drunkenness

Wine is a scorner, strong drink is riotous, and whosoever reels thereby is not wise.

—Proverbs 20:1

THE TRAGIC consequences of intoxication are depicted in the biblical account of Noah's life. The Flood had purged the world of its corruption, and to Noah was assigned the task of resettling the earth. He foolishly began the process of reconstruction by planting a vineyard. Savoring the fruit of his labor, he fell into a stupor. His youngest son, Ham, saw his intoxicated father and committed a vile act. The cycle of corruption thus started all over again.

Wine consumed in moderation is salutary, in excess, destructive. This dilemma has faced mankind ever since Genesis. Is the willpower of the average man strong enough to limit his drinking habit short of intoxication? The widespread prevalence of alcoholism proves that a considerable number of people lack such willpower.

Should society outlaw liquor for the sake of the weak and dissolute? Past experiments with legal prohibition of liquor have failed to attain the desired results. Islam has used the force of religion to impose abstention from liquor. Judaism has relied on moral persuasion to convince people of the wisdom of moderation. The fact that alcoholism was practically nonexistent in traditional Jewish society demonstrates the effectiveness of its policy.

The Bible does not ban the drinking of wine. Indeed, wine was used in the ritual libations of the Temple altar. The practice of using wine in the ritual of sanctification of the Sabbath and holidays was instituted by the rabbis in the first century (*Pesachim* 107a).

Wine's potential as a tranquilizer was highly valued in ancient society. The psalmist praised God for creating "the vine that makes glad the heart of man" (Ps. 104:15). Wine was served to mourners in their agony of bereavement (*Pirkei deRabbi Eliezer* 17). There was also a common belief that wine possessed medicinal properties. Samuel (3rd cent.) recommended the drinking of wine for the restoration of one's vigor after a blood-letting (*Shabbat* 124a). Rabbi Joshua b. Levi (2nd cent.) considered wine beneficial for lactation (*Ketubot* 65a).

Up until the destruction of the Second Temple (70 C.E.), mainstream Judaism, as well as its sectarian offshoots, did not favor temperance. There were a few notable exceptions. A Nazirite was forbidden to drink wine (Num. 6:3). This prohibition was inherent in the naziritic vow. The rabbis were not sympathetic to Nazirism and its ascetic leanings. They considered the self-imposed abstention from wine an unnecessary affliction (*Nedarim* 10a).

Priests under the influence of wine were forbidden to perform ritual functions in the Temple (Lev. 10:9). This prohibition was carried over by the rabbis into the post-Temple era with regard to priests who pronounce the Priestly Benediction in a synagogal service (*Taanit* 26a). For obvious reasons, judges who preside over judicial proceedings were similarly barred from drinking wine (*Eruvin* 64a).

Except for the above-listed prohibitions, there was no movement in ancient Israel favoring total abstention from liquor. Even the austere followers of the Qumran sect served wine at their communal dinner table (*Manual of Discipline* 6). A few isolated voices in opposition to the drinking of wine based their views on the need for teaching frugality to the young (*Chulin* 84a).

The main effort of the religious leadership was directed toward a campaign against excessive drinking. While the beneficial qualities of wine were extolled, its potential harm was strongly emphasized. "Wine measurably drunk and in season brings gladness to the heart and cheerfulness of the mind; but wine drunk with excess makes bitterness of the mind, with brawling and quarreling" (Ecclus. 31:28–29). When the apocryphal Tobit sent off his son Tobias on his journey, he is quoted as having said: "Drink not wine to make thee drunken, neither let drunkenness go with thee in the journey" (Tobit 4:15).

Philo of Alexandria (1st cent.), despite his leanings toward asceticism, did not favor total abstention from wine. His strictures were mainly addressed to those who exceed a reasonable limit. "The wise man never takes too much unmixed [unadulterated] wine. . . . Others have said that to be overcome with wine is appropriate even to the virtuous man, but that to behave foolishly is inconsistent with his character" (*About the Planting of Noah* 35). He expressed himself in somewhat stronger terms in another passage: "The wise man will never enter upon a contest of hard drinking. Unmixed wine is a poison which is the cause, if not of death, at least of madness" (ibid. 36).

The rabbis added their voices to the educational campaign against alcoholism. They depicted the effects of successive stages of increased intoxication in a graphic portrayal: "When a man drinks one glass of wine, he behaves like a lamb, modest and humble. When he drinks two glasses of wine, he fancies himself as mighty as a lion and shouts, 'No one can stand up to me.' When he drinks three or four glasses of wine, he acts like a swine that wallows in mud and refuse" (*Yalkut, Noah* 61).

Women, as a rule, did not indulge in excessive drinking of alcohol. The few who did evoked a strong revulsion. Liquor destroys feminism and weakens a woman's sexual inhibitions. In a parallel portrayal of the effects of successive stages of increased intoxication on women, it was declared: "One glass [of wine] is becoming to a woman; two are degrading; three, she solicits publicly; four, she solicits even an ass in the street and cares not" (*Ketubot* 65a).

The rabbis criticized with equal vigor a scholar who disgraces himself with drunkenness. They declared that the biblical aphorism "A ring of gold in a swine's snout" (Prov. 11:22) is an apt description of a drunken scholar (*Zohar, Vayera* 110).

Moderation was essential to society's approval of the drinking of wine. The appropriateness of the time of drinking was another essential factor. It was considered highly improper to drink in the daytime, when one must devote his full attention to study or work. "It is forbidden to drink [wine] in the afternoons . . . because it prevents one from studying Torah" (*Avot deRabbi Natan* 4). In another passage, Rabbi Dosa b. Horkinas (2nd cent.) declared: "Morning sleep and midday wine . . . put a man out of the world" (*Avot* 3:14).

A small temperance movement emerged shortly after the destruction of the Second Temple (70 C.E.). It considered the drinking of alcohol, which induces joy, inconsistent with its advocated state of perpetual mourning for the loss of the Temple (*Baba Batra* 60b). For practical reasons, the rabbis opposed a state of perpetual mourning and refused to ban the drinking of wine. However, beginning with the eleventh century, a tradition prohibiting wine in the nine-day period preceding the Fast of Tisha B'Av was widely accepted (Bloch, *The Biblical and Historical Background of Jewish Customs and Ceremonies*, p. 315).

Education

Thou shalt teach Jacob thy ordinances and Israel thy law.
—Deuteronomy 33:10

MODERN SOCIETY worships success. Education is the key to success in business and the professions. An education which is geared to the promotion of proficiency in one's career must of necessity stress technological and scientific competence. Philosophy and ethics are of little consequence within this framework. Regretfully, technology does not enhance a student's moral stance, and postgraduate degrees do not attest to perfection of character.

Fortunately, man's ethical heritage derives from various sources, independent of formal education. Many professionals find an opportunity to project their humane impulses in their chosen fields of endeavor. The dedicated social worker, the medical practitioner in the inner city, the lawyer who defends the poor, the teacher who remains after school hours to tutor students in need of help, and countless others in different fields, find self-fulfillment in acting out their moral perceptions.

Judaism has advocated the pursuit of education as a worthy goal in its own right, not for the material gain which it may produce. A rabbinic slogan which reflects this attitude was coined by Rabbi Zadok (1st cent.): "Make not the Torah a crown with which to aggrandize thyself, nor a spade with which to dig" (*Avot* 4:7). The rabbis and teachers of antiquity were unsalaried people who made their living by hard labor. Despite their lack of economic success, they received the highest degree of respect, admiration, and veneration.

Traditional Jewish society equated education with the study

99

of Torah, a compendium of ritual laws, civil laws, and ethical precepts. Experts and laymen alike were required to have a knowledge of this code. It was mandatory for every individual to set aside periods for study. The basic rule of national conduct with regard to education was formulated in the command to Joshua: "This book of the law shall not depart out of thy mouth, but thou shalt meditate therein day and night, that thou mayest observe to do according to all that is written therein" (Josh. 1:8). The purpose of education, spelled out in this command, is to teach the rules which one must translate into daily conduct.

Adulation of scholarship is prominently highlighted in the Bible, and the pursuit of knowledge was assiduously recommended. "The beginning of wisdom is: Get Wisdom. . . . Extol her and she will exalt thee; she will bring thee honor, when thou dost embrace her" (Prov. 4:7–8). "Better is a poor and wise child than an old and foolish king" (Eccles. 4:13). "Happy is the man that has not walked in the counsel of the wicked . . . but his delight is in the law of the Lord; and in his law does he meditate day and night" (Ps. 1:1–2). "My son, gather instruction from thy youth up; so shalt thou find wisdom till thine old age" (Ecclus. 6:18).

The priest was the principal source of knowledge throughout the biblical era (Mal. 2:7). His expertise lay mainly in the field of ritual law. The prophet supplemented the ministry of the priest by assuming the role of the guardian of the nation's conscience.

The conclusion of the era of prophecy (5th cent. B.C.E.) witnessed the emergence of academies and rabbinical scholars who challenged the priestly supremacy. In time the rabbi became the chief interpreter of the law and the source of developing perceptions of morality and ethics. The destruction of the Temple (70 C.E.) removed the priests from their position of influence and enthroned the rabbinic scholars as the sole religious leaders of the people. It was in this period that education and scholarship reached the zenith of popularity and prestige, which became the hallmark of Judaism.

The most far-reaching assertion of the importance of education was voiced by Rabbi Meir (3rd cent.): "Even a heathen who studies the Torah is [as exalted] as a high priest" (*Sanhedrin* 59a). The study of Torah was the core of traditional education, but other subjects were not excluded. A knowledge of science and languages was essential to the proper understanding of the Bible. Hillel, the noted sage of the first century, was said to have mastered all natural sciences (*Soferim* 16:9).

The rabbis set forth some useful guidelines as an aid to the pursuit of education. A student must never pretend that he understands a subject if in fact he does not. A teacher who does not know the answer to a given question should not feel embarrassed to admit his ignorance.

One should encourage and support the children of poor and uneducated families to pursue an education, if they show aptitude and promise. Scholarship is not a hereditary trait. The children of scholars are not necessarily scholarly, and the children of the ignorant may attain scholarship (*Nedarim* 81a).

The obligation to pursue knowledge transcends most other commitments. Nothing must be permitted to interfere with the orderly process of learning. Students may not be removed from their studies to volunteer their labor even for so exalted a task as the construction of the Temple (*Shabbat* 119b).

One may open a school in his home even if the neighbors object on the grounds that the noise disturbs their sleep (*Choshen Mishpat* 156:3).

Creditors who seize property in payment of debts may not remove textbooks used by the debtor's children at school (*Choshen Mishpat* 93:25).

No adult may engage a teacher in conversation during a lesson, if such conversation interferes with his teaching (*Sefer Chasidim* 124).

Education is a precious asset which once acquired must not be allowed to be frittered away through neglect (*Sifre, Devarim* 11).

The fact that one is incapable of gaining much knowledge does not diminish the value of education. Even the elderly, who no longer retain their lessons, should pursue learning (*Avodah Zarah* 19a).

Busy days and sleepless nights are frequently the price of an education. Rabbi Bisna (4th cent.) said: "No man on earth is entirely exempt from pain. If his eye hurts him he cannot sleep, a toothache keeps him awake all night. A scholar, too, if he engages in the study of the law, may spend a whole night in thoughtful meditation ... It is a blessing to suffer wakefulness over the study of the law" *(Tanchuma, Miketz)*.

The ancient educational guidelines have not lost their validity even in an age when the utilitarian aspects of education predominate in the curriculum.

Embarrassment and Insults

An undisciplined child embarrasses his mother.
—Proverbs 29:15

AN EMBARRASSED person suffers shame and discomposure. The same is true of the victim of insult. There is a significant difference, however, between embarrassment and insult, with regard to the hurt of the offended and the intent of the offender.

Embarrassment frequently results from careless acts or words performed or uttered in ignorance of their offensive implications. Such rudeness is extenuated, if not condoned, by the offender's lack of sophistication. There are instances when embarrassment is used deliberately as a corrective measure. It is common in the process of child training. "Did you say thank you to the nice lady?" "Did you say excuse me to the gentleman?" Most children bear embarrassment with equanimity, but they get the point of the reproach. There are times when one is constrained to use the same method with adults whose manners leave much to be desired.

Embarrassment is also a subjective state of mind that indirectly results from actions and words involving other people. Relatives of a convicted criminal feel embarrassed. A person who brings along an uninvited guest to a party may feel embarrassed when his friend proves to be a nuisance.

Civilized and well-behaved individuals may at times commit an inadvertent faux pas. When their error is called to their attention they feel deeply embarrassed.

An insulting person acts with malice aforethought and with a full awareness of the provocative character of his behavior. He most likely nurses a real or imagined grievance and finds relief

103

in administering an insult. There are also, on the other hand, prejudiced people whose insulting manner is gratuitous, without even a semblance of justification.

Judaism condemns insulting conduct and stresses the necessity of avoiding situations which create embarrassment.

"He who insults a person in public is morally as guilty as if he had shed blood" (*Baba Metzia* 58b). Rabbi Nachman (3rd cent.) found a physical manifestation which illustrates this moral dictum in a biological phenomenon common to victims of insults. Their faces turn red with onrushing blood, which is quickly drained, leaving the face all white (ibid.).

"He who insults a person in public . . . loses his share in the world-to-come" (Avot 3:11).

Rabbi Simon b. Yochai (2nd cent.) said: "Better had a man throw himself into a fiery furnace than publicly put his neighbor to shame" (*Baba Metzia* 59a).

One who calls a man by a derisive nickname, even if it is commonly used by others, is guilty of a grave offense (*Baba Metzia* 58b).

Rabbi Judah HeChasid (12th cent.) dealt at length with the subject of embarrassment and suggested ways to avoid it.

"If you are aware of an error in a teacher's lesson, do not tell him 'you are wrong,' because such correction may embarrass him. Inform his best friend, who will discreetly pass the information to him" (*Sefer Chasidim* 139).

"Do not ask your friend a scholarly question if you know that he is ignorant of the answer" (ibid. 312).

"A man who sees only out of one eye may be embarrassed by a conversation in which such a handicap is the topic of discussion" (ibid. 635). This moral perception is akin to the talmudic dictum: "Speak no evil of pagans in the presence of a former pagan who has converted to Judaism" (*Baba Metzia* 58b).

The Talmud suggests that one should avoid meeting a person at the time of his disgrace in order to spare him embarrassment (*Avot* 4:23).

People guilty of an insulting manner will rarely be deterred by ethical strictures. However, the hurt of a victim can be assuaged if other parties who are present at the scene rise to his defense.

Endangerment

Only take heed to thyself and guard thy soul diligently.
—Deuteronomy 4:9

MANY INJURIES result from accidents in the home. A loose window pane, a blob of fat on the kitchen floor, a torn rug, a slow gas leak, a broken chair, an exposed electric wire, and dozens of similar conditions are signals of potential danger to members of a household. Immediate repair of a dangerous condition would eliminate future trouble. Unfortunately such problems often fail to get prompt attention. It may be that the danger spot is not readily detected. It may also be that the well-intentioned head of family has other matters on his mind and promises himself "to take care of it the first thing in the morning." Regretfully, accidents do not wait for the next morning. The safety of the family was needlessly endangered.

Mishaps in the streets are also due to carelessness. A driver who exceeds the speed limit would not have injured a pedestrian had he observed the law. A driver under the influence of liquor would not have come to grief if he had the presence of mind to sober up before he entered his car. The person who slips on a banana peel would not have broken his leg if the banana eater had thrown the peel in the trash basket. Nor do we absolve other pedestrians who noticed the peel on the sidewalk and failed to remove it. They are responsible for endangering the health of a fellow man.

The safety of a family is sometimes endangered by an imprudent act of one of its members. A young man who attacks a neighborhood boy may invite a counterattack by the victim and his friends, who will exact revenge from the assailant's kin.

This is true even when the original attack was provoked by the victim.

The biblical account of the revenge taken by Simon and Levi against the people of Shechem, in retaliation for the dishonor suffered by their sister Dinah, illustrates the potential danger of a rash act. Jacob felt responsible for the security of his clan. He reacted with a sharp rebuke: "You have troubled me, to make me odious unto the inhabitants of the land . . . and I being few in number, they will gather themselves together against me and attack me; and I shall be destroyed, I and my family" (Gen. 34:30). Simon and Levi stood accused of endangerment.

People may be endangered by packs of wild dogs that roam the streets of our cities. It is the responsibility of the authorities to remove this hazard from inhabited areas. Prior to their settling in the Promised Land, the ancient Israelites were given the following assurance by God: "I will give peace in the land . . . and I will cause evil beasts to cease [their attacks] in the land" (Lev. 26:6). According to Rabbi Judah (2nd cent.), God did not promise to change the nature of wild beasts to make them docile. To make the streets secure the wild beasts would have to be physically removed (Sifre, Lev. 26:6).

The ethical obligation to correct dangerous conditions was enacted into biblical law. A person who digs a pit on property accessible to the public must cover it to prevent possible injuries (Exod. 21:33–34). Flat-roofed homes must have parapets to protect visitors from falling off (Deut. 22:8). This law was broadly interpreted by the rabbis to include all dangerous conditions which pose a danger to innocent people. Hence the prohibition of harboring dangerous dogs in a home or of placing a broken ladder against the wall of one's home (Ketubot 41b).

Containers of medicine normally carry a warning label which reads: "Keep out of reach of children." Consideration for the protection of children dictates reasonable preventive measures. However, it does not indicate a ban on medicine, which properly belongs in the home. What about poison, for which there is no common practical need? Does the occasional use of poison for exterminating purposes justify the risk which its presence entails? Josephus (1st cent.) was unequivocal in his objection.

"Let no Israelite keep any poison that may cause death, or any other harm" (*Antiq.*, bk. 4, 8:34). Poison may be used under proper safeguards to exterminate rodents. Whatever is left should be disposed of in a manner which will create no danger to man and animals alike.

Does the same ethical prohibition apply to the possession of guns in a private home? Rampant crime has produced a growing demand for guns for reasons of self-defense. There are instances where guns have proved useful in driving off criminals. Unfortunately, there are many more instances of guns falling into the hands of minors with tragic results. In urban areas, where police protection is available, the possession of a gun is a risk which should not lightly be assumed.

A rabbinic decree (2nd cent.) prohibited the sale of offensive weapons to individuals who are suspected of harboring a criminal intent (*Avodah Zarah* 16b). In modern societies licensing procedures have been instituted to keep guns out of the hands of criminal elements. Such procedures have proved woefully inadequate. There is a need for stricter gun-control laws. Ethical considerations make such legislation imperative.

Entrapment

In the net which they hid is their own foot taken.

—Psalm 9:16

TEMPTATION DOES not excuse sinful or criminal actions. Theology as well as secular criminal law is based on the notion that human beings must exercise self-control and restraint even in the face of the most powerful incentives to commit a wrong. Despite the demands for absolute rectitude, it is immoral and malicious to tempt an individual to perpetrate an illegal act. This is true even when the proffered temptation is merely a subterfuge as a means of testing a person's character and integrity. Such is the case when an employer deliberately leaves money unattended, within easy reach of an employee, so that he may find out whether the latter is capable of resisting a temptation to steal.

An entrapper is a moral accomplice to the criminal. The ancient rabbis expressed their loathing for entrapment by condemning it as a sin of greater gravity than murder (*Bamidbar Rabbah* 21:4).

The principal source of the prohibition of entrapment is the biblical verse: "Do not place a stumbling-block before a blind person" (Lev. 19:14). The blind person is not aware of the human intervention which caused his fall. In most instances of entrapment the individual who holds out the blandishments is known to his victim. Yet the attraction of the temptation is such that the victim is blinded to the true intent of the entrapper and the potential danger to his own welfare.

The young man who induces his friend to smoke marijuana by describing its blissful rewards is an entrapper. The person who persuades his buddy to join him on a stealing rampage because it is "a good way of making some easy money" is an entrapper. The young lady with a taste for expensive jewelry who is willing to offer her favors as soon as the young man proves his love with lavish gifts is an entrapper.

The rabbis' objection to entrapment was extended also to the creation of opportunities for entrapment, even where none was intended. Thus they looked with disfavor upon lending money when the transaction is not done in the presence of witnesses or if no receipt is demanded. A debtor pressured for money might be tempted to deny the loan under such circumstances.

An individual who deliberately offers misleading advice for selfish reasons of personal gain was considered guilty of violating the law against entrapment. The recipient of his advice, who has confidence in the sincerity of the adviser, is blinded to the trap laid before him (Sifra, Lev. 19:14).

Provocation, like temptation, may impel an individual to commit a wrong. Both are equally immoral and mischievous. One of the serious offenses severely condemned in the Bible is the striking of a parent (Exod. 21:15). Fathers were strongly cautioned by the rabbis against striking an adult son, regardless of the merits of the case. An adult son, struck by his father, might be provoked into hitting back. The striking son is guilty of a major crime, but his father is equally guilty for having entrapped him (Moed Katan 17a).

Is entrapment morally acceptable when performed by governmental agencies in the course of a criminal investigation? A promise of leniency in exchange for a confession must be adhered to, if it is not to constitute an entrapment. An undercover agent who bribes an individual in order to prove his corruption is guilty of the blatant act of entrapment. Any prosecution of the bribe-taker renders the government an accomplice to the crime.

Envy

. . . their hatred and their envy is long ago perished.
—Ecclesiastes 9:6

ENVY IS generally associated with a hostility that is born of jealousy. This assumption is not entirely correct, because it fails to differentiate between several grades of envy. In its mild form, envy heightens the discontent of a person who is less fortunate than his friend. He does not, however, begrudge his friend's happy state or dislike him for it. In its severe form, envy breeds ill-will and induces a strong desire to bring about a friend's downfall.

The term "envy" is also loosely used as an expression of admiration and praise. In this linguistic metamorphosis, envy is stripped of its unethical connotations. Indeed it projects a laudable form of flattery.

As a rule of thumb, envy of a neighbor's material wealth smacks of hostility. Envy of a person's fine traits expresses approval and gratification. Beware of a person who says: "I envy my neighbor's beautiful home." Applaud the person who says: "I envy my neighbor's cheerful disposition." In effect he betrays a secret wish to be like him.

Envy, even if it emanates from impure motives, is not always baleful. The ancient rabbis tolerated envy among scholars because it promotes knowledge (*Baba Batra* 21a). Encouragement of competition in schools or the business world employs envy as a subtle means of producing desirable results.

The fact that envy stimulates emulation makes it doubly imperative to caution people against envying the success of criminals. Warnings against envy of the wicked are a recurrent biblical theme. "Envy not the man of violence, and choose

110

none of his ways" (Prov. 3:31). "Let not thy heart envy sinners" (Prov. 23:17). "Be not envious of evil men, neither desire to be with them" (Prov. 24:1). "My steps had well nigh slipped, for I was envious of the arrogant, when I saw the prosperity of the wicked" (Ps. 73:2–3).

Envy exacerbates strife. Philistine envy of the success of Isaac in finding water led, according to the Bible, to discord and an end to friendly neighborly relations (Gen. 26:14). In the agony of her childlessness, Rachel expressed her envy of the fertility of her sister Leah (Gen. 30:1). The result was a strain on their sibling relationship.

Ethical condemnation of envy mandates an obligation to avoid creating situations which are likely to provoke envy in other people. Parents who single out one child for more favorable treatment are guilty of generating sibling rivalry, envy, and hatred. Jacob, for reasons of his own, made Joseph an object of favoritism. The Bible describes the unhappy consequences. "When his brethren saw that their father loved him more than all his brethren, they hated him and could not speak peaceably to him" (Gen. 37:4).

Drawing the proper conclusion from this incident, Rav (3rd cent.) issued a timely warning: "Let no man show favoritism in the treatment of his children" (Shabbat 10b). Parents may properly reward a child for a meritorious act but should not habitually offer one child preferential treatment in a discriminatory manner. Similarly parents have a right to punish a child who is guilty of wrongdoing. However, they should refrain from imposing a penalty which will irretrievably attach a stigma to the child for the rest of his life. Parents who disown a child in their will in a moment of great vexation sow the seeds of chronic envy and hostility among siblings.

Prosperity and good fortune frequently excite envy in less fortunate people. A successful person can do much to eliminate such envy by refraining from flaunting his success in an ostentatious and arrogant manner. Rabbi Aaron of Barcelona (13th cent.) touched on the subject of public adulation of a popular scholar which regretfully overlooks another scholar of equal merit. "When two scholars arrive in a city and only one is received with great honor, let him make sure to praise and show honor to his colleague who was ignored and thus forestall envy and frustration" (*Sefer Chinuch* 359).

Exposing children to luxuries which parents cannot afford to provide may also lead to envy and unhappiness. Elijah Gaon (18th cent.) was the most renowned talmudic scholar of his generation. He was also among the poorest people of that generation. Prior to his leaving on a journey, which he hoped would take him to the Holy Land, he left a letter of moral instructions with his wife. One of the instructions addressed to his wife stated: "Do not take your daughter to the synagogue, where she will see girls of her age dressed in finery of which she is deprived. This may produce envy and gossip."

Self-isolation is neither feasible nor desirable in an open society. Modern media of communication expose even the neediest to the luxuries available to the most privileged. If one is thereby stimulated to raise his standard of living, the resulting envy can be converted into a constructive force.

Equity

He will minister judgment to the peoples with equity.
—Psalm 9:9

JUSTICE, BY its very definition, must treat all people with equal impartiality, rich and poor, powerful and humble. The Bible explicitly prohibits favoring the poor or giving preference to the rich (Lev. 15:9). Yet equality before the law does not always meet the ends of justice. The loss of a small financial claim will not significantly affect a rich person but it may destroy a man in need.

The universality of law precludes the kind of flexibility which allows for wide judicial discretion. This renders the law helpless to prevent occasional miscarriages of justice. To remedy this situation, courts of equity came into existence in medieval England. Equity judges gave liberal interpretations to the letter of the law in order to arrive at equitable decisions. However, even courts of equity were bound by legal principles which did not permit judges to entirely ignore the letter of the law.

The layman's interpretation of equity, as it is widely understood in modern times, is not constrained by technicalities, as was the case when equity was part of the national juridical system. In common parlance equity is synonymous with fairness. The determining factor of fairness is ethics, not law. The burden of equity is the responsibility of all individuals in every walk of life. The standard of behavior of equitable people must be measured on the scale of fairness rather than legality.

Fairness is a highly elastic quality. A higher degree of perfection and refinement is demanded of educated people than of the ignorant. A person in a position of leadership is expected to live up to higher ethical standards than what is normally demanded

113

of the average man and woman. The test of civilized behavior is not whether a given act is permissible under the law but whether it is fair in the eyes of the public.

The layman's concept of equity is an integral part of biblical ethical guidelines. Thus the injunction "to do that which is good and fair" (Deut. 12:28) was interpreted by Rabbi Akiva (2nd cent.) to mean "that which is good in the eyes of heaven and fair in the eyes of men" (*Sifre*, Deut. 12:28). Accordingly, the duty to act fairly is an obligation imposed on all people. This was also the basis of the mandate empowering rabbinic courts to render decisions, whenever necessary, in the spirit of equity rather than law.

The rabbis of the third century coined the phrase "beyond the prescription of the law" (*lifnim mishurat hadin*) to define the moral principle of equity (*Baba Kama* 89b). There are two biblical sources from which this principle derives; one is in the Pentateuch, and the other in the Hagiographa. The Pentateuchal source reads: "And thou shalt teach the statutes and the laws, and shalt show them the way wherein they must walk and the deeds they must perform" (Exod. 18:20). The text appears to imply that abiding by the law is essential but there are additional paths beyond the law which also need to be pursued. According to Rabbi Joseph (3rd cent.), "deeds" refers to conduct within the letter of the law, "they must perform" refers to acts beyond the prescription of the law (*Baba Metzia* 30b).

The Hagiographical source of equity is a verse in the Book of Proverbs: "That thou mayest walk in the way of good men and keep the paths of the righteous" (Prov. 2:20). The rabbis assumed that only persons who are motivated by ideals of equity may be considered good and righteous (*Baba Metzia* 83a).

The principle of equity is reflected in many decisions and rules promulgated by the talmudic sages. Rabbi Yochanan b. Zakkai (1st cent.) suspended the biblical ritual for testing a wife suspected by her husband of adultery. He ruled that the test is effective only if the conduct of the husband is above reproach (the ancient doctrine of clean hands). He obviously considered it inequitable to subject wives to a ritual test of morality in a generation when the moral stance of husbands was under a cloud of suspicion (*Sotah* 47a).

Rabbi Ishmael b. Jose set a personal example of equitable conduct. On one of his walks he came across a man who needed assistance in lifting a bundle unto his back. According to the Bible such help must be extended by any person present at the scene. However, elderly or sick people are exempted from this obligation. Scholars are also exempted if the performance of this task is considered by the public unbecoming to a man of great dignity. Rabbi Ishmael was definitely covered by this exemption. Nevertheless, he felt impelled by the dictates of equity to offer his assistance. However, he was reluctant to defy public opinion, which regarded such as work unbecoming to a man of his standing. As a way out of the dilemma, Rabbi Ishmael purchased the bundle from its owner and then left it at the side of the road for anyone to claim (*Baba Metzia* 30b).

Equity was also applied to legal statutes of limitations which barred financial claims after the expiration of a limited period of time. A buyer who was overcharged by the seller by more than one-sixth of the value of the merchandise had a right to return the merchandise and to claim his money back. The claim had to be made within a limited time period. However, the rabbis urged merchants to act in the spirit of equity and return the money to the buyer even if his claim was made after the expiration of the period of limitation (*Baba Metzia* 49b).

Porters who negligently damage property in the course of their work are legally liable for damages. Despite this law, Rav (3rd cent.) refused to order porters employed by Rabbah to pay damages for negligently breaking a barrel of wine. When Rabbah protested that the law was on his side, Rav retorted that a man of his stature must govern his acts by the dictates of equity rather than the law. For the same reason, Rav also ruled that Rabbah pay the porters their full wages because of their dire need (*Baba Metzia* 83a).

The rabbis condemned communities where the prevailing custom was to abide by the law but not beyond the prescription of the law. A lack of equity corrodes the fabric of civilization. In

assessing the conditions which had undermined the independence of Judea and led to the loss of the Temple in Jerusalem,
Rabbi Yochanan (3rd cent.) alleged: "Jerusalem was destroyed
because they [the people of that generation] based their judgments upon biblical law and did not extend themselves beyond
the requirements of the law" (*Baba Metzia* 30b).

The rabbinical assessment of the equitable behavior of ancient communities is equally relevant to the conduct of nations
in our time. The stability of modern societies depends upon
law and order. However, the quality of their civilization rests
upon their willingness to act in the spirit of equity.

False Impressions and Deception

Commend not a man for his beauty; neither abhor a man for his outward appearance.

—Ecclesiasticus 11:2

FALSE IMPRESSIONS can be highly damaging to one's good reputation. Even innocent acts may engender unfounded gossip if one is not alert to the potentially wrong conclusions that people may draw from them.

A lady waiting for a bus on a freezing night accepts a lift from a passing motorist, an old friend of the family. Her coworkers, unaware of the relationship, regard her action as a breach of conventional propriety. It should come as no surprise to her if the telephone wires are buzzing that evening with reports of her tryst with a stranger. The unfortunate gossip could have been avoided had she had the presence of mind to introduce the motorist to her friends. Regretfully, she must now suffer the consequences of her heedless conduct.

False impressions are at times deliberately created for self-serving reasons. It is done without any intent to harm other people but merely to satisfy one's ego. Joe is pressed for funds and his friends are eager to help him. An old acquaintance meets Joe's next-door neighbor and hands him some money with a request that he give it to Joe without revealing the name of the donor. The neighbor delivers the money but fails to mention that the gift was given by an anonymous friend. Although the neighbor did not specifically profess that the money was his, he deliberately created that impression to enhance his own image. Such conduct is unethical and deceptive.

The worst kind of false impression is one that is fostered for self-gain at the expense of another party. An individual who affects a blind man's disguise when soliciting money is guilty of unethical conduct and outright fraud.

It is the false impression that is inadvertently created, without any deceptive intent, that is most frequently illustrated in the Bible. The other two categories, perpetrated for reasons of prestige or financial gain, required little elaboration because they are specifically banned by biblical injunctions prohibiting all forms of deception. "And if thou sell aught unto thy neighbor, or buy of thy neighbor's hand, thou shalt not deceive one another." "And thou shalt not deceive one another, but thou shalt fear thy God" (Lev. 25:14, 17). According to rabbinical interpretation, the ban covers all misleading words and acts, even if not perpetrated for financial gain (*Baba Metzia* 58b).

Moses made effective use of the objection to the creation of false impressions in his intercession with God on behalf of the people. He forcefully argued that the destruction of the Hebrews in punishment for the worship of the golden calf would lead the Egyptians to the wrong conclusion that the death of the freed Hebrew slaves was premeditated by God at the time of the exodus (Exod. 32:12). Additionally, the intended punishment might also create the false impression that God was impotent to deliver the land which he had promised to Abraham (Deut. 9:28).

In Ezekiel's prophecy, God confirmed that it was indeed the likelihood of creating a false impression that moved him to yield to Moses' plea for mercy. "But I wrought for my name's sake, that I should not be profaned in the sight of the nations" (Ezek. 20:9).

The practical wisdom of preventing unfounded gossip was evinced by Boaz when the Moabite Ruth came uninvited to the threshing-floor where he had been asleep alone. She had come to seek help for herself and Naomi, the mother of her deceased husband. Upon waking at midnight, Boaz was startled by Ruth's presence. Reluctant to send her away in the dead of night, Boaz urged that she leave before daybreak. "Let it not be known that the woman came to the threshing-floor" (Ruth 3:14).

The rule forbidding acts which might lead to false impressions was given the talmudic name of *marit haayin* ("for appearances' sake"). This rule had many halachic implications. Thus the owner of a house with two separate entrances was ordered to light two Chanukah lamps, one in front of each entrance. This law was based on the rule of *marit haayin*. Pedestrians passing the house might wrongly assume that the two entrances lead to two separate apartments and that one of the tenants had failed to observe the ritual of lighting a Chanukah lamp (*Shabbat* 23a).

Another illustration of the halachic application of the rule of *marit haayin* is the case of the person whose clothes got wet when he crossed a stream on the Sabbath. The person was forbidden to spread his clothes to dry in the sun for fear that some people might wrongly assume that he had washed his clothes on the Sabbath, an act prohibited by religious law (*Shabbat* 146b).

Rav (3rd cent.) was strict in the enforcement of prohibitions based on the rule of *marit haayin*. He ruled that "whatever the sages forbade for reasons of *marit haayin* [in public] is forbidden even in one's innermost chambers [though no outsider sees it]" (*Shabbat* 64b).

Is a law prohibiting the creation of false impressions justifiable when no one but the heedless person suffers thereby? If a party is in fact innocent of wrongdoing and is insensitive to the consequences of baseless gossip, why stop him? Obviously the rabbis considered an individual who plants seeds of doubt and suspicion in the minds of other people guilty of entrapment. Those who are led to suspect him without cause are morally guilty of a serious breach of ethics (*Yoma* 19b). The individual who contributes to their wrongdoing is an accomplice to the offense.

The rabbinic guidelines on proper conduct lean heavily on the rule of *marit haayin*, as is shown by the examples that follow.

"Rav Judah said in the name of Rav [3rd cent.], 'Anyone who is not a scholar and parades in a scholar's cloak [to receive the honor accorded to scholars] is not admitted to the circle of the Holy One' " (i.e., God is displeased with him; *Baba Batra* 98a). This guideline embraces all self-serving affectations in mannerism or language for the purpose of creating a false impression.

One may not inquire of a merchant the price of an item (thus creating the impression that he is interested in buying it) if in fact he has no intention of buying anything (*Tanchuma, Vayera* 53).

A person who brings food to the house of a mourner should not carry it in an oversized bag to give the wrong impression that he is giving an imposing gift (*Chulin* 94a).

One should not enter without permission a neighbor's premises to retrieve a lost animal lest one be taken for a thief (*Baba Kama* 27b).

When instructing students or conversing with people, it is important to use simple language which does not require further elucidation or interpretation. One should not assume that upon careful consideration people will in the end understand the true import of his words. Chances are that they may arrive at a wrong conclusion (Maimonides, *Avot* 2:4).

It is wrong to request a person to do a favor "for the sake of God" if he is known to be a kind-hearted individual who is happy to help people because of his innate humane inclinations. Some might get the wrong impression that he would refuse to be of help if God's name had not been invoked (*Sefer Chasidim* 1093).

When an individual seeks to redress a grievance, it is best to get disinterested people to take up his cause. Interceding relatives may create a wrong impression that their efforts are motivated by kinship rather than justice (*Sefer Chasidim* 1106).

Those who deliberately create false impressions for ulterior purposes are denounced in postbiblical and rabbinic literature as deceivers. The Second Book of Maccabees recounts the story of Eleazar, a highly respected elderly sage, who was pressured by an agent of King Antiochus to eat the flesh of swine. If he ate the forbidden food all other Jews would follow his example and thus hasten their conversion to paganism. In the face of Eleazar's adamant refusal to comply with the request, even under the threat of death, the Greek official suggested a compromise. Eleazar would pretend to eat the forbidden food but in reality eat kosher food which would be kept out of sight of the Jewish guests. Eleazar rejected the compromise with disdain, declaring that he would rather die than create a deceitful impression (II Macc. 6:18–31).

Rabbinic censure of creating self-serving false impressions was articulated by Rabbi Akiva (2nd cent.): "He who puts bandages over his eyes or on his hip and proclaims 'help a blind man' or 'help a man afflicted with leprosy' will in the end be punished for his dissimulation by suffering from the condition which he falsely pretends to have" (*Avot deRabbi Natan* 3:1).

Coloring of merchandise to give it an artificial appearance of freshness or better quality is forbidden. It is similarly forbidden to cover fruit of an inferior grade with a top layer of fruit of higher quality. This is true even if the price is not raised as a result of the deception, which is used merely to attract the attention of buyers (*Choshen Mishpat* 228:9–10).

The modern advertising industry, an essential arm of business enterprise, is particularly vulnerable to the charge of creating false impressions. Official regulations have substantially curbed the practice of irresponsible advertising dissimulation. However, there is still a murky area, within the bounds of law, where illusion and reality intermingle.

Official propaganda agencies are also prone to manipulate the truth by creating false impressions. In a democracy, public opinion and a free press act as a brake on runaway misrepresentations. In a dictatorship, propaganda is as deadly as it is unethical.

Preelection campaign oratory is another area where false impressions are created with impunity. Victorious cynical candidates shrug off promises made to the electorate by fostering the notion that promises made in the heat of a campaign are not taken seriously by the voters. However, such a notion is as false as the promises which were never intended to be kept. No amount of cynicism can absolve a misleading candidate from the charge of a breach of trust and ethics.

To some degree there are areas in humn relationships which are normally colored by false impressions. The romantic period of courtship is a case in point. Young people of both sexes make an effort to exhibit their best qualities and to conceal their faults. To the extent that such behavior is instinctive and mutually tolerated, one must not be rash in applying moral judgment. However, false impressions which conceal major faults that go to the very heart of the future happiness of the couple cannot be condoned.

The temptation to create false impressions in every walk of life is strong and pervasive. It is only the cumulative effect of the persistent denunciation of this practice in the ethical litera-ture of all nations that keeps civilized society from accepting or even endorsing it.

Filial Obligations

Honor thy father and thy mother.

—Exodus 20:12

YOUNG CHILDREN depend upon the love and care of their parents for survival. The Talmud spells out the scope of parental responsibilities. The Bible, however, does not touch upon this subject in its ethical admonitions. There was obviously no need for cautioning parents to fulfill their obligations to their children. Parental love is spontaneous and instinctive. On the other hand, filial duties to parents are given great emphasis in biblical literature. Indeed, the inclusion of this responsibility in the Decalogue testifies to the overriding importance assigned to it in Judaic ethical injunctions.

Prior to the enactment of modern wide-ranging social legislation, which put the onus of care of the aged upon the state, children were held legally responsible for the maintenance of indigent parents. This is no longer the case at present. However, socioreligious traditions still shape the scope of proper filial attitudes with regard to parents.

Biblical and apocryphal texts stress the abstract qualities of reverence and honor of parents. They also urge children to conduct themselves in a manner which will reflect well upon their parents and to avoid misconduct which will disgrace their ancestry. It was left to the Talmud to outline the specific filial obligations which translate the biblical "honor" and "reverence" of parents into concrete deeds.

A variety of rationales may be suggested in explanation of the stringent demands made of children in implementation of the spirit of the fifth commandment.

123

1. Honor of parents is honor of God; dishonor of parents is dishonor of God.

"Rabbi [Judah HaNasi, 2nd cent.] said: 'Honor of father and mother is dear to him who created the world [God], for he equated honor and reverence for them with honor and reverence for him, and cursing of parents is like cursing him'" (Exod. 20:12, *Mechilta*).

The exalted status of parents is inherent in their biological kinship to their children. Philo the Alexandrian (1st cent.) expressed this view in the following passage: "Parents are human, they are born and die, but they are also divine because they created life" (*On the Ten Commandments*). Philo's words are not to be taken literally as an attribution of divinity to the personage of a parent, a belief prevalent in some ancient cults. He is merely stating that parents possess divine qualities. The ability to create life is a divine power which they share with God, the creator of all life. By honoring the divine qualities of parenthood one also honors God, who bestowed these powers upon them. By the same token, if one dishonors his parents he also dishonors God. In the words of Ben Sira (2nd cent. B.C.E.) "He that forsakes his father is a blasphemer" (Ecclus. 3:16).

The traditional link between parenthood and God helped create the father-image of God in a spiritual and physical sense. According to tradition, it is God who implants the soul in the body. He is therefore the spiritual father of the human race. Beyond that, it is God's established law of nature which makes it possible for the human embryo to grow and develop. In the words of the psalmist: "For thou hast made my reins, thou hast knit me together in my mother's womb" (Ps. 139:13). This concept provided the basis for the talmudic statement that "there are three partners in the creation of man, God and father and mother" (*Kiddushin* 30b).

The father-image of God was an essential ingredient of the prophetic messages of hope and confidence. To the despairing Jews of the sixth century B.C.E., overwhelmed by the cataclysmic destruction of the Temple and national independence, the prophet proclaimed: "But now, our Lord, thou art our father. . . .

Be not angry overmuch, O Lord, neither remember iniquity for ever" (Isa. 64:1, 8). "As one whom his mother comforteth, so will I [God] comfort you, and you will be comforted in Jerusalem" (Isa. 66:13).

Jeremiah also used the father-image of God in a message of hope: "And I said, thou shalt call me my father and shalt not turn away from me" (Jer. 3:19). To the people weeping in distress, he said: "I will cause them to walk by rivers of water, in a straight way wherein they shall not stumble, for I am become a father to Israel" (Jer. 31:9). The psalmist declared his trust in God's infinite mercy: "Like as a father has compassion upon his children, so has the Lord compassion upon them that fear him" (Ps. 103:13).

The father-image of God also inspired the prophet Malachi in his quest for equal justice for all. "Have we not all one father? Has not one God created us all? Why do we deal treacherously every man against his brother, profaning the covenant of our fathers?" (Mal. 2:10).

Veneration of father was transmuted into veneration of God, the father of all human beings. This process strengthened the faith of the people as well as their morale in times of stress.

2. Honor of parents is essential to their assigned task of transmitting religious and cultural values to succeeding generations.

Instruction of one's children is the only parental duty mentioned in the Bible (Deut. 6:7). Children who are respectful of their parents will readily accept their guidance and instructions. The biblical command "You shall fear every man his father and his mother" is concluded with the statement "I am the Lord your God" (Lev. 19:3), i.e., parents whose children fear them are able to implant reverence for God in the hearts of their children. The verse following this command warns against the worship of idols. The link between parental honor and the preservation of the faith is thus clearly implied. This connection is explicitly emphasized in the Book of Proverbs: "The fear of the Lord is the beginning of knowledge. . . . Hear, my son, the instruction of thy father, and forsake not the teaching of thy mother" (Prov. 1:7–8).

It may be added parenthetically that parental honor solidifies family bonds. The survival of Jewish society as a religious and cultural community rests upon the foundation of stable family units.

3. Honor of parents brings many rewards.

The biblical command to honor one's parents is coupled with the promise "that thy days may be long and that it may go well with thee" (Deut. 5:16). A similar comprehensive reward was promised to those who observe all of God's statutes and commandments (Deut. 4:40). The reward for parental honor was thus equated with the reward in store for those who observe the Torah in its entirety.

Ben Sira (2nd cent. B.C.E.) listed several other rewards granted to those who honor their parents. "Whosoever honors his father makes an atonement for his sins" (Ecclus. 3:3). This doctrine is not repeated in rabbinic sources. Nevertheless, it might have served as an added incentive for the strict observance of the fifth commandment.

Ben Sira listed an additional reward for parental honor. "Whosoever honors his father shall have joy of his own children, and when he makes his prayers, he shall be heard" (Ecclus. 3:5). This particular reward is not grounded in theology but is, rather, based on an educational principle. The example set by a son who honors his parents will be dutifully followed by his own children, who will honor him in turn. Thus they will bring him much joy.

4. Parental honor is dictated by a sense of gratitude.

Most children are naturally attached to their parents and honor them without regard to any conscious obligation deriving from a sense of gratitude. Yet the element of gratitude is undoubtedly a latent component of filial attitudes toward parents. Moralists of all ages have occasionally appealed to children to be mindful of their indebtedness to their parents. They might have addressed their exhortations to children whose honor of parents does not measure up to ethical standards.

The author of the apocryphal Tobit (2nd cent. B.C.E.?) enlarges on the theme of filial gratitude: ". . . despise not thy mother, but honor her all the days of her life, and do that which will please her, and grieve her not. Remember, my son, that

she saw many dangers for thee, when you were in her womb"
(Tobit 4:3–4).

Philo (1st cent.) wrote in the same vein: "Honor of parents is
incumbent on children so that they may reciprocate the many
services rendered by their parents" (*On the Ten Commandments*).

Rabbi Aaron of Barcelona (13th cent.) also regarded gratitude as one of the rationales for parental honor. "The basis of
this commandment is the need for appreciation to one's benefactor and that one must not manifest indifference and ingratitude to him. Such an attitude is utterly despised by God and
men. . . . One must honor them [the parents] and be helpful to
them in any way possible because they brought him into the
world and endured hardships for his sake when he was in his
infancy" (*Sefer HaChinuch* 33).

An analysis of the various rationales and their sources indi-
cates that the Bible and Talmud emphasized the theological
implications of parental honor, while the Apocrypha and the
Hellenist Jewish writers added a social motivation. Post-talmudic rabbinic moralists adopted a combination of rationales,
establishing the socioreligious basis of the fifth commandment.

The following selection of rabbinic moral ordinances pertaining to proper filial conduct is culled from the religious code
(*Yoreh Deah* 240).

One must not occupy a pew in the synagogue which is
normally reserved for his father when he worships (occupying
his place is considered a disrespectful act).

One must not sit in a chair which his father uses when he
dines (a man's regular seat is a symbol of his status as head of
the family).

One must not disagree with or contradict his father to his
face (a child may not embarrass his parent).

One should not address his father by his first name or refer
to him by name after his death (such intimacy lessens parental
dignity).

A child must rise when his parent enters his home (the Bible
regards the act of rising as a gesture of respect).

Children must provide their needy parents with food, drink,

and garments. They must help them in and out of their home (if they are infirm). The expense burden should be borne equally by all the children. In the event that some of the children are rich and some poor, the burden should be shouldered by those who can best afford it.

It is the duty of grandchildren to honor their grandparents.

One should not speak disparagingly of a pagan in the presence of his son who has converted to Judaism. This law is relevant in our own time. One should not malign a criminal in the presence of his son. The natural respect that a child has for his parent is not diminished by the disrespect in which he is held by society. It is painful for children to hear their parents reviled.

A son must not criticize or reprimand his father in a rude manner. If a father violates a religious law, his son should not tell him "you committed a wrong." Instead, he should call his attention to the law and acquaint him with its provisions.

Senile parents must be treated with respect and infinite patience. If a senile parent destroys his child's property, he is not to be reprimanded or put to shame.

A son should not see his father in the nude.

Stepfathers and stepmothers are entitled to parental honor.

All laws pertaining to the honor of a father are equally applicable to the honor of a mother.

Senior siblings should be honored by junior siblings. Older children frequently take on parental duties and responsibilities. They earn the respect of their younger brothers and sisters.

Rabbi Judah HeChasid (13th cent) listed some additional moral perceptions of the fifth commandment.

When a son acts at the bidding of his mother in the performance of a task which is displeasing to his father, he should not reveal to him that it was his mother who requested this act. Rabbi Judah obviously felt that the cause of domestic harmony justifies the withholding of a full revelation of all facts from a parent (*Sefer Chasidim* 336). This recommendation is not to be taken as a license to tell an outright lie under similar conditions. The talmudic sage Rav (3rd cent.) was tormented by a spiteful wife. When he asked for a meal of lentils she would prepare peas, and vice versa. When their son, Chiyya, grew up, he came to resent his mother's vexing habit. To please his father, he resorted to a deceitful strategy. When Rav asked for lentils he would tell his mother that his father had asked for peas, and in keeping with her habit, she served lentils. Surprised by his wife's change of heart, Rav queried Chiyya, who sheepishly confessed his strategy. Whereupon Rav warned him not to resort to lies in the future (*Yevamot* 63a).

A son who feuds with his siblings brings sorrow to his parents. He is therefore in violation of the fifth commandment, even if he respects and honors his father and mother (*Sefer Chasidim* 571).

A child who embarks on a journey which is fraught with danger has an obligation to communicate with his parents to let them know that he is out of danger. He is not relieved of this duty even when such communication entails a substantial expense (*Sefer Chasidim* 575).

Biblical law condemns to death a son who strikes a parent, causing a flow of blood (Deut 25:3). A son who is a physician should avoid medical treatment of a parent, if it entails a surgical operation. However, if another surgeon is not available, the son may perform the necessary operation (*Sefer Chasidim* 48).

There are some wealthy parents who out of miserliness fail to provide an adequate diet for themselves. It is the duty of considerate children to supplement their parents' diet (stinginess is to be treated as an illness; *Sefer Chasidim* 582).

Whatever help is extended to parents must be given joyfully. Even the most lavish gift given grudgingly is in violation of the fifth commandment (Jer. *Kiddushin* 1:7).

The following are some modifications of the stringent laws of parental honor:

Married daughters are exempt from rendering a service for their parents if it interferes with their duties to their families (*Kiddushin* 30b). However, if a husband suggests that his wife take time out to help her parents, she may do so (*Sefer Chasidim* 335).

A child should not heed a request of parents that he commit a wrong or violate a religious law (*Baba Metzia* 32a).

A son may ignore parental objections to the prospective bride of his choice if he does not consider their objection justifiable (*Yoreh Deah* 240:25).

A request of parents that their son remain single so that he may have more time to devote to them should be ignored (*Sefer Chasidim* 564)

Jewish ethical literature does not deal with the problem of abused or neglected children, an alarmingly growing phenomenon of modern society. Do abused children have any filial obligations toward their parents when they are grown? The omission of this subject in the classical works of Judaic ethics is testimony to the fact that there were no abused children in the traditional Jewish milieu. It is the loosening of the family structure and the rising number of one-parent families that is responsible for the emergence of the abused-child problem. A parent who willfully neglects his child has no claim upon that child's love or support.

An analysis of the rabbinic guidelines crystalizes the magnitude of the dimensions of parental honor. Yet filial obligations must be viewed within the framework of practical wisdom, which denies parents the right to make exorbitant demands of their children. Josephus (1st cent.) went beyond the spirit of the rabbinic guidelines in his comment on the near-sacrifice of Isaac by his father, Abraham. His statement that Isaac "would have been unjust if he had not obeyed, even if his father alone [without God's command] had so resolved" (*Antiq.*, bk. I, 13:4) is an unwarranted opinion, not in line with Jewish ethical thought.

Many anecdotes about extraordinary honor of parents have been preserved in the Talmud. Rabbi Tarfon (2nd cent.) used to get down on his hands and knees so that his mother could use him as a stepping stool when she climbed into bed (*Kiddushin* 31b). The father of Rabbi Avimi (3rd–4th cent.) asked his son for some water. Rabbi Avimi rushed to get the water, but when he came back his father was asleep. He remained at his side for several hours so that he might hand him the water as soon as he awoke (*Kiddushin* 31b).

There are many anecdotes of this genre in the Talmud. They were preserved as an inspiration for the enhancement of the fifth commandment. Their standard is much higher than what is expected of the average man. Yet even the moderate standard which Judaism has adopted in its code sets a high norm unique in the annals of Western civilization.

Flattery

A man who flatters his neighbor spreads a net for his steps.
—Proverbs 29:5

FLATTERY IS defined as an "undue, or insincere, compliment" *(Funk & Wagnalls Dictionary)*. This definition leaves out the main ingredient which gives flattery its ugly connotation. It is the exaggerated praise prompted by an ulterior self-serving motive that makes flattering a morally repulsive practice. A flatterer who is solely interested in pleasing a friend may be a fool. One who flatters for self-gain is a knave.

Most people who resort to flattery are not necessarily morally insensitive. It is a commonplace practice legitimized by a need to ingratiate oneself with another individual.

There is no lack of situations in which flattery appears attractive. An employee flatters his employer in the hope of obtaining a desired promotion. A salesman flatters a prospective customer in the hope of concluding a deal of questionable value. A social climber flatters a socialite in the hope of wangling a social invitation. Similar occasions arise in every walk of life.

Few flatterers pause to analyze the unethical components of flattery. To flatter is to lie. Even people who do not normally lie condone a lie which comes in the form of praise.

Flattery constitutes a verbal bribe, morally as despicable as a financial bribe.

A flattering employee who seeks preferential treatment deprives another employee of an advancement opportunity to which he is entitled. This makes him guilty of theft.

A flatterer who persuades another person to form an inflated opinion of his ego is guilty of having created a false impression.

132

A recipient of undue adulation who is astute enough to see through the flatterer's guile develops a skepticism which will inevitably color his reactions even to people who deserve his trust.

The evil of flattery did not escape the biblical moralists. The author of Proverbs denounces the flatterer as a "smooth-tongued" individual. Harlots were branded as flatterers who attract men with honeyed words (Prov. 5:3). He also points out that flattery is highly destructive. "A flattering mouth works ruin" (Prov. 26:28).

Ecclesiasticus cautions against the wiles of a hypocritical flatterer. "An enemy speaks sweetly with his lips, but in his heart he plots how to throw thee into a pit" (Ecclus. 42).

In the talmudic lexicon a flatterer is described as one "whose lips and heart are not as one" (*Pesachim* 113b). Society is in desperate shape, according to a talmudic maxim, if its leader resorts to flattery (*Devarim Rabbah* 5). It was apparently the opinion of the rabbis that a flattering leader covers up his inefficiency with sweet and soothing words. They also cautioned against resorting to flattery even if the purpose is to obtain a free meal (*Derech Eretz Rabbah* 2).

When the self-serving motivation is removed from flattery, it becomes a tolerable practice. It is even prudent if the exaggerated praise is intended to help an individual overcome a sense of inferiority or a state of depression. There are some occasions when flattery, in its benign connotation, is an approved pro forma expression of friendship. Mutual flattery between a courting couple is a romantic necessity. The Talmud recommends that wedding guests vocally admire the beauty of the bride, even if her appearance belies such praise (*Ketubot* 17a).

In some people's minds flattery is synonymous with fulsome praise. If their praise is devoid of cynicism, they deserve no reproach.

Forgiveness

But he, being full of compassion, forgives iniquity and destroys not.

—Psalm 78:38

"TO ERR is human; to forgive, divine" (Pope) is an aphorism widely quoted and admired. Are there any circumstances under which forgiveness is less than divine? Is an erring person who manifests no regret or remorse entitled to forgiveness? The wicked generation that was doomed to perish in the Flood received no divine forgiveness. The same was true of the Sodomites. Why not?

Moses was the first biblical figure to assert the crucial importance of forgiveness in God's relationship with man. The worshippers of the golden calf were initially condemned by God to death. Moses was distressed by God's decree, which did not leave the door open to forgiveness. Addressing the people, he said: "You have sinned a great sin, and now I will go up unto the Lord; perhaps I shall obtain forgiveness for your sin" (Exod. 32:30). Moses' forceful argument in his plea to God formulated the theological doctrine of forgiveness as a permanent factor of divine judgment.

The doctrine which emerged out of the dialogue between God and Moses established the principle that forgiveness is a conditional privilege which only those who are worthy of divine compassion may expect. This principle was clearly spelled out in a divine proclamation: "The Lord, the Lord God, merciful and gracious, long-suffering and abundant in goodness and truth. Keeping mercy unto the thousandth generation, forgiving iniquity, transgression, and sin" (Exod. 34:6–7). Forgiveness, according to this proclamation, is rooted in divine com-

134

passion, which is consistent with truth. In other words, forgiveness is not an emotional reaction but a rational judgment based on truth and justice.

What must an offender do to deserve divine compassion and forgiveness? The basic condition is an admission of wrongdoing and an expression of penitence. This is the import of the biblical passage in Leviticus: "And they shall confess their iniquity . . . in the treachery which they committed against me . . . if then perchance their uncircumcised heart shall be humbled . . . then will I remember my covenant with Jacob" (to protect his offspring; Lev. 26:40–42).

The emerging doctrine of forgiveness was succinctly formulated in the Book of Proverbs: "Whoso confesses and forsakes [his evil ways] shall obtain mercy" (28:13). That admission of wrong and repentance are absolute prerequisites of divine forgiveness is a basic tenet of Judaism. Nonrabbinic writers similarly adopted this tenet as a cardinal principle of Judaism. The Qumran Scrolls express the same view: "I [God] will harbor no angry grudge against those that indeed repent, but neither will I show compassion to any that turn from the way" (Gaster, *The Dead Sea Scriptures*, Hymn of the Initiants).

The required sequence of penitence, divine compassion, and forgiveness is the burden of the message of the Book of Jonah (8th cent. B.C.E.). The Ninevites are warned of their impending doom. As an expression of his faith in God, the king declares a fast and proclaims: "Let everyone repent his evil way and desist from the rudeness that is in their hands" (Jonah 3:8). Jonah's personal conviction that criminals should not go unpunished is in conflict with the judgment of God, who is merciful and forgiving to those who are truly penitent (Jonah 4:2).

Why was divine forgiveness denied to the generation of Noah and to the people of Sodom? One may suggest that absolution by penitence was a divine concession first granted to Moses. One may also rationalize the absence of early forgiveness by the prevalence of extreme corruption which destroyed man's ability to perceive wrong, to confess to it, and to experience penitence. Biblical texts seem to support this view. The sentence "and the earth was filled with violence" (prior to the Flood,

Gen. 2:11) seems to convey the enormity of the corruption. The description of the Sodomites. "Their sin is exceedingly grievous" (Gen. 18:20), similarly depicts extreme depravity.

The Talmud agrees with the view that divine forgiveness was always available to man if only he mended his ways. Penitence would have saved the victims of the Flood and the people of Sodom. Rabbi Jose of Caesarea offered the following scenario: "Noah rebuked them, urging 'Repent, for if not, the Holy One, blessed be he, will bring a deluge upon you'" (Sanhedrin 108a). Josephus included a similar scenario in his history of the Jewish people: "And [Noah] being displeased at their conduct urged them to change their disposition and their actions for the better" (Antiq. III:1).

The institution of the solemn Day of Atonement made the theological doctrine of penitence and forgiveness central to Judaism. However, the Day of Atonement primarily relates to religious offenses against God. It is an axiomatic rabbinic maxim that "offenses against God are forgiven [on Yom Kippur], but offenses against a fellowman are not condoned unless one receives the forgiveness of his victim" (Rosh HaShanah 17b). It is important to bear in mind that a violation of the rights of a fellowman constitutes a double offense, against man and against God. Consequently one must secure the forgiveness of both.

The steps leading to human forgiveness are somewhat different than those preceding divine forgiveness. In place of penitence, a term which has a theological connotation, it is preferable to demand an expression of regret and remorse. The sequence preceding human forgiveness is as follows: An admission of guilt, an expression of regret, an apology, and a request for forgiveness. There must also be an offer to make restitution for whatever damage was done. This applies to physical damage as well as to the mental suffering of the injured party.

Is there an ethical obligation to forgive an offender once the above-listed conditions have been fulfilled? The temptation to withhold forgiveness is at times overpowering. Damage to one's reputation, a betrayal of trust, and other similar grave offenses are not easily forgotten. Nevertheless, Judaic ethics make human forgiveness mandatory because man must emulate the ways of God.

Ecclesiasticus (2nd cent. B.C.E.) stresses the ethical imperative of forgiveness. "Forgive thy neighbor the hurt that he has done unto thee, so thy sins also be forgiven when thou prayest. . . . If he that is but flesh nourishes hatred, who will entreat for pardon of his sins?" (Ecclus. 28:2).

The Talmud criticizes persons who stubbornly refuse to be forgiving. Rabbi Jose b. Chanina (3rd cent.) said: "One who asks pardon of his neighbor need do so no more than three times" (*Yoma* 87a). After that one may look to God's forgiveness even in the absence of the forgiveness of the injured party, provided, of course, that restitution has been made. In another talmudic statement, the rabbis labeled an individual who withholds forgiveness "a cruel person" (*Baba Kama* 92a).

The Talmud also deals with the problem of situations where human forgiveness is no longer obtainable as a result of the criminal's action. Such is the case of a murderer. An earthly tribunal will impose a punishment. Can the murderer, however, hope to obtain divine forgiveness in the absence of human forgiveness? Murder is a crime which may not deserve a pardon. What about death resulting from another man's negligence? Can the guilty person be forgiven?

To meet this dilemma, the rabbis devised a religious ritual. The killer must assemble ten persons at the graveside of the victim and say: "I have sinned against the Lord, the Lord of Israel, and against this one whom I have hurt" (*Yoma* 87a). By making his admission of guilt public, he has met the most important condition to satisfy the requirement for divine forgiveness.

The ethical aspect of forgiveness has received universal attention in the post-Nazi era. The continuing search for Nazi criminals who have escaped punishment for their barbaric crimes has met with some opposition, even among those who were deeply outraged by the Nazi atrocities. An oft-expressed opinion holds that with the passage of years it is both humane and ethical to forget and forgive. A prominent member of the clergy articulated this sentiment in a brief statement: "We must forgive them, they will come before the High Tribunal of God."

Judaic ethical perceptions do not envision the forgiveness of criminals who deny their guilt and express no regrets or compassion for the tortured victims. To forgive an unregenerated criminal is to perpetuate evil. Politicians may find it expedient to erase the past. To camouflage expedience with moral sanctity is a travesty of justice.

To repeat the aphorism with which this essay was begun: "To err is human; to forgive, divine." The Nazi error was not human, it was beastly. To forgive them is not divine, it is blasphemy.

Friends and Friendship

A faithful friend is a strong defense, and he that has found one
has found a treasure.

—Ecclesiasticus 6:14

A DEVOTED friend is a good companion, a trusted confidant, a
reliable adviser, a staunch defender, and a sympathetic com-
forter. The price of friendship is reciprocity. Whoever receives
friendship must also give it.

Friendship entails mutual responsibilities far beyond the
normal obligations of man to man. Every person has a duty to
respect the rights of his fellowman, to assist him when his life
is endangered, and to treat him in a manner which does not
insult his dignity. In a relationship between friends, both must
take a personal interest in each other's welfare. They must
share one another's grief and rejoice in one another's happiness. If necessary, each must be prepared to make substantial
sacrifices to help out his friend. A friend is entitled to the
privileged position of a beloved member of one's own family.

A lack of reciprocity ruins the most noble of friendships. A
man who readily accepts an unsecured loan from a good friend
has a moral obligation to act in kind when that friend is in need.
One who permits his friend to expose his private life to him has
a duty to be just as forthcoming and candid with him. To fall
short of these and similar implicit commitments of friendship is
to be guilty of an unethical betrayal of confidence and trust that
makes one's claim of friendship a hollow pretense. A one-sided
friendship inevitably disintegrates into mordant hostility.

The term "friend" in common parlance has an elastic quality.
It ranges the gamut of relationships, from a close and intimate
companion to a stranger who is not one's enemy. Thus speak-

139

ers who address a large audience, most of whom are strangers, normally use the salutatory "friends." An individual who wants to make clear that a specific person is an intimate friend generally adds a clarifying adjective, such as "my good friend" or "close friend." A similar ambivalence is found in the Bible.

The Hebrew term for friend is re-a. The root meaning of this word is "a person in whose company one delights" or "a very desired person." By its very definition, re-a originally designated an intimate friend. The word re-a appears for the first time in the Bible in the description of the relationship between Judah and Hirah the Adullamite (Gen. 38:20). Hirah was obviously an intimate friend of Judah. He was privy to Judah's amorous adventure with Tamar. Hirah was also the man whom Judah entrusted with the delicate mission of retrieving the pledge which he had left with Tamar and suppressing news of an incident which might prove embarrassing. Hirah was described as a re-a of Judah.

The term re-a appears next in Exodus (11:2). The Hebrew slaves were instructed to accept "every man from his [Egyptian] friend" silver and gold jewels. Here the word re-a is no longer used in its original etymological sense of an intimate friend but rather in its broader connotation of a neighbor or any friendly person. It is in this sense that re-a is used thereafter in the Bible. Thus the text of the Golden Rule, "Love thy neighbor [re-a] as thyself" (Lev. 19:18), mandates love of all people.

The broadening of the term "friend" to include every human being reflects a generous and civilized impulse. However, it did not erase the distinction between various grades of friendship. When one finds it important to underline that a particular person is a very close friend, a descriptive phrase is added. Thus in the biblical admonition against undesirable influences of an intimate friend, the text reads: "thy friend who is as thy own soul" (Deut. 13:7).

The rewards of friendship are great, and the Bible encourages people to cultivate it. There are exceptional people who are loners, either by choice or by chance. For most people, the acquisition of friends is a practical necessity. The biblical phrase that "It is not good for man to be alone" (Gen. 2:18) is as applicable to a man without friends as to a man without a wife. Ecclesiastes advocates the assiduous pursuit of friends (Soncino, Eccles. 11:2). Ben Sira informed his readers that "sweet language will multiply friends" (Ecclus. 6:5). He cautioned, however, that "if thou wishest to get a friend, prove him first and be not hasty to credit him" (Ecclus. 6:7). He also warned, "Open not thy heart to every man, lest he repay thee with a shrewd turn" (Ecclus. 8:19).

While the advantages of friendship are obvious, there are also pitfalls that should not be ignored. Biblical moralists were fearful of the influence of undesirable friends. The Pentateuch warns against the enticements of friends who seek to alienate people from their faith (Deut. 13:7). The relevance of this warning is well understood by modern parents whose children have made friends with members of various cults and as result have deserted their parental homes and traditions. It is, of course, a major parental duty to approve of the friends their young children choose.

Considering the inherent dangers of misguided friendships, the rabbis regarded with misgivings a fraternization pursued exclusively for social ends. They preferred associations which promote morality and wisdom. The term re-a, basically a social friend, disappeared from the rabbinical lexicon. Instead, they popularized the term chaver ("one who joins, a companion").

Chaver is a biblical noun which first appears in the post-Pentateuchal Scriptures. It is mentioned in the Book of Judges (20:13) to denote a nation united by common resolve. Isaiah (8th cent. B.C.E.) used this term in a derogatory sense to describe a band of thieves (1:23). The Book of Proverbs used it in the same vein (28:24). However, all later references to chaver connote a positive sense. The psalmist exclaimed: "I am a companion [chaver] of all them that fear thee" (Ps. 119:63). Malachi (5th cent. B.C.E.) calls the wife of one's youth "her husband's companion" (chavertecha, 2:14).

Unlike re-a, chaver is devoid of social overtones. In talmudic terminology, a chaver is a scholar who joins a fellow student for the pursuit of knowledge. A scholarly circle was known as a chavurah (Berachot 9b) or, in its Aramaic rendition, chavrutah (Yevamot 96b).

Some of the social aspects of re-a were retained in a

chavurah. Thus it was said that one must join his *chaver* at mealtime. They must read, study, and live together, and share their secrets (*Avot deRabbi Natan* 8).

The virtue of acquiring a *chaver* was extolled by the rabbis. Rabbi Joshua b. Perachyah (1st cent. B.C.E.) said: "Provide thyself with a teacher and get thee a *chaver*" (*Avot* 1:6). Rabbi Elazar (2nd cent.) recited a daily prayer: "May it be thy will, O Lord our God, to cause to dwell in our midst love and brotherhood, peace and friendship . . . and help me obtain a good *chaver*" (*Berachot* 16b).

The rabbis listed rules of conduct essential to the cementing of proper companionships.

"On the day of his [the companion's] success, rejoice with him" (*Kohelet Rabbah* 7).

"Consider the slightest wrong committed against a *chaver* a major offense, and treat a major service rendered for a *chaver*, as but a small favor" (*Avot deRabbi Natan* 41).

Rabbi Eliezer [2nd cent.] said: "Let thy friend's honor be as dear to you as your own" (*Avot* 2:15).

Like the biblical moralists, the rabbis continued to warn against joining a *chaver* of low character (*Avot* 1:7).

The rabbinical advocacy of scholastic associations did not keep social friendships from flourishing in the talmudic era. The rabbis coined a new word to designate a social friend. They called him *ohev*, an individual who likes another person. There was a tinge of admiration for a man who is able to make friends. They noted that it was much easier to acquire enemies than to make friends (*Yalkut, VaEtchanan* 845). Indeed, "Blessed is he who can convert an enemy into a friend" (*Avot DeRabbi Natan* 23).

The term *ohev* did not gain wide circulation. Most people preferred to call their friend a *chaver*. This common usage is frequently reflected in the pages of the Talmud. In post-talmudic literature, *chaver* is the only term used in describing friends of every nature.

Meiri (13th cent.) summed up the subject of friendship with a pithy maxim: "Do not consider a single enemy too few and a thousand friends too many" (Commentary on *Avot* 1:8).

Gambling

A gambler trespasses all the Ten Commandments.
—Leon of Modena, *Sur Mera*

THE DEPREDATIONS of gambling are no less deadly than the ravages of drug addiction. Despair, poverty, domestic discord, violence, and crime lurk behind gamblers to exact a horrible price. Society's attitude to gambling has been marked by flexibility, depending upon the climate of permissiveness prevailing at any given time. Social small-scale gambling has always been regarded as an innocent pastime. Indeed, people with little interest in music and art find the distraction of an absorbing game most helpful in dispelling the boredom of idleness.

The Bible and the Apocrypha are silent on the subject of gambling. Gambling was unknown in the ancient Hebrew community. It was first introduced in Palestine in the first century, one of the dubious benefits bestowed by the Greek and Roman cultures. Within the century, games of chance and pigeon-racing spread from the Hellenized segment of the population to the rest of the community. The emergence of this fad met with the strong disapproval of the rabbinic leadership.

The introduction of card playing in the fifteenth century, a highly popular form of amusement, similarly evoked firm rabbinical opposition. The rabbis regarded card playing per se, even when gambling was not involved, as highly objectionable. The inordinate amount of time consumed by card games was considered by them a detrimental waste, without any redeeming social value. In most traditional homes the possession of cards was taboo. Yet social card games, played in the privacy of one's home, persisted and eventually gained a passive acceptance in some modern traditional circles.

Strong talmudic opposition to gambling was responsible for a rabbinic law which put the integrity and trustworthiness of gamblers into question. As a result, gamblers were barred from appearing as witnesses in most judicial proceedings. Technically, their right to testify in a court was placed on a par with the eligibility of women, whose right to testify was limited for other reasons. Specifically, gamblers were not accepted as witnesses in civil cases involving financial claims (*Rosh HaShanah* 22a). The impaired credibility of gamblers constituted a public stigma strong enough to discourage all but addicts from gambling.

Rabbi Judah (2nd cent.) eased somewhat the stringency of the law of the ineligibility of gamblers. According to him, the law applies only to gamblers "who have no other means of livelihood [i.e., professional gamblers]. If they have another gainful occupation, they are eligible" (*Sanhedrin* 24b). The divergence of rabbinic views stemmed from two distinct perspectives of the evil of gambling, the legal and moral aspects. Rabba bar Chana (4th cent.) based the rule of disqualification of gamblers on the principle that money gained by gambling is tainted with the smell of robbery.

The biblical definition of robbery is limited to the forceful appropriation of money without the consent of the owner. Acceptance of gambling gains does not constitute robbery in the biblical sense of the word. After the spread of gambling the rabbis broadened the definition of robbery to include money won by gambling. They justified the broader definition by the fact that gamblers do not truly and willingly consent to the giving up of their money. Gamblers enter a game with hopes of winning. A gambler's agreement to forfeit his money if he loses is qualified by mental reservations. One lives up to the terms of the agreement under conditions which amount to quasi compulsion. It is therefore proper to regard money won by gambling as tainted with the smell of robbery.

Individuals guilty of violent robbery (the biblical definition) are wholly disqualified from ever giving testimony in court (Exod. 23:1). Individuals accepting gambling profits (rabbinical definition of robbery) are only partially deprived of their eligibility.

Rav Sheshet (4th cent.) disputes the legal premise of the

opinion which holds a gambler culpable of rabbinically prohibited robbery. In his view, gambling agreements are entered into
voluntarily and hence are legal, though not necessarily enforced by the courts. However, gambling is morally wrong
because it is against public policy. It is God's wish that people
engage in constructive work which contributes to the welfare of
society. A professional gambler is a parasite who does not serve
the interests of the community. A social gambler, on the other
hand, if he has a gainful occupation, is surely not guilty of a
parasitic mode of life and hence does not incur the penalty
which bars him from testifying in a court of law.

The medieval rabbis based their opposition to gambling on a
fusion of the legal and moral aspects discussed in the Talmud.
Social gambling is wrong and should not be permitted. However, violators incur no penalty. A professional gambler is an
antisocial person who lives off the sweat and hard labor of other
people. Such money is tainted with the smell of robbery, and he
who takes it will be penalized accordingly.

Civil laws prohibiting gambling have been relaxed in many
modern societies. A pressing need for revenue has dulled the
age-old objections to gambling and created a liberal approach to
this problem. Players who win millions in lotteries and similar
fund-raising schemes run by the state become overnight heroes greatly popularized by the media. Gambling is thus glam-
orized in the eyes of the public, and its morality is no longer
discussed. The treatment meted out by the talmudic rabbis
stands out in stark contrast. Demoting the eligibility of professional gamblers to the level of the limited rights of women
carried a symbolically significant message. The work force in
ancient society consisted primarily of men. Gamblers were not
a part of this work force. Unlike women, who rendered essential domestic services, the gambler was an unproductive pariah
who was not to be trusted.

Oddly, the initiative for the liberalization of antigambling laws
originated with religious institutions, many of which have
come to depend on income from games like bingo to support
their religious and charitable work. The legalization of bingo
has considerably contributed to the climate which makes the
official licensing of gambling casinos possible.

Gluttony

Be not among bibbers of wine, among gluttonous eaters of meat.

—Proverbs 23:20

GLUTTONY IS harmful to the human body and also degrades one's character. A reckless surrender to excessive appetites reflects greed, the pursuit of self-gratification, lack of self-control, and, above all, ill-manners.

Gluttons are easily recognizable. A group of friends are invited to sit down at a dinner table to help themselves from a tray of food centrally placed within easy reach of all. The glutton is the first to lunge for the food. He takes the largest portion, or even two, without the slightest care that he may be depriving others of their share.

The Bible regards gluttony as a sympton of deep-seated and pervasive corruption which may eventually seek an outlet in criminal activities. This assessment gave rise to the unique biblical law of the "rebellious son." This law is expounded in the following passage: "If a man has a stubborn and rebellious son, who does not heed the voice of his father, or the voice of his mother, and though they chasten him, will not listen to them. Then shall his father and his mother get hold of him and bring him to the elders of his city . . . and they shall say to the elders of his city: 'Our son is stubborn and rebellious, he does not obey us, he is a glutton and a drunkard.' And all the men of the city shall stone him with stones" (Deut. 21:18–21).

The severity of the punishment of the glutton puzzled the rabbis and evoked intense rabbinic discussion. Rabbi Jose Hagalili (2nd cent.) wondered whether a boy was to be executed merely for the crime of gluttony. He resolved the question by attributing the biblical stringency to a psychological insight into the anatomy of gluttony. "The Torah foresaw his [the rebellious son's] ultimate destiny. For in the end, after dissipating his father's wealth, he will seek to satisfy his gluttonous appetite, but being unable to do so, he will go forth at the crossroads and rob" (*Sanhedrin* 72a). Obviously, the normal child with an excessive sweet tooth is not a potential "rebellious son."

Mortal judges cannot be credited with divine prescience. It is beyond their ken to distinguish offensive from criminal gluttony. The rabbis therefore felt that the law of the "rebellious son" was academic, intended to express the Bible's moral repugnance toward gluttony. Built-in legal technicalities, incorporated in the biblical law, rendered a judicial verdict of guilt a practical impossibility. Indeed, according to rabbinic testimony, there was no record of even a single conviction of a "rebellious son" (*Sanhedrin* 71a).

By conceding their inability to implement the biblical anti-gluttony law, the rabbis enhanced its moral force. They used the law as a means of warning parents to moderate a child's untrammeled appetite for food, lest it end as criminal covetousness for money and sex.

In addition to condemning gluttony, the rabbis criticized bad table manners, which give an appearance of gluttony. "No one should grasp food with all his fingers, when eating his meal, so as not to give the appearance of a glutton" (*Kallah Rabbati* 10). Swallowing big mouthfuls of food or drinking a glass of wine in one gulp is gluttonous (*Chinuch* 248).

Traditional rituals associated with the blessing recited over bread were instituted to make people aware of appearances of gluttony. Thus, upon the completion of the sanctification prayer over two loaves on the Sabbath (*Kiddush*), one should slice first only one loaf. An immediate slicing of both loaves may give the appearance of gluttony (*Abudrahim, Betziat Hapat)* The slices must not be too thin, lest he appear stingy. They must not be too thick, lest he appear gluttonous (ibid). Guests receiving a slice of bread each must not begin to eat until the host has had a chance to take a bite first (*Berachot* 47a).

Gossip and Slander

Keep thy tongue from evil and thy lips from speaking guile.
—Psalm 34:14

THE GIFT of speech, which distinguishes man from all other living creatures, is the most vital instrument in the evolutionary process of civilization. At the same time, it is also a most formidable weapon for the destruction of society. In the words of Proverbs: "Death and life are in the power of the tongue" (Prov. 18:21).

The positive and negative potentials of speech are reflected in the opening chapters of Genesis. Two quotations of the statements of each of the principal actors in the drama of the Garden of Eden, Adam, Eve, and the serpent, are recorded in the Bible. Adam's first spoken words proclaimed the establishment of the family unit as the basis of civilized society (Gen. 2: 23–24). On the other hand, in his second statement, Adam disclaimed responsibility for his own wrongdoing by placing the blame on Eve (Gen. 3:12).

The first recorded words of Eve conveyed a sense of pious submission to the will of God, who had forbidden the "fruit of the tree which is in the midst of the garden" (3:2–3). In her second statement, Eve, like Adam, sought to escape punishment, blaming the serpent for her transgression (Gen. 3:13).

The serpent, portrayed as the incarnation of evil, used from the very beginning its power of speech to express blasphemous innuendos and to question the motives of God's prohibition of the fruit (Gen. 3:1). In its second statement, the serpent openly accused God of harboring sentiments of jealousy (Gen. 3:5). The rabbis regarded this verse as history's first slanderous expression and used it as an illustration of the frightful

148

consequences of slander. Adam and Eve were deprived of their immortality. The serpent was condemned to become an object of man's deep loathing (*Tanchuma, Bereshit* 8).

The frequency with which the Bible denounces gossip and slander attests to the persistence of this habit in society. Gossip is motivated by malice, arrogance, love of mischief, idle garrulity, and boredom. People who would normally shrink from inflicting physical injury on anyone else may have no scruples about slinging poisonous verbal arrows at their fellow-men.

The biblical injunction "Thou shalt not go up and down as a talebearer among the people" (Lev. 19:16) is a comprehensive prohibition of malicious calumny as well as idle tattling. Truth is no defense against the sin of talebearing. The second half of the verse which prohibits gossip reads as follows: "neither shalt thou stand idly by the blood of thy neighbor." The sequence is highly significant. It is a dire warning of the potentially deadly consequences of gossip.

There is an additional biblical injunction relating primarily to malicious slander. "Thou shalt not take up [or circulate] a false report" (Exod. 23:1). According to rabbinical interpretation, this injunction is mainly addressed to those who lend a willing ear to false rumors (*Mechilta* 196; Onkelos, Exod. 23:1).

The nefariousness of gossip is enlarged upon in great detail in the Hagiographa. Talebearers create discord among friends (Prov. 16:28). They destroy their neighbors (Prov. 11:9). They readily reveal confidential secrets (Prov. 11:13, 20:19). He who has slander on his tongue cannot be close to God (Ps. 15:1, 3).

Ben Sira (2nd cent. B.C.E.) penned many memorable lines in the continuing campaign against slander. "Many have fallen by the edge of the sword, but not so many as have fallen by the tongue" (Ecclus. 28:18). He exhorts gossipers to give up their habit for their own good. "Honor and shame is in talk, and the talk of man is his downfall. Be not called a whisperer, and lie not in wait with thy tongue; for a foul shame is upon the thief, and an evil condemnation upon the double tongue" (Ecclus. 5:13–14). "He that controls his tongue shall live without strife, and he who hates babbling shall have less evil" (Ecclus. 19:6).

The *Manual of Discipline* of the Qumran sect (ca. 1st cent. B.C.E.) condemned slander as a serious breach of discipline. "If a man slanders his neighbor he shall be regarded as outside of the communal state of purity" (VII:15).

The strongest condemnation of gossip and slander was expressed by the talmudic sages. It was part of the ongoing process of rabbinic interpretation and development of biblical legal and moral perceptions. However, it is likely that political conditions motivated the rabbis to broaden the scope of slander in order to protect the safety of the Jewish community.

The loss of national independence left the Jewish population at the mercy of the officials of a hostile government. An irate victim of baseless gossip might be tempted to seek revenge by turning informer. In the heat of anger, an informer might very well lodge fictitious charges of Jewish revolutionary activities. The belief that the destruction of Jerusalem resulted from false charges brought to the Roman authorities by a disgruntled individual who was insulted by his neighbor (*Gittin* 65a) reinforced the fears of the rabbinic leadership.

The rabbis coined the metaphor *lashon hara* ("evil tongue") as a comprehensive designation of gossip and slander. Their condemnation of talebearing was couched in much more vehement terminology than what is found in the Bible. The following rabbinic dicta illustrate the forcefulness of their moral preachments.

"A gossiper is like unto him who denies the existence of God" (i.e., habitual slanderers end up by slandering God; *Arachin* 15b).

"Slanderers and I [God] cannot coexist in the same world" (ibid.).

"Gossipers, receivers of gossip, and those who bear false testimony deserve to be thrown to the dogs" (*Pesachim* 118a).

"The Exodus generation was doomed to perdition because they listened to slander" (*Arachin* 15b).

"Penitence obtains divine forgiveness of sin, except for the sin of slander" (*Zohar, Vayikra* 53).

It is the duty of man to be forgiving, when his forgiveness is requested, except for the sin of slander (Jer. *Baba Kama* 8:10). This opinion may have been based on a rabbinic psychological insight that the hurt of a victim of slander persists even after he professes forgiveness (*Bereshit Rabbah* 98:19).

The rabbis offered some advice for those who would like to keep from or break the habit of gossip. If one is a scholar let him engross himself in the study of Torah (he will find no time for gossip). If a person has no cultural interests, let him humble himself (by discovering his own faults he will refrain from maligning other people; *Arachin* 15b). Talebearing is a contagious habit. It is best to keep from socializing with friends who are gossips (*Elijah Rabbah* 12).

Under the broad rabbinical definition of slander, deliberate disparagement of the quality of plants and minerals is sinful (*Arachin* 15a). Slander of an unnamed individual, whose identity is recognized by the listener, is forbidden (Jer. *Peah* 1).

A new category, named by the rabbis "dust of slander," was added to the list of biblical prohibitions (*Baba Batra* 165a). Thus a slanderous statement repeated not as a fact but in a humorous vein as a joke is forbidden (Maimonides, *Hilchot Deot* 7:4). Innocuous statements which may provoke other people to engage in slander are forbidden (*Arachin* 16a). Thus one should not praise an individual in the presence of his enemy. The latter will instinctively retort with a calumny (Maimonides, *Hilchot Deot* 7:4). Post-talmudic moralists even cautioned against the mere mention of an individual's name to that person's enemy.

It is noteworthy that despite the harsh condemnation of slander, the rabbis permitted the defamation of contentious individuals whose divisive influence threatens communal harmony (Jer. *Peah* 1). The prohibition of slander, aimed at the protection of society, should not be used as a shield to protect those who seek to destroy it.

Despite the numerous moral interdictions of slander, the rabbis realized that their measures alone would not eradicate the habit. One must also pray to God for help in resisting the temptation of slander. Mar the son of Ravina (3rd cent.)

composed the following prayer which he recited every morning: "My God, keep my tongue from evil and my lips from speaking guile. May my soul be silent to them that curse me, and may my soul be as dust to all" (*Berachot* 17a). This prayer was incorporated into the daily liturgy.

Greed and Miserliness

He who loves silver shall never have his fill of silver.
—Ecclesiastes 5:9

MAN IS endowed with a variety of appetites, some instinctive and some acquired. The appetite for food is present at birth. The appetite for sex comes with puberty. Both are stimulated by powerful inner drives. The craving for material wealth, developed by most people, is merely incidental to the need for satisfying one's basic appetites.

Nature in its wisdom renders the process of gratifying one's hungers a pleasurable experience. Thus it makes sure that man will meet his biological needs. However, nature's bonus of pleasure also poses a danger. Some people develop insatiable appetites in their pursuit of pleasure to the point where they can no longer satisfy their hungers without doing irreparable damage to their own welfare.

The process of acquiring money is not pleasurable per se. People work hard to earn money because it is a necessary means to an end. There are some, however, to whom money is an end in itself. Such people are not driven by natural appetites but by greed.

The first-century Hellenist philosopher Philo the Alexandrian analyzed the desire for money as follows: "The bad man considers the acquisition of money as the most perfect good possible, but the good man, only as a useful and necessary thing" (*On the Allegories of the Sacred Laws* 2:6).

The symptoms of greed may appear early in life. Two little boys get money on their birthdays. One rushes out to buy candy or toys. The other puts his money away and does not spend it. Both boys may be sending signals of danger. One may grow up to be a spendthrift, the other a hoarder and a miser.

153

The transgression of Adam and Eve in the biblical account of the Garden of Eden is a classical example of greed. They had at their disposal all the fruits in the garden, but they were greedy for the forbidden fruit.

Greed and miserliness are among the vanities decried in Ecclesiastes. "There is one that is alone . . . yet is there no end of all his labor, neither is his eye satisfied with riches; for whom then do I labor and deny my soul all pleasure?" (4:8). "There is an evil which I have seen under the sun . . . a man to whom God gives riches, property, and honor . . . yet God gives him not power to eat thereof" (6:1–2).

The tenth commandment, against covetousness, is Judaism's fundamental condemnation of greed. The commandment considers man capable of resisting the temptation of greed. Judaism denies that it is God who "gives him not power to eat thereof." It is up to man to tame his greed. According to Philo, this was one of the aims of the institution of Yom Kippur. "After the harvest, there might be a tendency to proceed at once to begin devouring the bounty. Moses looked upon that as an act of greediness; he therefore regarded the fast of Yom Kippur as an act of piety to tame greediness" *(On the Ten Festivals, The Ninth Festival)*.

The tenth commandment has to be read in the context of previous commandments which prohibit murder and theft. The association reveals a philosophic insight into the evil of greed. The wealth of the world is God's gift to humanity. Every person has a right to take a share which will meet all his needs. The greedy man, who grasps a share in excess of his needs and does not put his wealth in productive ventures, robs other people of their opportunity to get their due. In their perversity, greedy people are dissatisfied with what they have and desire the property of others. They are a constant source of dissension within the community. In the words of the Book of Proverbs: "A greedy person stirs up strife" (Prov. 28:25).

Poverty and wealth are relative terms. A greedy person, no matter how rich, does not consider himself wealthy. "Who is wealthy?" asked the rabbis, "he who is contented with his lot" (*Avot* 4:1).

Hate and
Grudge-Bearing

The Lord hates the man of blood and of deceit.

—Psalm 5:7

HATE IS a reflexive emotion which manifests itself in early life. Children hate their doctor because he inspires fear and occasionally causes pain. Young students hate teachers who are strict disciplinarians. Theoretically, if a child could be raised in a benign environment, free of pain and unpleasantness, he would never experience hate. Such a hypothesis, of course, is purely academic. Pain-free environments exist only in utopia.

When a child matures and acquires sophistication, he reacts to the intent of the people whom he encounters rather than their acts. He soon comes to realize that the doctor is his friend despite his pain-causing manipulations. On the other hand, he will not be taken in by the man who wears a perpetual smile to mask his inner hostility.

The most common hates which the average individual experiences are of the mild and passive category generally described as dislikes. Sooner or later man adjusts to his dislikes and learns to live with them. Those who dislike some items of food quietly exclude them from their diet. Those who dislike the rude manners of some of their friends simply avoid their company. In contrast to the mild dislikes, the hate with which one reacts to people who intentionally hurt him is both violent and aggressive. Indeed, there are many categories of hate, ranging between dislike and detestation.

In addition to emotional hatreds, there are reasoned, albeit irrational, hatreds induced by hostile propaganda or environment. Thus one may acquire a hate for people of other faiths or races, even though he has never met them or experienced personal unpleasantness at their hands. Reasoned hate is invariably much more violent than the emotional type. Indeed, the fewer the rational grounds to account for one's hate, the greater the belligerence of one's hostility.

Is hate intrinsically an unethical and repugnant emotion, a barbaric vestige of man's primitive past? If hate of antisocial people is instinctive, can such a reaction be regarded as immoral, for which one should feel guilty?

The basic biblical injunction against hate is found in Leviticus: "Thou shalt not hate thy brother in thy heart" (19:17). Is this a blanket prohibition of hate of people under all circumstances? The phrase "thy brother" appears significant. It seems to imply that individuals who normally act in a brotherly fashion and pose no threat to society do not merit the hate of their fellowmen, even in the event that they commit an occasional wrong. Such people are generally amenable to correction, and they are entitled to be given a chance to make amends, when amends are possible. Their opportunity for rehabilitation is prejudiced by the hate of society. It is highly significant that the injunction against hate is coupled with another injunction: "thou shalt surely rebuke thy neighbor" (ibid.). The intent of this verse is rather clear. So long as a wrongdoer accepts rebuke and is willing to restore friendly relationships, he must not be hated.

It is noteworthy that the qualifying phrase "thy brother" does not appear in the negative injunctions of the Decalogue (Exod. 20:13–14). One may not kill or rob any person, saint or sinner. This obviously is not the case with regard to hate. A habitual and incorrigible criminal may, and indeed should, be hated by society, individually and collectively.

The rabbis took note of an additional phrase in the injunction against hate, which further limits the intent of this verse. The prohibited hate is the kind which is "in thy heart" (Lev. 19:17). Hate can find an outlet in violent reactions, or it can remain quiescent in the heart. A prohibition of overt acts is feasible. However, what is the practical effect of a divine prohibition of an emotion? How can one control his heart to exclude from it an instinctive reaction of hate? Hate is part of man's psyche and will not disappear because it is outlawed.

The rabbinical answer to these questions amended the scope of the prohibition of hate. In the opinion of the rabbis, the phrase "in thy heart" changes the framework of the prohibition. In effect, the principal aim of the verse is to warn against keeping a grudge bottled up "in the heart," i.e., one must not keep his grudge secret. "Thou shalt surely rebuke thy neighbor." A discussion of one's grievance is therapeutic and desirable. The rabbis regarded as particularly reprehensible any pretense of "business as usual," and needless to say an appearance of friendship, at a time when one bears a grudge in his heart (*Bereshit Rabbah* 84). The new interpretation stresses the need for purging one's hate rather than prohibiting the initial experience of hate.

The expression of an opinion that comes closest to favoring a prohibition of hate is attributed in the Talmud to Beruriah (2nd cent.), the scholarly wife of Rabbi Meir. The rabbi was sorely vexed by a lawless band of highwaymen operating in his neighborhood. In a moment of great despair, Rabbi Meir uttered a prayer to God that he bring destruction upon the criminals. Beruriah overheard her husband's prayer and demurred. She was aware that his prayer followed closely the text of a verse in the Book of Psalms: "Let sinners [*chataim*] cease out of the earth, and let the wicked be no more" (104:35). However, Beruriah remonstrated that the Hebrew term *chataim* is a double-entendre. It means "sinners" but also "sins." She felt that her husband should direct his hate against the crime rather than the criminals. He should therefore pray that the sins of the criminals should come to an end and in this manner "the wicked will be no more" (*Berachot* 10a). It is not clear, however, whether hate is always immoral in the opinion of Beruriah. Conceivably, she had a better insight into the psychology of the street gangs and felt that they were not beyond reform.

The rabbinic censure of animosity was mainly centered on the causeless hate (*sinat chinam*) that stems from blind prejudice. The Hebrew phrase *sinat chinam* was based on a verse in the Book of Psalms: "May those who for no reason are my enemies not rejoice over me; as for those hating me without cause [*sonei chinam*], let them not wink the eye" (35:19).

The rabbis attributed the destruction of the second sanctuary (1st cent.) to the prevalence of causeless hatred in society (*Yoma* 9b). They added for emphasis: "That teaches you that groundless hatred is considered of equal gravity with the three sins of idolatry, immorality, and bloodshed together" (ibid.). Rabbi Joshua (1st–2nd cent.) warned that groundless hate is self-destructive. "Hatred of one's fellowman puts one out of the world" (*Avot* 2:16).

A glaring example of causeless hate prevailing in the post-Temple era, when academies of high learning assumed a dominant position, was the deep animosity which separated the ignorant from the educated classes (*Pesachim* 49b). The rabbis issued a stern warning: "Let no one say, 'I love scholars and hate ignorant people,' but say, 'I love them all, and I hate the perverters of religion and the inciters' " (*Avot deRabbi Natan* 16).

The rabbis felt that there was ample reason for hating inciters who sought to subvert the Jewish religion. Judaic monotheism was a small island in an ocean of paganism. It had to wage a perpetual struggle to keep from being submerged. In Christian Europe, ever since the fourth century, Jews were exposed to Christian missionary activities. At the same time, missionizing by Jews became a capital offense. Conditions under Islam were not much better. It is not surprising that Jews regarded with utmost gravity the efforts of missionaries, be they former Jews or non-Jews, to undermine the structure of the Jewish community. Hate of a missionary was a potent self-defensive weapon in the Jewish arsenal.

The power of church over state has undergone a radical change in modern times. This is particularly true in countries where religion and state are separated. However, freedom of religion has not induced Jews to resume missionary activities after a hiatus of seventeen centuries. Furthermore, Jews lack any incentive for gaining converts, in view of their belief that all followers of monotheism are equally in the grace of God. An old rabbinic slogan proclaims that "religious people of all faiths have a share in the world-to-come" (Tosefta, *Sanhedrin* 13). As a result, Jews are still open to missionary blandishments and activities which pose a danger to Jewish survival. Jews regard such efforts as offensive and hateful.

There are other objectionable situations to which hate was considered an appropriate and justifiable reaction. It is permissible to hate immoral people (*Pesachim* 113b). God was portrayed as hating hypocrites and those who withhold testimony which is needed by another person to prove a claim (ibid.). In both instances the offender is shielded by a screen of secrecy and cannot be called to account by society for his unethical conduct.

An enemy engaged in war is a legitimate object of hate. The biblical verse "A time to love and a time to hate" (Eccles. 3:8) was interpreted as follows: " 'A time to love'—when peace prevails; 'a time to hate'—when an enemy is at war" (*Kohelet Rabbah* 3).

Despite the legitimacy of hate of an enemy, the Bible warns the victor not to gloat when the enemy has fallen. "Rejoice not when thy enemy falls, and let not thy heart be glad when he stumbles" (Prov. 24:17). This perception is an example of morality at its highest level. The sight of suffering is saddening even if it is the enemy who suffers.

No epoch in history has left a greater heritage of hate than the Hitler era. The Nazis gloried in their hate and in turn were detested by civilized mankind. However, some moralists were troubled by the widespread hate for the Nazis. Their misgivings were based on the inconsistency of hate, even of Nazi degenerates, with the Golden Rule. Martin Buber, himself a victim of Nazi persecution, is quoted as having said: "We hate Nazism but not Nazis." A moralist of lesser stature expressed the same sentiment more forcefully: "I love Hitler but despise Hitlerism."

It is indeed admirable when moralists can master their emotions to the point where they are able to eradicate hate from their hearts. Few people are possessed of such strength. Judaism does not demand a moral stance which the overwhelming mass of people is incapable of attaining. The expression "I love Hitler" might have been a calculated choice of phraseology for its shock effect, but it smacks of cynicism. From a practical point of view, a moral stance which goes beyond an accepted norm of ethics is in most instances counterproductive. Does kindness shown to a Nazi have a humanizing effect on him? Experience has proven otherwise. Indeed, the Nazis themselves would have branded any of their victims who did not react with hate as a weakling and a subhuman who deserved to be exterminated.

It is wrong to dissociate an unregenerated criminal from his crime. A perpetrator of evil deeds is an evil person. A refusal to hate him is an open invitation to future crimes and holocausts.

Hospitality

Deal thy bread to the hungry, and bring the poor that are cast out to thy house.

—Isaiah 58:7

HOSPITALITY WAS widely practiced in primitive societies, particularly in the Near East. Unlike the modern hospitality for social entertainment of friends, ancient hospitality was a charitable function to aid strangers in need of food and shelter.

The hospitability of the ancients is amply illustrated in the Bible. The sight of strangers passing his tent sent Abraham scurrying after them with an urgent invitation to dinner (Gen. 18:3). Abraham's nephew, Lot, residing in the midst of the Sodomites, risked his life by offering shelter to strangers (Gen. 19:2). Josephus attributed Lot's hospitability to the influence of Abraham (*Antiq.* I:11). It was more likely a tribal tradition. Rebecca, a kin of Abraham residing in far-off Mesopotamia, extended hospitality to Eliezer in a most gracious manner (Gen. 24:25).

The Midianites, a Semitic tribe descended from Abraham and Keturah (Gen. 25:2), were also a hospitable people. When Jethro, the priest of the Midianites, learned of the presence of a stranger, he ordered his daughters to invite him to dinner (Exod. 2:20).

Hospitability continued to be a folk trait of the Hebrews after they changed their nomadic existence and settled down to a national life in permanent homes. More than seven centuries after Rebecca, Manoah pleaded with a stranger (the disguised angel who predicted the birth of Samson): "I pray thee, let us detain thee that we may make ready a kid for thee" (Jud. 13:15). About a century and a half later, a Shunammite host-

161

ess ran after the itinerant prophet Elisha with an offer of board and lodging (II Kings 4:8).

Despite the fact that ancient hospitality was an act of charity, no mention of it is made in the various biblical injunctions dealing with the subject of charity. Most of these commandments provide for the sharing of agricultural products with the poor (Lev. 19:9, Deut. 24:28, etc.). To a farming nation agricultural products were the most available commodities for distribution to the needy. The indigent beneficiaries were local residents who carried the distributed food to their own homes for consumption. The number of wayfarers was too small to create a visible need of official provision for the accommodation of strangers away from home. Pilgrims on the way to Jerusalem carried their own food and did not depend on hospitality.

The economic structure of Palestinian Jewry changed after the colonization of Palestine by the Persian and Roman empires. The introduction of commerce filled the highways with travelers. Frequent wars between competing dynasties sent roving masses of uprooted people through the countryside in search of new homes. The establishment of academies in various parts of the country attracted great numbers of students who were too poor to set up temporary living quarters in the vicinity of the school. The resulting urgency for large-scale hospitality is reflected in various talmudic legal and moral dicta.

A rabbinic ordinance of the second century permitted the clearing on the Sabbath of warehouses filled with straw to make room for visitors and students who could not be accommodated at the school (Shabbat 126b). The demand for space was so extensive that on some occasions large farm tracts had to be cleared of sheaves to make room for temporary student lodgings (ibid.). These measures reflect the developing conditions which made hospitality an urgent social need.

It was not until the era of the Crusades, with the dislocation of numerous Jewish communities in its wake, that hospitality became an absolute necessity for survival. The growing need for welcoming strangers into one's home is further reflected in the various customs and institutions developed by medieval Jewry.

The basic talmudic passage exalting the merit of hospitality dates from the third century. Rabbi Yochanan was quoted as saying: "There are six acts the fruit [reward] of which man eats in this world, while the principal remains for him in the world-to-come [i.e., he is rewarded again in the hereafter]: hospitality to wayfarers, visitation of the sick, etc." (*Shabbat* 127a). An earlier passage in a Mishnah lists three meritorious deeds which bring a reward here and hereafter: "Honor of parents, the practice of loving deeds, and making peace between man and his fellows" (*Peah* 1:1). Hospitality, not mentioned in the first passage, ranks first in the later list. It appears that the need for hospitality grew more urgent in the interval of time between the two passages.

The following are some of the talmudic quotations lauding hospitality.

1. "Yose the son of Yochanan of Jerusalem [2nd cent. B.C.E.] said: 'Let thy house be open wide, let the poor be members of thy household' "(*Avot* 1.5).

Meiri, a thirteenth-century scholar and moralist, commented on the significance of the phrase "let the poor be members of thy household." A poor person should repeatedly be invited to one's home so that he should get to feel at home and come to be regarded as a member of one's family. He also noted that by establishing a close relationship with his needy guest, the host will assume a responsibility for securing work for him, in the same spirit as one would try for a "member of the household" (*Bet HaBechirah. Masechet Avot*).

Rabbi Israel Meir Kahan (Chafetz Chaim, d. 1933), the outstanding modern rabbinic moralist, added another ethical perception in his comment on the phrase "a member of thy household." He noted that there are people of modest means who are reluctant to invite strangers because the appearance of their homes and the simplicity of their meals are below the standards of more affluent families. This reluctance could be overcome by regarding the guest as a "member of the household." A host does not strive to impress his family, nor is he embarrassed by maintaining a standard of living which is within his modest means (Chafetz Chaim, *Masechet Avot*).

2. The virtue of a dining table which provides food for the

poor was compared by Rabbis Yochanan and Resh Lakish (3rd cent.) to that of the sacrificial altar in the Sanctuary. "At the time when the Temple was in existence [in Jerusalem], the altar used to make atonement for a person; now a person's table makes atonement for him" (*Chagigah* 27a).

3. "Make sure that the door to your home is not locked when you sit down at the table to eat" (i.e., permit hungry people to join you; *Derech Eretz Zuta* 9).

4. Rav Huna (4th cent.) made it a habit to go outside his house at mealtime to announce: "Whoever is in need let him come and eat" (*Taanit* 20b). Rav Huna's slogan was eventually incorporated into the Haggadah as an invitation to all who are hungry to enter and participate in the Seder.

It is reported that the sight of an inscription on a Jewish home inviting the hungry to enter and eat influenced Lord George Gordon, an eighteenth-century English convert, to take an interest in Judaism.

Rabbinic efforts to promote hospitality in the Jewish community also led to the formulation of rules of proper conduct for visitors.

An invited guest may not bring along with him an uninvited guest (*Baba Batra* 98b).

Guests must beware of overstaying their hospitality (*Chulin* 84a).

An ethical guest admires the quality of the meal and appreciates the host's efforts on his behalf. An unethical guest is critical of the food and dismisses the efforts of the host as having been made primarily to please his own family (*Berachot* 58a). However, the rabbis cautioned guests not to sing the praises of their host in public for fear that they might be overwhelmed by too many requests for hospitality.

Medieval Jewry, faced with the problem of a growing number of wayfarers in need of lodging, permitted the use of synagogues and schools as hostelries. The ritual of *Kiddush*, the sanctification of the Sabbath, normally performed at home, was introduced into the Friday Eve service for the sake of visitors who spend the Sabbath away from their homes. For a similar reason, congregations built a communal sukkah to accommodate visitors spending the festival on the road. At the same time the custom of inviting strangers to one's home to partake of Sabbath and festival meals became widespread.

Modern conditions have eliminated the need for hospitality as a charitable function. Yet to some extent, the traditional hospitality still serves a spiritual need, though it is no longer characterized as charity. Modern travelers who observe the religious laws of kashrut still appreciate an invitation to a kosher home for a Sabbath meal. The same is true of out-of-town college students who occasionally crave the warmth of a meal in a home environment. To young people in the military service, an invitation to a family dinner may well be the highlight of their social lives. To all such people the traditional Jewish hospitality still provides a genuinely meaningful and enriching experience.

Humility

A man's arrogance shall bring him low, but he that is humble shall attain honor.

—Proverbs 29:23

HUMILITY IS the reverse of arrogance. An arrogant individual has a high opinion of himself. A humble individual thinks little of himself. Arrogance is born of conceit, humility flows from an innate sense of modesty.

A humble person is free of illusions of superiority. He is aware of his achievements but does not believe that they entitle him to preferential treatment. However, humility which results from self-denigration is a harmful trait, destructive of human dignity. Humility is most virtuous when it does not distort one's judgment of oneself. It must not be tinged with a sense of false modesty nor with a sense of inferiority.

Judaism regards humility as the crown of man's ethical stature. The Bible singles out the humbleness of Moses as his most laudable trait (Num. 12:13). The Talmud points to Hillel's meekness as the quality most worthy of emulation (*Shabbat* 31b).

The early biblical figures set a proper tone of modesty. When Abraham questioned the justice of God's condemnation of Sodom, he made sure to disclaim any stance of arrogance, "for I am but dust and ashes" (Gen. 18:27). Jacob's expression of gratitude for God's help was heightened by the disarming acknowledgment that he was unworthy of such generous consideration (Gen. 32:11). David rejected the rebuke of his wife, Michal, for his participation in the dance of the common people on the occasion of the arrival of the Ark of God. He protested

166

that he would continue to be lowly in his own eyes (II Sam. 6:22).

Isaiah proclaims that "the humble shall increase their joy in the Lord" (29:19). The Book of Proverbs declares: "Better it is to be of lowly spirit with the humble than to divide the spoil with the proud" (16:19). The Book of Psalms describes the great promise in store for the meek. "The humble shall inherit the land and delight themselves in the abundance of peace" (37:11).

The apocryphal Ecclesiasticus continued to preach the virtue of modesty. "My son, go on with thy business with meekness, so shalt thou be beloved of him that is approved. The greater thou art, the more humble thyself, and thou shalt find favor before the Lord" (3:16–17). "The mysteries of God are not revealed to the renowned but to the meek" (3:19). The Qumran sect (ca. 1st cent. B.C.E.) declared humility to be a prerequisite for atonement of sin (*Manual of Discipline*).

The Talmud extols the virtue of humility in most lavish terms. Rabbi Levitas of Yavneh said: "Be exceedingly lowly of spirit, since the hope of man is but the worm" (*Avot* 4:4). It was a pointed reminder that in the end the arrogant share the fate of the humble.

Rabbi Meir (2nd cent.) asserted that the test of true humility is man's conduct in the presence of all kinds of people, including the boorish and the ignorant (*Avot* 4:12). A later Midrash elaborated upon this theme. "A man should be humble with his parents, teacher, and wife, with his children, with his household, with his close and distant relatives, even with the heathen in the street, so that he will become beloved on high and looked up to on earth" *(Tanna devei Elijah)*.

Rabbi Chanina b. Ida suggested that only the truly humble can attain scholarship. There is substantial logic behind this assumption. An arrogant person never admits to a mistake, and as a result the truth will always elude him. Rabbi Chanina expressed his opinion in a homiletical passage. "Why are the words of the Torah likened unto water, as it is written 'Ho, everyone who is thirsty [for knowledge], come for water' [Isa. 55:1]? This is to teach you, just as water flows from a higher level to a lower level, so too the words of the Torah endure only with him who is humble" (*Taanit* 7a).

Rabbi Joshua b. Levi (1st–2nd cent.) said: "He who has a humble mind is regarded [by God] as if he had offered all the ritual sacrifices [humility is a spiritual sacrifice which atones for his sins], and his prayers are received with great regard" (*Sotah* 5b).

The preeminence of humility is stressed in the following passage from a late Midrash. "One should pray first for humility, then for intelligence, and after that for a livelihood" (*Schochar Tov* 20:5). The sequence reflects the order in which morality should be instructed in the various stages of human development. The virtue of humility should be instilled in the very young. With maturity one is ripe for the acquisition of intelligence. The assumption of economic responsibility comes in the last stage of growth.

Humility and intelligence are essential qualifications for any person who presumes to pass judgment on others. "A judge must possess wisdom and humility so that the minds of men shall be pleased with him" (*Sanhedrin* 88b).

The rabbis provided some rules of conduct as a test of one's humbleness.

"One must not walk about with a stiff bearing" (*Berachot* 43b). The same objection applies to any bearing which reflects aloofness and a mien of superiority.

When an individual is invited to lead a congregational service, he should at first decline the honor (*Berachot* 32a). Honor is bestowed only upon individuals who deserve it. A humble person, therefore, should always question whether he is deserving of honor.

People should not accept exaggerated praise. Every person who is aware of his inadequacies is best able to judge which praise is unwarranted. He must therefore voice his reservations (*Chovat HaLevavot, Shaar HaChinuch* 7).

The dictates of human dignity and of humility may clash at times and result in a conflict. The rabbis were careful to establish a balance between dignity and humility so that each receives its due.

A humble individual should refrain from responding to insults and must urge his family and friends to do likewise (*Sefer HaChinuch* 650). However, if his reputation is at stake, considerations of humility are put aside and he must preserve his dignity by reacting properly to the insult (*Sefer HaChinuch* 674).

An unemployed person who declines an offer of menial work because it is beneath his dignity, and prefers to humble himself and accept charity, commits a folly (*Baba Batra* 110a; Luzzatto, *Mesilat Yesharim* 11).

A scholar who engages a colleague in debate must not fret if his opponent demonstrates superior knowledge. It is more important to learn the truth than to seek the satisfaction of victory (*Sefer HaChinuch* 42).

Nachmanides, the most revered scholar of his generation (13th cent.) sent a moralist testament from Acre, Palestine, to his son in Spain. The letter has become a treasured contribution to Judaic ethical literature. The central theme of the message is the importance of cultivating humility. He admonished his son to "humble yourself so God will exalt you . . . consider other people more worthy than yourself . . . when people address you, do not respond in a loud voice, but only in a gentle tone, like a student speaking to his teacher" (*Iggeret HaRamban*).

Dignity and humility are important elements of man's religious outlook. Above all, they are essential to man's proper social behavior.

Hypocrisy

They speak falsehood everyone with his neighbor; with smooth words and with a double heart do they speak.

—Psalm 12:3

IT IS said that every man has some larceny in his heart. If there is any truth to this cynical remark, one may properly add that there is some hypocrisy in every man's mind. Surely people who pretend in public to adhere to a strict code of integrity and morality but fail to live up to their professed high standards of behavior in the privacy of their homes suffer from a touch of hypocrisy.

Mild hypocrisy is generally motivated by a desire to make a good impression and to gain the respect of one's fellowman. Moralists do not condone even the mildest form of hypocrisy, but they accept it as a common human weakness. They are not so charitable when it comes to aggressive hypocrisy directed against other people, mostly for selfish reasons.

An individual who secretly disregards the law when it serves his needs but persists in attacking others for their lawlessness is a despicable hypocrite. An individual who is secretly lax in his religious observances but sanctimoniously berates his friends for their lack of religious fervor is a detestable hypocrite. An individual who seldom supports worthy causes but criticizes others for their skimpy contributions to charity is a mean hypocrite. It is a known fact that vigilante groups engaged in moral crusades attract a high number of hypocrites to their ranks.

In addition to the common classes of passive and aggressive hypocrites, there is another category of self-exculpating hypocrites. Chief among these are people who seek to camouflage their record of unethical activities with a screen of respectability and high-minded social consciousness. A thief who ostentatiously donates part of his ill-gained wealth to charity, a loan-shark who supports worthy causes, an exploiting employer who sets up philanthropic foundations, are all engaged in a hypocritical coverup. Institutions which accept tainted largess are inadvertently aiding an unconscionable process of whitewashing.

All types of hypocrisy are deceitful, banned under the biblical prohibition of deceit (Lev. 25:14). Self-exculpating hypocrisy, sweetened by the bait of civic-mindedness, is singled out in the Bible as unacceptable. A harlot's offering, acquired by immoral acts, must be rejected out of hand by the officials of the sanctuary (Deut. 23:17). The same is true of offerings brought by thieves (Rashi, Lev. 1:2; *Sukkah* 30a).

The prophet Malachi (5th cent. B.C.E.) was contemptuous of unethical people who pollute the altar with their hypocritical offerings. "You have brought that which was taken by violence, thus you bring the offering. Should I accept this of your hand?" (1:13). The legal principle which bars the laundering of blemished money is based on the rabbinic maxim: "A precept [good deed] fulfilled through a transgression" is not acceptable (*Sukkah* 30a). The end does not justify the means.

The prophet Isaiah (8th cent. B.C.E.) strongly inveighed against all hypocritical behavior. The prayers of people who have shed blood will not be heeded by God (1:15). He railed against hypocrites "who swear by the name of God . . . but not in truth nor in righteousness" (48:1). He ridiculed the hypocrites who indulge in fasts to obtain atonement but persist in their wickedness (58:4). The prophet Micah (8th cent. B.C.E.) condemned judges who accept bribes and priests whose judgment is influenced by money. "They lean upon the Lord and say: 'Is not the Lord in the midst of us?' " (3:11).

The Book of Proverbs abounds in denunciations of hypocrisy. "The sacrifice of the wicked is an abomination to the Lord" (15:8). "Burning lips and a wicked heart are like an earthen vessel overlaid with silver dross. . . . When he speaks fair, believe him not, for there are seven abominations in his heart"

(26:23, 25). Ben Sira (2nd cent. B.C.E.) points to the paradoxical situation of the hypocrite who feels insecure even when he abides by the law. "A wise man hates not the law, but he that is a hypocrite is a ship in a storm" (Ecclus. 33:2).

The Talmud continued to give emphasis to biblical strictures against hypocrisy. Resh Lakish (3rd cent.) was the author of a forceful maxim: "Correct thyself and only then correct others" (*Baba Metzia* 108b). This maxim effectively deflates hypocritical critics who habitually pass judgment on others while blithely ignoring their own faults.

In their campaign against hypocrites, the rabbis used the threat of divine displeasure as a powerful deterrent. "Three [individuals] the Holy One, blessed be he, hates; he who is a hypocrite . . ." (*Pesachim* 113b). "There are four classes of men who are not admitted into the presence of God; the mockers, the hypocrites . . ." (*Midrash Tehilim* on Ps. 51:7). "Hypocrites bring [divine] anger upon the world . . . their prayers are unheeded" (*Sotah* 41b).

Rabbi Chiya (2nd–3rd cent.) strongly urged that hypocrites be publicly exposed. The unmasking of hypocrites is necessary in order to forestall unfair reflections on God. Should misfortune befall an individual whose hypocrisy is unknown to the general public, some may baselessly question the justice of God (*Midrash Tehilim* on Ps. 52:2).

The hypocrisy of ordinary people is deplorable, but hypocritical leaders pose a much greater danger to the welfare of society. Their true disposition may not be discovered in time to allow the community to take some protective measures. The best advice the rabbis had to offer to these people projected a tone of helpless resignation: "When a community perceives its leader to be a hypocrite, it is well advised to fly into space" (i.e., to move away; *Devarim Rabbah* 5). Happily, under a democracy, society has recourse to other remedies.

Hypocritical scholars and self-appointed religious leaders were singled out as targets of severe rabbinic strictures. "Hypocritical individuals pretend that they can read the Scriptures and the Mishnah, but in fact are ignorant, don a tallit, put on tefillin, and proceed to oppress the poor. . . . It is up to me

[God] to punish them, as it is written [Jer. 48:10]: 'Cursed be they who do the work of the Lord deceitfully' " (*Kohelet Rabbah* on Eccles. 4:1).

Rabbi Gamaliel (1st–2nd cent.), head of the academy, opened school with a daily announcement: "Students whose inside is not like their outside [hypocrites] may not enter the academy" (*Berachot* 28a). In this manner, he sought to weed out young men of undesirable character from joining the ranks of scholars.

Rava (4th cent.) said: "A scholar whose inside is not like his outside is no scholar" (*Yoma* 72b). This statement is more than an impugnment of the moral stature of a hypocritical scholar. It denies his standing as a scholar. A hypocrite, motivated by selfishness, has no capacity for objective research. Rava's colleague, Abaye, used even stronger language. A hypocritical scholar, he said, is an abomination (ibid.).

We have discussed elsewhere the widespread slanderous New Testament allegations which smear the talmudic rabbis with a taint of hypocrisy (Bloch, *The Biblical and Historical Background of Jewish Customs, and Ceremonies*, p. 367). The Bible and the Talmud are remarkably frank in exposing the weaknesses of even the most prestigious Jewish leaders. Yet not a single religious leader or scholar has ever been accused of hypocrisy. King Alexander Jannaeus (2nd–1st cent. B.C.E.), an avowed opponent of the rabbinic leadership, acknowledged the sincerity of the rabbis. He is quoted as having told his wife, Queen Alexandra, in a deathbed statement: "Fear not the Pharisees, or the non-Pharisees, but the hypocrites who ape the Pharisees" (*Sotah* 22b). According to Josephus, it was Jannaeus who cynically advised his wife to pretend that she was a loyal follower of Rabbinic Judaism (*Antiq.* XIII:15).

Hypocrisy by its very nature is easily concealed. It is the extreme effort of some hypocrites to convince people of their sincerity that occasionally betrays them. Rabbi Moses Kobriner, a Chasidic leader of the nineteenth century, was the author of a pertinent parable. An old mouse sent her young son to fetch some food. "Be careful of our enemy," she prudently warned him. The young mouse came upon a rooster and ran back to his mother in great panic. "I saw a creature which appears so haughty and wears a prominent red comb on his head." His mother reassured him. "He is not our enemy." On his second trip, the mouse encountered a turkey. Overcome with fright, he fled once again to his mother. "I saw a puffed-up creature with the mean look of a killer." "He is not our enemy," the mother repeated. "Our enemy keeps his head down in a show of humility. He is smooth and soft-spoken, friendly in appearance, and looks like the kindest of creatures. Of him you must beware" (Newman, *Hasidic Anthology*, p. 192).

A concise rabbinic passage relating to hypocrisy was adopted as a prayer and included in the daily liturgy: "At all times let a man fear God, as well in private as in public, acknowledge the truth, and speak the truth in his heart" (*Tanna devei Eliyahu* 21).

Idleness and Indolence

Sweet is the sleep of the laboring man.

—Ecclesiastes 5:11

RETIREES, THE unemployed, and incapacitated individuals must sooner or later cope with the problem of idleness. Prior to the enactment of modern social legislation, the primary concern of people out of work was one of economics. Social security and pensions have removed the specter of starvation from homes where the head of the family is no longer in a position to earn a livelihood.

The partial solution of the economic problem has accentuated the social problem of boredom, which is bred by idleness. Young children, idle all day, while away their time by playing or by acting out their fantasies in a world of make-believe. Even then, they frequently react to boredom by plaguing their mothers with the plaintive question: "What should I do now?" Idle adults ponder over the same question with greater frequency, and unfortunately, the outlets afforded in childhood disappear in later life.

The effects of boredom on adults could be very devastating. Psychologists have discovered that retired people, with no interests or diversions to occupy their minds, have a shorter life-span than what their physical condition has led them to expect. Young people, bored by idleness, not infrequently drift into antisocial and criminal adventures.

The problem of idleness received little attention in the Scriptures. This omission is not due to a lack of interest in the problem. It rather reflects the fact that there was little idleness in the primitive agrarian society of the biblical era. The divine rebuke of Adam, "Cursed is the ground for thy sake; in toil shalt thou eat of it, all the days of thy life" (Gen. 3:17), was an accurate prognostication of the hard life of a farmer. The lot of ancient women was not much easier.

The farmer's workday extended from sunrise to sunset, with nighttime sleep providing the only break. The psalmist meditated on the long and wearying hours of hard-working people and warned them that even their sleep is filled with anxiety, except for those who put their trust in God. "It is vain for you that you rise early and sit up late, you that eat the bread of toil; so he [God] gives [rest] unto his beloved in sleep" (Ps. 127:2).

The institution of the Sabbath, a day of abstention from work, did not create a problem of boredom. The primary purpose of the Sabbath was to allow man and beast some needed physical rest. A period of rest between stints of labor was never considered a waste of time. It is as essential to the regeneration of energy as the respite of refreshing sleep in the hours of the night. A tired person, relaxing after hard labor, is never troubled by the restlessness which results from idleness. It is possible that the physiological needs of man do not normally require a full day of rest. The rabbis therefore urged that part of the Sabbath day, after one has rested, be set aside for study and intellectual stimulation (*Gittin* 58b).

Judaism regards the study of Torah as a lifetime religious commitment. "This book of the law shall not depart out of thy mouth, but thou shalt meditate therein day and night . . . and then you will act wisely" (Josh. 1:8). Theoretically, this comprehensive injunction commands man to utilize every free moment of his day for the enlargement of his knowledge. Indeed, educated people relax after a day's work with a book or other reading material in their hands. The problem of boredom is thus blissfully eliminated for persons immersed in intellectual pursuits. That is likely the implication of a comment by Rabbi Samuel bar Nachmani (3rd cent.): "This [the order to read the Torah] is neither a duty nor a command but a blessing" (*Menachot* 99b).

Intellectuals have always been a minority. Individuals of average education cannot be expected to devote their after-work hours to the reading of scholarly works. The introduction of a forty-hour work week has produced longer periods of leisure. It is up to each individual to spend his free time doing the things which he finds most relaxing. Most people spend their evenings watching television programs or playing social games. Uncompromising rabbinic moralists still decry such pastimes as intellectually sterile and wasteful. However, any legitimate diversion which keeps people from boredom serves a good purpose and should not be considered unethical or improper.

Retirees have done much to relieve the problem of boredom through membership in senior-citizens organizations which plan a great variety of programs. Those who have developed hobbies utilize their newly gained freedom to indulge in activities which stimulate their interests. Many volunteer their services to worthy charitable institutions and thus find fulfillment and dignity in contributing to the public welfare.

In addition to people who are forced into idleness, there have always been individuals who court idleness due to laziness. Understandably, such people enjoy their idleness and are never bored by it. The Bible condemns laziness not because it produces boredom but because it is innately antisocial and unproductive.

The Book of Proverbs is most assertive in its denunciation of laziness. Sluggards are advised to learn diligence from the ant (6:6). They are warned that lazy people end their lives in poverty (6:9–11). Their paths are full of thorns (15:19). Even the threat of starvation does not normally stir the lazy to mend their ways (19:24). They invent ridiculous excuses to justify their slothfulness (22:13). Their property deteriorates through neglect (22:30–31).

The rabbis noted that lazy people do not take their obligations and promises seriously. They therefore ruled that one is not to recite his prayers in a moment when he is strongly possessed by a mood of laziness (*Berachot* 31a). Laziness hampers the process of acquiring knowledge. He who studies regularly, a little at a time, ends up with a great deal of knowledge. He who procrastinates and alleges "I will study tomorrow" ends up with no knowledge at all (*Yalkut, Mishle* 945).

The economic base of the Jewish community changed in the

talmudic era from mainly agrarian to a mixed economy of farming and commerce. Merchants enjoyed greater leisure than farmers and artisans. The emergence of a class with more free time made it possible for gambling to take root. The rabbis condemned gambling as an antisocial activity (*Rosh HaShanah* 22a). Generally, idlers were denounced on religious grounds for their neglect of the study of Torah (*Shabbat* 32b).

The problem of boredom as a social evil was also discussed by the talmudic rabbis. Wealthy married women could afford the luxury of idleness because they were not part of the work force nor were they required to study Torah. They were also exempt from doing house chores, if their husbands waived that duty or if they brought along, as part of their dowry, several maidservants. Legally, such women "may lounge in an easy chair" (*Ketubot* 59b). Despite their legal exemption, the rabbis opposed such idleness because it produces boredom with its undesirable consequences. Rabbi Eliezer (2nd cent.) said that boredom dulls the mind.

Modern society has brought the privilege of leisure to the poor as well as the rich. If it is not properly used, it may not be the blessing it is commonly believed to be.

In-Laws

And he shall be unto thee a restorer of life, and a nourisher of thy old age; for thy daughter-in-law, who loves thee, who is better to thee than seven sons, has borne him.

—Ruth 4:15

EVER SINCE its inception, the institution of marriage has had to contend with in-law problems. The most troubled area of conflict is confined to the mother-in-law and daughter-in-law relationship. Some mothers perceive the dual loyalties of their married sons as an alienation of affection. In addition, mothers who have spoiled their sons with doting attention resent the refusal of daughters-in-law to spoil their husbands.

In societies with tight family units, where mothers retain a powerful role in the lives of their children, the conflict was less likely to rise to the surface. A bride accepted from the outset a subservient role in the knowledge that someday she would become a dominant figure, when her mother-in-law was no longer on the scene. In societies with loose family structures, a bride normally asserts her independence as soon as she enters matrimony. Conflict is likely to surface soon after the wedding band is placed on her finger.

Biblical accounts of domestic life in the Jewish society of that era do not reflect any strain in family relationships. The story of Naomi and her daughter-in-law Ruth is an inspiring tale of love which has been held up as a model for Jewish youth. The memorable dialogue between the two women has become an immortal testament to human devotion. Prior to her return to her native Palestine, Naomi pleaded with her daughters-in-law: "Go return, each of you, to her mother's house; the Lord deal kindly with you, as you have dealt with the dead [husbands] and with me" (Ruth 1:8). Ruth retorted: "Entreat

179

me not to leave you, for whither thou goest, I will go, where thou diest, I will die, and there will be buried; the Lord do so to me . . . if aught but death part thee and me" (Ruth 1:16–17).

When the ethical standards of the family deteriorated in the rising prosperity of the eighth century B.C.E., the prophet Micah expressed his outrage at the breakdown of respect for the older generation. "The son dishonors the father, the daughter rises up against her mother, the daughter-in-law against her mother-in-law" (Mic. 7:6). He could but recall with grief the passing of the good old days when daughters-in-law were as respectful as daughters. The regard of Moses for his father-in-law, Jethro, was noted in the Bible. When Jethro visited Moses in the Sinai desert, "he [Moses] went out to meet his father-in-law and bowed down and kissed him, and they asked each other of their welfare" (Exod. 18:7).

When the apocryphal Tobias married Sarah, he promised his father-in-law that he would stay with him for fourteen days and thereafter return to the home of his parents. Subsequently, Tobias was asked to tarry a little longer. Tobias refused the request because he felt that his duty to his parents took precedence over his new obligations to his in-laws. His father-in-law wished him well and took leave of his daughter with the following instruction: "Honor thy father-in-law and thy mother-in-law, who are now thy parents, that I may hear good reports of thee" (Tobit 10:12).

Rabbinic Judaism placed honor of in-laws on the same plane with parental honor. "Man is obligated to honor his father-in-law as much as his father" (*Midrash Tehilim* on Ps. 7:5). The rabbis noted that David addressed his father-in-law, King Saul, as "my father" (I Sam. 24:12). Likewise, "man calls his son-in-law 'son,' and his daughter-in-law 'daughter,' " (*Bereshit Rabbah* 84:21). The close relationship evidenced by such appellations gave rise to a new ritual custom. When a husband or a wife loses a parent the spouse joins in the observance of mourning rites. This practice was instituted primarily as an expression of sympathy for one's mate. The custom continued in force for many centuries, until the late Middle Ages (*Moed Katan* 26b).

Notwithstanding rabbinic preachments, in-law conflicts were not uncommon in the Jewish society of the talmudic era. Indeed, the rabbis mentioned a shocking and extreme case of an in-law treated worse than an outlaw. "A certain mother-in-law hated her daughter-in-law. Said she to her: 'Go and anoint yourself with balsam oil' [which is highly flammable]. She went and anointed herself. On her return she said to her: 'Go and light the lamp.' She went and lit the lamp, a spark landed on her, and she was burned" (*Shabbat* 26a).

The rabbis examined the root of in-law frictions and came up with the following analysis. A mother-in-law believes that her daughter-in-law squanders her savings (and will eventually squander her husband's inheritance). A daughter-in-law hates her mother-in-law because she reports to her son all that she does (*Yevamot* 117a). Curiously, this ancient analysis is still valid today.

The Talmud took judicial notice of the existence of strife between in-laws and considered it widespread enough to warrant the enactment of a special law. Thus testimony of a daughter-in-law that her father-in-law died in a distant country and that her mother-in-law is now free to remarry was not admitted in a court of law. The exclusion of the testimony was based on the suspicion that a hating daughter-in-law may give false evidence in order to get her mother-in-law in trouble. For the same reason, a mother-in-law was barred from testifying that her daughter-in-law was free to remarry (*Yevamot* 117a).

Conflicts with in-laws occasionally prompt a wife or a husband to object to visits to their home of any member of the spouse's family. The medieval rabbis upheld the right of a spouse to make such objections, particularly when it is claimed that the visits exacerbate domestic tranquility. However, neither the wife nor the husband has a right to forbid a spouse to visit his or her relatives (*Tur* Code, *Even HaEzer* 74).

Rabbi Judah HeChasid (12th cent.) touched upon the proper stance of a husband whose wife quarrels with his parents. He considers it proper for a husband to remain neutral if his intervention might trigger domestic discord. Such neutrality must not be taken by anyone as proof of his sympathy. When a husband is aware that his wife's grievances are justifiable, he must not be angry with her for voicing her complaints, for the sake of pleasing his parents (*Sefer Chasidim* 563–564).

In-law strife is not endemic to the institution of marriage. Misunderstandings are the result of a failure to exercise goodwill and common sense. The parents-in-law and the new bride must have a common clear perception of the rights and duties of each party. Parents are entitled to the love and respect of a newcomer to the family. The newcomer is similarly entitled to the love and respect of her husband's family. She is also entitled to complete freedom from interference or direction by her in-laws. At the same time she must learn to differentiate between well-intentioned advice and interference. The willingness of all parties to make reasonable concessions and to adjust to new conditions will eliminate most causes of conflict.

Jealousy

For jealousy is the rage of a man, and he will not spare in the day of vengeance.

—Proverbs 6:34

JEALOUSY IS defined as a state of apprehension of being displaced by a rival. All types of human relationships, religious, economic, and domestic, are susceptible to attacks of jealousy.

The first commandment, "Thou shalt have no other gods before me" (Exod. 20:3), is reinforced with the declaration "for I the Lord thy God am a jealous God" as a warning that God is vigilant in the protection of monotheism from pagan encroachments.

Top executives are jealous of underlings who scheme to replace them in their dominant positions. They react to such threats with sharpened alertness and undisguised hatred.

Husbands and wives are jealous of rivals who attempt to steal the affection of a spouse. A threatened mate reacts with a heightened sense of suspicion and vindictiveness.

Most people regard jealousy as a legitimate and justifiable reaction, if facts and circumstances warrant it. Unfortunately, jealousy is an explosive emotion which thrives on suspicion more often than on facts. This is particularly true of jealousy arising from romantic involvements. A biblical verse warns of its dangerous intensity. "For love is strong as death, jealousy is cruel as the grave; the flashes thereof are flashes of fire" (Song of Songs 8:6).

Groundless jealousy is an emotional aberration which does not respond to logic or moral admonitions. An unreasonably jealous individual is not impressed by charges of unethical conduct. On the contrary, his conviction that he is motivated

183

by moral dictates for the preservation of chastity is progressively hardened and insulated by a sense of self-righteousness.

Psychologists attribute extreme jealousy to an inferiority complex. This diagnosis offers little hope for short-range relief. In ancient Israel, jealous husbands were offered an opportunity for a quick resolution of their suspicions by means of a ritual procedure which tested the guilt or innocence of a wife suspected of infidelity.

The biblical "ordeal of jealousy" was discontinued by the rabbis in the first century. However, modern Jews will find a reading of this passage still rewarding because it sheds light on the developing attitude of Judaism to the legitimacy of jealousy.

We quote the biblical text with an interpolation of rabbinical interpretations. "If a man's wife go aside, and acts unfaithfully against him. And a man lie with her carnally, and it be hid from the eyes of her husband, she being defiled secretly . . . [that is the gist of the husband's accusation but he has no evidence to prove it]. And the spirit of jealousy come upon him, and he is jealous of his wife [he warns his wife in the presence of witnesses against clandestine meetings with a particular man], and she be defiled [testimony by a single witness of her secluding herself with the man whom the husband considers a rival is sufficient to prove her guilt] the wife is declared an adulteress and the marriage must end in divorce.

"Or if the spirit of jealousy come upon him, and he be jealous of his wife [he warns her in the presence of witnesses against secret meetings with a particular individual] and she be not defiled [there is no evidence of seclusion with the rival], then shall the man bring his wife to the priest" (Num. 5:13–15). The text proceeds to describe the ritual which confirms or disproves the husband's suspicions.

The text, as interpreted by the rabbis, stresses several facts. The husband's jealousy has become public knowledge, a condition which imposes a greater degree of circumspection upon the wife. His objection is not addressed to men in general but to a specific man whom he does not trust. The wife apparently disregards her husband's warnings. These circumstances spell out a case of justifiable jealousy, and no censure of his behavior is reflected in this passage.

One rabbinic school came to a different conclusion. The phrase "if a spirit of jealousy come upon him" drew the attention of the School of Rabbi Ishmael (2nd cent.). "A man is not jealous of his wife unless a 'spirit' enters into him" (*Sotah* 3a). Apparently they took the term "spirit" to mean an emotional disturbance. They obviously felt that under certain circumstances jealousy is understandable but not morally proper. Later rabbis offered opposing definitions of the term "spirit." "The rabbis declare it as a spirit of impurity [a negative emotion], but Rav Ashi [4th–5th cent.] said it is a spirit of purity [a positive emotion]."

In another difference of opinions, Rabbi Ishmael declared that the biblical phrase "and he be jealous of his wife" is voluntary. On the other hand, Rabbi Akiva said it is mandatory (*Sotah* 3a). Rabbi Ishmael did not consider jealousy helpful to the restoration of domestic peace. He also did not regard it as an essential tool for the preservation of family purity. Well-founded suspicions are best solved by a discussion of the facts and an elimination of the causes.

In the absence of incriminating circumstances, jealousy is ugly and destructive. The rabbis defended the integrity and reputation of all married women and criticized men who lightly impugn women's presumption of morality and respectability. An individual named Judah b. Papus who kept his wife under lock when he was not at home was held up for ridicule and derision (Jer. *Kiddushin* 4:4).

Jealousy is as endemic to women as it is to men. In the polygamous society of ancient times, the law took little cognizance of a wife's jealousy. While a husband's extramarital affairs were forbidden, a wife could not legally stop her husband from taking an additional wife. However, a sole wife had the right to demand a divorce if her husband terminated his monogamous marital state.

Joyfulness and Depression

Light is sown for the righteous, and joy for the upright in heart.
—Psalm 97:11

JOYFULNESS IS a pleasurable emotion which enhances one's sensation of physical and mental well-being. Its antonym, depression, is a distressing emotion which aggravates one's sensation of malaise. Both emotions are infectious. A jovial person exhilarates people who come in contact with him. A sad person feeds on grief and depresses people who share his company.

The contagiousness of depression raises a moral question. Is an individual who depresses his family and friends guilty of an unethical disposition? Should he shun all social intercourse or hide his gloom behind a mask of mirth? Unless one's sadness is self-induced or affected, it seems unfair to charge him with a breach of ethics any more than one would blame a disfigured person whose sight evokes a painful reaction.

It may be argued that unlike physical disfiguration, a depressed person can and should control his emotion to avoid causing discomfort to other people. But can he? Will sadness yield to a rational command to evanesce? Joyfulness and depression are merely symptoms of underlying causes over which people may have little control.

A variety of events, major or even trifling, may trigger a cheerful disposition. The completion of a mission, the bestowal of honor, a compliment, a whisper of love, a friendly smile, a happy family event, are among the common causes which brighten up a face with joy. The holder of a winning

186

lottery ticket, even if the prize is minuscule, will add buoyancy to his gait.

A reporter preparing material for a profile of a New York congressman noted his subject's odd practice of dropping dimes on his way to Congress. When queried, the congressman explained that pedestrians who picked up his scattered coins felt happy for the rest of the day. It was a cheap price to pay for a day's happiness of some strangers.

Depression is brought on by sickness, disappointment, death of a kin or friend, loss of money or security, a reprimand and an insult, or a host of other traumatic events. Depression is to the psyche what pain is to the body. Physical pain cannot be willed away. It will respond to anesthetics, but lasting relief is attained only by removal of the cause which is responsible for the pain. Does the same hold true for depression? Time heals most depressions. Psychiatrists have suggested various remedies for overcoming depressions, particularly the ones which stem from grief. Is it also possible to relieve one's depression by an exercise of willpower?

Except for pathological depressions, highly motivated individuals can do much to allay their sadness. Religion is one of the forces which can provide such motivation. People of deep piety and zeal have been able to suppress all manifestations of sorrow and depression on Sabbaths and festivals because sadness is incompatible with the joyous spirit of those days.

Religious people have several motivations at their disposal for overcoming depression. Hope is an important ingredient of faith. When a distressing condition, such as sickness or privation, is potentially reversible, one finds relief in the hope that God will bring about an improvement. This theme is recurrent in the Bible. "I found trouble and sorrow, but I called upon the name of the Lord" (Ps. 116:3–4). "The hope of the righteous is joy" (Prov. 10:28). "For I will turn their mourning into joy, and I will comfort them and make them rejoice from their sorrow" (Jer. 31:12).

When a tragedy is beyond repair, such as a death in the family, a pious individual takes refuge in a resignation which recognizes God's superior wisdom and does not question his sense of justice. "Shall we receive good at the hands of God, and shall we not receive evil?" (Job 2:10). "The Lord gave and the Lord has taken away; blessed be the name of the Lord" (Job 1:21).

Obedience to God is a source of infinite joy to the pious. The observance of daily mitzvot, which set the standards of proper conduct, provides a sense of achievement and gratification. This ever-replenished joy cannot but relieve the severity of depression. A mourner's recitation of *Kaddish* has a therapeutic effect even in the darkest hour of bereavement.

The chanting of prayers, under nonstressful conditions, should be a joyous experience, according to the Bible. "Serve the Lord with gladness, come before his presence with singing" (Ps. 100:2). "Even them [the righteous of all nations] will I bring to my holy mountain, and make them joyful in my house of prayer" (Isa. 56:7).

The Talmud emphasized the need for cultivating a happy disposition. "Our rabbis taught: 'One should not rise to recite the Tefillah [the Silent Prayer] while immersed in sorrow, or idleness, or laughter [levity], or chatter, or frivolity, or idle talk, but only while still rejoicing in the performance of a religious act" (*Berachot* 31a). To make sure that one will enter upon that prayer in a happy mood, one should precede the recitation of the Tefillah with the reading of a biblical passge that offers a comforting message. In the same vein, the rabbis alleged that the divine presence does not rest upon a man of gloom (he is not able to commune with God) but only on a man who rejoices in the performance of a (religious) precept (*Shabbat* 31a). Obviously, one must distinguish between a man of gloom and a man in distress.

A rabbinic view advocating the joyous acceptance of suffering emerged in the second century (*Sanhedrin* 101a). Rabbi Joshua b. Levi (3rd cent.) expanded on this theme. "He who joyfully bears his suffering brings salvation to the world" (*Taanit* 8a). Rabbi Joshua lived in Palestine in a period of great political ferment. Anti-Roman agitation was rife, and the authorities reacted with severe repression. The rabbi's words might have been addressed to the exigencies of his time.

A more extreme view advocated the acceptance of suffering with greater joy than normally attends good fortune (*Tanchuma, Jethro* 16). This recommendation was based on the belief that suffering atones for sin. Additionally, suffering was alleged to be ordained by God to alert man to his need for penitence and improvement of character. The righteous King Hezekiah was unable to influence his son, Manasseh, to desist from evil. It was not until Manasseh took ill that he changed for the better. "Thus you learn how precious is suffering" (*Sanhedrin* 101a). Hence Rava's conclusion: "If man sees that painful suffering afflicts him, let him examine his conduct" (*Berachot* 5b).

Despite these rabbinic exhortations, the average man could hardly be expected to welcome pain, let alone accept it with joy. Even so eminent a sage as Rabbi Yochanan (3rd cent.) was no exception. When he fell ill and a visiting colleague asked him: "Are your sufferings welcome to you?" he retorted: "Neither they nor their reward" (*Berachot* 5b).

Rava (4th cent.) composed a private prayer which he appended to the daily liturgy. "May it be thy will, O Lord my God, that I sin no more. May you wipe out in thy great mercies the sins which I committed before thee, but not through suffering or disease" (*Berachot* 17a). Notwithstanding the natural reluctance to welcome pain, the assumed divine purpose in causing pain was widely known, and such knowledge surely relieved the intensity of the sufferer's depression. For further discussion of this subject, see "Suffering and Pain."

The cultivation of spiritual joy as the moving force of religious ecstasy was vigorously pursued by the Chasidic movement after its emergence in the eighteenth century. Spiritual joy is based on a consciousness of the presence of God and a total dedication of one's energies to the fulfillment of his commands. Chasidism decries the pursuit of physical pleasure as an end in itself but welcomes it as a means for putting man in a happy frame of mind so that he can serve God out of joy. Spiritual joy is a dominant force which can exist even in the midst of privation and distress.

Isaiah culminated his comforting prophecies with a vision of a new era in which abundance and righteousness will blend to create a happy life (chap. 55). To Jews suffering the interminable privations of the diaspora, Isaiah's vision was a promise yet to be fulfilled. To Chasidism, however, the promise of happiness is within every person's reach because joy born of the pursuit of righteousness transcends the sadness of privation. The Alexanderer Rabbi (19th cent.) took for his text Isaiah's verse, "For you shall leave with joy" (55:12). "If you cultivate joy, you will leave all tribulations behind you."

For a discussion of related topics, see "Asceticism" and "Contentment and Discontent."

Labor

The earth is full of the fruit of thy labor.

—Psalm 104:13

THE BIBLE and the Talmud hold labor in high regard. "When thou eatest the labor of thy hands, happy shalt thou be, and it shall be well with thee" (Ps. 128:2).

A laborer contributes to the welfare of society and is instrumental in advancing God's design for building up the world. "Six days shalt thou labor and do all thy work, but the seventh day is a Sabbath" (Exod. 20:8–9). In the view of Rabbi Judah HaNasi (2nd cent.), these verses convey a dual command. "Just as Israel was instructed regarding the Sabbath [when they must rest], so were they instructed regarding work [that they must work the rest of the week]" (*Mechilta deRabbi Simon b. Yochai* on Exod. 20:9). Ben Sira had expressed the same view several centuries earlier: "Hate not laborious work, neither husbandry, which the most high commanded" (Ecclus. 7:15). Labor was thus invested with the theological virtue of the performance of a mitzvah.

The Judaic attitude to labor was shaped by two divergent socioreligious motivations: a strong opposition to idleness and an equally deep opposition to any servitude which diminishes man's freedom of action. The labor of self-employed people was highly lauded, but exploitation of other people's work for one's own interests was severely criticized and curtailed.

Abhorrence of idleness was forcefully asserted in the Bible and Talmud. "Everyone that is slack in his work is a brother to him that is a destroyer" (Prov. 19:9). "Rabbi Judah b. Bateira said: 'If one is not occupied by any work, what shall he do? If he has a yard which is in disrepair, or a pasture which has been

191

neglected, let him go and repair it [so as not to be idle], for it is written: "Six days shalt thou labor, and do all thy work" [Exod. 20:9]. What is the implication of "and do all thy work" [a redundant phrase]? To teach us that he who has a neglected yard or pasture shall busy himself with it' " (*Avot deRabbi Natan* 11).

The censure of idleness was coupled with praise of labor. "He that tills his ground shall have plenty of bread, but he that follows vain things is void of understanding" (Prov. 12:11). "Sweet is the slumber of the laborer" (Eccles. 5:11). "Better is he that labors and abounds in all things than he that boasts himself and wants bread" (Ecclus. 10:27). Even the unskilled worker is God's favorite. "Again, there is another [laborer] that is slow and has need of help, wanting ability and full of poverty; yet the eye of the Lord looks upon him for good, and sets him up from his low estate, and lifts up his head from misery, so that many who saw it marveled at it" (Ecclus. 11:12).

The Talmud similarly lavished praise upon laborers. "A man who lives from labor is greater than the one who fears heaven" (but looks to charity for his sustenance; *Berachot* 8a). "Man must labor and produce with his hands, and God will bestow his blessings upon him" (*Tanchuma, Vayetze* 13). No work, regardless of how menial, may be considered beneath human dignity. "Rav [3rd cent.] said to Rav Kahana: 'Dress a carcass in the street to earn a living and say not, I am a great man and the work is degrading to me' " (*Baba Batra* 110a). Rav Kahana was an eminent scholar who commanded great respect. His position in the community entitled him to some privileges. Scholars, for instance, were exempt from the biblical injunction to lead a lost animal through the streets in search of its owner (Exod. 23:4) because doing so was not becoming to men of public stature (*Baba Metzia* 30b). Nevertheless, when one is faced with a choice between dependence on charity and doing menial work, even if he is a scholar he must choose the latter.

The second socioreligious motivation, an innate reaction against servitude, even if entered voluntarily, was an outgrowth of the impact of the biblical account of the Exodus from Egypt.

The long and painful struggle against bondage that preceded the birth of the nation left an indelible mark upon its social outlook. "For unto me [God] the Children of Israel are servants, they are my servants whom I have brought forth out of the land of Egypt" (Lev. 25:55). To which the rabbis added: " 'For unto me the Children of Israel are servants,' and not servants unto servants" (*Baba Kama* 116b).

Servitude, which but remotely had the appearance of slavery, was frowned upon. Long-term labor contracts were viewed with disfavor as a surrender of freedom (Rema, *Choshen Mishpat* 333:3). This may sound odd to modern workers in a free society. In the absence of powerful unions and appropriate government regulations, the ancient worker was at the mercy of his employer. The rabbis of the talmudic era had good reason to disapprove agreements which were too restrictive of a worker's freedom of action. Ben Sira (2nd cent. B.C.E.) had the same concern in mind when he proclaimed: "Let thy soul love a good servant and defraud him not of liberty" (Ecclus. 7:21).

Sensitivity to the preservation of the worker's dignity was circumscribed, however, by the recognition of the legitimate rights of the employer. Judaic labor laws therefore have a dual purpose. The freedom of laborers is carefully protected. At the same time, employers are guaranteed a day's work for a day's pay. Despite the sentimentality in favor of workers, a sluggard was not coddled. Diligence was praised and demanded. However, when a worker sought to terminate his employment in the midst of his work, the law was generally sympathetic. Freedom was too cherished an ideal to permit its erosion.

Prompt payment of a worker's wage was the prime concern of the law. "Whoever withholds the wages of a hired laborer transgresses five biblical negative injunctions . . . and one positive command: 'Thou shalt not oppress thy neighbor; neither rob him' [Lev. 19:13]; 'Thou shalt not oppress a hired servant that is poor' [Deut. 24:14]; 'The wages of him that is hired shall not abide all night with thee' [Lev. 19:13]; 'At his day shalt thou give him his hire; neither shall the sun go down upon it' [Deut. 24:15]" (*Baba Metzia* 111a).

The combined weight of all these injunctions assured compliance with the imperative of prompt payment of wages. A rabbinical dictum lent additional moral emphasis to these injunctions. "He who withholds a worker's wages is as though he deprived him of his life" (*Baba Metzia* 112a). The rabbis also warned employers that the withheld wages would not enrich them. On the contrary, their transgression would result in the loss of their estates (*Bamidbar Rabbah* 11).

The biblical allegation that a worker "sets his soul upon it" (his wages; Deut. 24:15) was interpreted literally by the rabbis. "Why did the man ascend the ladder, suspend himself from the tree, and risk death itself; was it not that you should pay him his wages?" (*Baba Metzia* 112a).

Despite the biblical admonitions, the Jewish kings of the First Commonwealth used conscript labor. The prophet Samuel predicted this practice and used it as the basis for his opposition to a monarchy (I Sam. 8:12–13). Jeremiah (6th cent. B.C.E.) railed against this flagrant abuse of power: "Woe unto him that builds his house by unrighteousness, and his chambers by injustice; that uses his neighbor's service without wages, and gives him not his hire" (Jer. 22:13). It is small wonder that the rabbis made exploitation of labor the prime target of their labor legislation,

In deference to the traditional opposition to servitude, the rabbis permitted laborers who work for a fixed price to break a verbal working agreement and quit in the middle of the day (*Baba Kama* 116b). This right was not withheld even when payment of wages was made in advance. Of course, the unearned portion of the pay had to be returned (*Chosen Mishpat* 333:3).

There were other privileges enjoyed by ancient laborers. Farm workers could not be restrained by the owner from eating the produce of the farm or vineyard where they were employed (Deut. 23:25–26). Local custom determined whether employees were entitled to free meals as part of their emolument. If such a benefit was specifically included in an agreement, the employer was obligated to provide high-quality food. This law attests to the dignity of labor and the respect it commanded. The following talmudic anecdote is aptly illustrative. "Rabbi

Yochanan b. Mathia said to his son: 'Go out and engage laborers.' He went and agreed to supply them with food. On his return to his father, the latter said: 'My son, should you even prepare for them a banquet like Solomon in his glory, you cannot fulfil your promise, for they are descendants of Abraham, Isaac, and Jacob' " (and must be treated like nobility; *Baba Metzia* 83a).

Local custom determined the length of the workday. Employers cannot compel workers to work overtime. Even if his scale of wages is higher than the going rate, an employer cannot claim that the extra pay is contingent on extra time (*Baba Metzia* 83a)

The favorable position of the ancient Jewish worker did not relieve him of the obligation to deal honestly with his employer. The rabbis took cognizance of the fact that "it is the habit of workers to labor diligently for two or three hours and then slacken as the day wears on" (*Bereshit Rabbah* 70:18). The employer's right to honest work is as important as the worker's claim to freedom of action. Rabbinic measures against diminished productivity were so stringent that they appear excessive in the less exacting atmosphere of modern labor rights.

Moonlighting is currently an acceptable practice. The Talmud did not go along with this view. It forbids laborers to do heavy work, on their own or for hire, in their free time because their efficiency is bound to suffer (Jer. *Demai* 7:3). Considering the long working hours of ancient laborers, a failure to get proper rest would eventually affect their performance. For the same reason, workers were warned not to deprive themselves of proper food, even when motivated by a noble desire to leave some extra food for the family. An undernourished person makes a poor worker (ibid.). Indulging in voluntary fasts, normally an act of piety, was also forbidden.

A laborer working on top of an olive tree (where he has a firm footing) may recite his prayers at his place of work. Normally, one is required to offer prayers on the ground or the floor of a synagogue or home. A laborer is excepted from this rule so that he need not take the extra time for climbing down and up the tree. Surely, the lesson of this exception was not lost on the average worker. Unnecessary use of working time for purposes other than work is dishonest.

Abba Helkiah (1st cent.) a scholar distinguished for his great piety, made it a practice to refrain from responding to people's greetings when at work for an employer (*Taanit* 23b). While such conduct is normally considered rude, the sage believed that his responsibility to the employer did not justify any interruptions for the sake of civility. Most rabbis for practical reasons refused to go to such extremes.

Workers were exempt from the biblical injunction which commands people to rise in the presence of a scholar or elder as a sign of respect (Lev. 19:32). It was ruled that this deferential gesture was not required of workers because it conflicted with their obligation to perform uninterrupted work. Scholars were aware of this rule and consequently did not feel offended (*Kiddushin* 33a).

The taking of rest breaks beyond the number sanctioned by common practice or mutual agreement was prohibited (*Choshen Mishpat* 337:20). These and other restrictive rules do not reflect a bias in favor of employers. They merely emphasized the ethical dictates of honesty. One is tempted to add that many modern civil servants are rarely troubled by such moral considerations.

The basic aim of Judaic labor laws is to safeguard the security and dignity of workers and to protect the legitimate rights of employers. It is a serious breach of ethics to treat an employee with disrespect. It is equally a breach of ethics to treat an employer with disrespect.

Love

He executes justice for the fatherless and widow, and loves the stranger, in giving him food and raiment.

—Deuteronomy 10:18

LOVE IS man's most sublime emotion. Love of God is a mainstay of religion (Deut. 11:1). Love of the stranger is the mark of civilized society (Lev. 19:34). Mother-love is the breath of life (II Kings 3:26). Love of one's spouse is the cement of family cohesiveness (Eccles. 9:9).

True love is not conditioned upon reciprocity or reward. He who gives love for ulterior motives is doomed to disappointment. Indeed, selfish people are incapable of love.

The Golden Rule is based on the Pentateuchal pronouncement: "Love thy fellowman as thyself" (Lev. 19:18). Rabbi Akiva (2nd cent.) cautioned against regarding this verse as a mere rhetorical flourish. According to him, it reflects "a fundamental principle of the Torah" (Jer. *Nedarim* 9:4). All biblical social laws, affirmative and negative, stem from a basic obligation to love one's fellowman.

The Golden Rules of all major faiths are couched in paraphrased versions of the Pentateuchal verse, some in affirmative form and some in the negative. Christianity adopted the former. "All things whatsoever you would that all should do to you, do you even so to them" (1st cent.). On the other hand, Buddhism phrased the rule in the negative. "Hurt not others in ways that you yourself would find hurtful" (5th cent. B.C.E.).

One may justly wonder why the Leviticus text has no parallel in the religious literature of other faiths. The term "love" is uniformly omitted from their Golden Rules. Even in Judaism, the eminent sage Hillel (1st cent.) deemed it useful to para-

197

phrase the biblical text in the following manner: "What is hateful to you, do not to your fellowman" (*Shabbat* 31a). This version is close to the Buddhist text.

Hillel did not originate his maxim. He was not conversant with Buddhist literature, and we must rule that out as one of his sources. However, he was probably familiar with the apocryphal Tobit (assumed to have been written between 200 and 50 B.C.E.), in which a similar maxim appears: "Do that to no man which thou hatest" (Tobit 4:15). The Targum attributed to Jonathan b. Uziel, a disciple of Hillel, repeats Hillel's paraphrased version of the Golden Rule. In its exegesis of Leviticus 19:18 it states as follows: "You shall love your friend because what is hateful unto you, do not unto him" (on Lev. 19:18).

Ben Sira (2nd cent. B.C.E.) describes in several chapters of Ecclesiasticus some of the proper relationships between good neighbors. "Every man loves his neighbor" (13:15). "The mercy of man is toward his neighbor" (13:18). "Be faithful to thy neighbor in poverty" (22:23). "Forgive thy neighbor the hurt he has done unto thee" (28:2). "He that is merciful will lend unto his neighbor" (29:1). Despite his affirmative style, none of his dicta attains the sublime height of the Pentateuchal Golden rule.

The ancient Hebrew scholars apparently felt that the high moral stance of the biblical Golden Rule was too exacting to be established as the norm of human conduct. Furthermore, the syntactic construction of the Golden Rule appears to be inconsistent with the commonly accepted interpretation of its text.

The popular use of the phrase "thy neighbor" in many of the translations of the Golden Rule is misleading. It creates an incorrect impression that only neighbors, with whom one is acquainted, are entitled to man's love. This, of course, is absurd in view of the specific instruction to love the stranger (Lev. 19:34). The root meaning of the Hebrew re-a is "one who is joined in love or friendship." In the course of time the term re-a has assumed a comprehensive connotation, embracing any member of the human race. In a moral sense all men are friends. The ninth commandment, "Thou shalt not bear false witness against thy neighbor" (as most translators render the Hebrew *re-a-cha*), surely did not limit the prohibition to friends and neighbors only.

The correct rendition of the term *re-a-cha* in the Golden Rule, "your fellowman," presents a problem. Love, in the sense of an emotional attachment to an individual or idea, cannot develop without the existence of a specific object to which the love is directed. How can one love an individual whose existence is unknown to him? Yet the broad injunction "Love thy fellowman" appears to enjoin such sweeping love.

The second half of the Golden Rule, "as thyself," is equally in need of clarification. Does the average individual love himself? Even if we leave out the remote narcissistic implications, most people would deny the charge that they love themselves. Human beings naturally crave the joys and pleasures of life and abhor pain and suffering, but that does not amount to self-love. What then is the intent of the Golden Rule, which enjoins man to love his fellowmen as he loves himself?

There is another question relating to the Golden Rule which requires attention. Is an order to love someone, based on religious or social considerations, feasible? Subjective emotions, such as love and hate, are spawned in one's heart and mind and are not amenable to external discipline. The Golden Rule, basic as it is, was not included in the Ten Commandments because technically it is not the proper subject of a command. Yet how effective can it be even if it does not appear within the framework of the Decalogue?

Nachmanides (13th cent.) argues that it is unrealistic to expect man to love his fellowman as himself. Furthermore, he questions the ethicality of such an expectation in view of Judaic morality, which permits man to give precedence to his own life over the lives of other people. The selfsame Rabbi Akiva who declared the Golden Rule a fundamental principle of the Torah also asserted man's right to look to his own life first.

Nachmanides took note of the syntax of the Golden Rule, which is inconsistent with the traditional rendition of that verse. "Love" is a transitive verb which takes a direct object. In the Hebrew text of the Golden Rule, "thy fellowman" (*le-re-acha*) is the indirect object of "love." It differs from the

Deuteronomic verse (11:1), in which God is the direct object of man's love. In effect, the Golden Rule does not command one to love his fellowman but merely to have as loving an attitude toward other people as he has toward himself. This means, according to Nachmanides, that one should rejoice as much when another person has cause to be happy as he would if he himself had cause to celebrate (on Lev. 19:18). This interpretation of the Golden Rule comes closest to the Taoist maxim: "Regard your neighbor's gain as your own gain and your neighbor's loss as your own loss."

Hillel's maxim, "What is hateful to you, do not to your fellowman," reduces the Golden Rule to its minimal dimension, a stance within the capacity of most individuals to attain. He uttered this maxim in response to a heathen who had expressed a desire to convert to Judaism. The heathen had requested that he be given first a quintessential summation of the Torah. Hillel thereupon offered his maxim and added: "That is the whole of the Torah, while the rest is the commentary thereof; go and learn it" (*Shabbat* 31a). Hillel might have felt that an affirmative paraphrase of the Golden Rule might have frightened off the heathen. However, the preservation of this maxim in the Talmud reflects a desire to reassure the average person that even if he merely abides by the minimal standard of Hillel's dictum, he is in compliance with the spirit of the Golden Rule.

Love of one's fellowman was considered so meritorious by the rabbis that they held that God gives a reward even to members of a wicked society so long as they love each other. Thus the wicked people of the Tower of Babel, who lived in harmony with each other, were not destroyed but merely dispersed (*Avot deRabbi Natan* 12).

The merit of love does not rule out the legitimacy of hate when the occasion calls for it. A morality which demands that one love an attacking enemy is imprudent and self-destructive. In their comment on the verse in Ecclesiastes, "A time to love and a time to hate" (3:8), the rabbis noted: " 'A time to love,' in peacetime; 'a time to hate,' when at war" (*Kohelet Rabbah* 3).

Lust

Lust not after her beauty in thy heart.

—Proverbs 6:25

JOE AND his wife Jane walked leisurely down the avenue on their way to a senior-citizens club. An attractive young lady, walking in the opposite direction, caught Joe's attention and elicited an admiring comment.

"At your age, Joe, you still look at every pretty woman who passes your way," Jane remarked, half in jest and half in earnest.

"You should be glad I do. It shows that I am still young at heart," Joe responded triumphantly.

This good-natured banter, frequently exchanged by elderly loving couples, reflects a masculine pride in lustful longings and a feminine acceptance of the facts of life. Boys will be boys.

A biological attraction between the sexes is a boon to society. It is only when the attraction turns into lust that it becomes a social and moral problem. Judaism, in its role of guardian of morality, condemns lust as a corrosive agent which contributes to the dissolution of inhibitions and the transformation of secret desires into overt illicit acts.

Society is able to impose restraints upon human behavior. However, it cannot control man's thoughts. It is not surprising that moralists have seen their efforts to tame temptation as the most promising remedy against the perpetration of illegal and immoral acts.

The Decalogue prohibits adultery and theft (seventh and eighth commandments). As an added reinforcement of these prohibitions, the tenth commandment also forbids lusting after a neighbor's wife or property (Exod. 20:13–14). Fear of retribution and exposure to shame is a potent deterrent against a breach of the seventh and eighth commandments. The tenth commandment, addressed to man's innermost thoughts, immune to detection and censure, is not amenable to enforcement.

Religious and moral training undoubtedly bars some evil desires from the heart. Indoctrination, however, may prove ineffective in squelching cravings born of powerful human drives. The hunger drive, for instance, generates an irresistible desire for food, and most people would readily steal to satisfy their hunger. Indeed, it would be vain and even hypocritical to preach morality to a hungry person.

Sexual drives generate appetites which are nearly as powerful as the craving for food. Lust, in varying degrees of intensity, is present in most human hearts. Religious influences and an ingrained sense of morality constitute strong suppressants of illicit desires. Yet experience has proven that even in most pious societies, religion must lean on the secular arm to enforce its moral dictates. The secular arm has no sway over man's lust.

Theologians have generally regarded lust as a manifestation of man's inner evil impulses. Some have attributed these impulses to Satan, who implanted them in man in order to disrupt God's design for an orderly world. According to the belief of the Qumran sect (ca. 1st cent. B.C.E.), man's evil impulses do not stem from natural human traits but rather from man's submission to external evil forces. "God created man to rule the world, and appointed for him two spirits after whose direction he was to walk until the final inquisition. They are the spirit of truth and perversity. All who practice righteousness are under the domination of the Prince of Light . . . whereas all who practice perversity are under the domination of the Angel of Darkness" (*Manual of Discipline* 3).

The apocryphal Shealtiel (ca. 1st–2nd cent.) similarly believes that man's evil impulses do not flow from his natural traits. God created a perfect man who in a moment of weakness "wrapped himself in the evil tendency." Ever since that day, "the Torah and the source of evil struggled together in the people's hearts" (trans. of Nicholas de Lange, *The Apocalypse of Ezra*).

Philo the Alexandrian (1st cent.) also leans to the view that an external force is responsible for man's illegal desires. He speaks of man's "natural inclinations toward virtuous actions." However, the "evil counsellor" frustrates his natural inclinations and causes him to surrender to immoral tendencies (*Treatise on the Creation of the World* 24).

Rabbinic Judaism believes that man was initially endowed with good and evil tendencies (*Berachot* 61a). As a rational being, he must convert his evil impulse into a constructive force to serve the needs of society. In a midrashic interpretation of the Pentateuchal verse "And God saw everything that he had made, and behold, it was very good" (Gen. 1:31), a rabbi alleged that "everything" is inclusive of the evil impulse. Had it not been for the evil impulse (lust), man would not take a wife, he would not procreate, and he would not establish a home (*Shochar Tov on Ps.* 9:1). One must therefore learn to serve God with both impulses, the good and the evil (*Berachot* 54a).

The talmudic term for lust is *yetzer hara* ("evil tendency"). It was based on the Pentateuchal verse: "for the tendency of man's heart is evil from its youth" (Gen. 8:21, *Kiddushin* 30b). The noun *yetzer hara*, popularized by moralists of all ages, appeared for the first time in the talmudic literature of the second century (*Berachot* 16b, *Shabbat* 105b, *Sotah* 47a). It encompasses all kinds of desires; the lusting after false beliefs, other people's property, and illicit sex (*Chagigah* 11b, *Shir HaShirim Rabbah* 7). However, in common parlance the term was soon associated exclusively with sexual desires. The practice of separating sexual lust from other types of lust is reflected in the Bible. The original version of the Decalogue outlawed convetousness of sex and property in a single prohibition (Exod. 20:14). The Deuteronomic version of the Decalogue prohibits the two types of lust in two separate injunctions (Deut. 5:18).

Despite the strictness of the Jewish moral code, the ancient rabbis evinced a sympathetic understanding of the inordinate effort frequently entailed in man's resistance to sexual temptation. They were impressed by the fact that even the Bible made a concession to man's powerful sex drive in a situation where an absolute prohibition would only provoke defiance. The law regarding a heathen female captive of war, offering a psychological outlet for the sake of preserving the virtue of all parties involved, is a concession to human weakness (Deut. 21:10–14, *Kiddushin* 21b).

In an allegorical talmudic passage, the Jewish people is depicted as pleading to God for forgiveness because "you have created in us an evil inclination which is the cause of our sins" (*Shemot Rabbah* 46). In another passage, God is described as admitting the validity of this plea. "If I had not created an evil impulse in him [man], he would not have rebelled against me" (*Bereshit Rabbah* 7). According to Rabbi Levi (3rd cent.), God regretted the creation of the *yetzer hara* (ibid.).

Talmudic law took into account the compelling force of sexual temptation. Thus the rule which permits a married victim of rape to resume marital relations with her husband, was extended by Rava (4th cent.) to the case of a woman who had submitted to an attacker under duress but, once her passions were aroused, became a consenting partner. Rava considered the force of her passion a sequel and continuation of the initial duress (*Ketubot* 51b).

Rabbi Simon b. Eleazar (2nd cent.) cautioned against combating sexual immorality with extremist antisexual rhetoric which is critical of all sexual activities. Such tactics may lead to celibacy, which is inimical to social welfare (*Sotah* 47).

The rabbis preferred the adoption of preventive measures, in place of strident denunciations, as a more effective method of strengthening man's resolve to master his passions. People of known virtue were frequently extolled and given heroic stature. Joseph's rebuff of the blandishments of the wife of his Egyptian master was held up as a model for all to follow. An apocryphal romance, Joseph and Asenath, embroidered the biblical story with fanciful details to impress the youth of the nation.

Rabbi Yochanan (3rd cent.) said: "Concerning three does the Holy One, blessed be he, make proclamations [of commendation] every day: A bachelor who lives in a large town without sinning . . ." (*Pesachim* 113a). Surely few believers would risk forfeiting this divine commendation.

To avoid the pitfalls of temptation, the rabbis advocated early marriages (*Avot* 5:26). Above all, the rabbis advocated the need for preventing sexually provocative situations. One should not gaze at beautiful women with a prurient intent (*Midrash Aseret Hadibrot*). One should not be confined alone with a woman in private quarters (*Avodah Zarah* 36b). Men and women should be segregated in public assemblies (*Sukkah* 52a). Seductive attire and the baring of provocative parts of the body were strictly prohibited (*Berachot* 24a).

Some of the above-mentioned preventive measures have been relaxed by many modern Jews. The perception of what constitutes sexual provocation differs with time and geographic location. However, the underlying principle that provocative attire and behavior contribute to sex crimes is as valid today as it was in ancient times.

The rabbis recommended the study of Torah as an effective barrier to carnal desires. According to an old maxim, there is no lust in a house of study (*Berachot* 5a). Preoccupation of any kind leaves little time for lustful distractions. Religious studies in particular were deemed helpful in reinforcing one's moral restraints. As a last resort, the rabbis advised people possessed of lust to remember the day of death, when all human appetites cease.

Idleness and boredom contribute to lust and sin. Due to the consideration of this fact, the rabbis imposed a duty on every wife to engage in some manner of domestic work. The law that exempts women who are wealthy in their own right and have many maids at their command from doing domestic chores was superseded by a moral law which prohibited wives from sitting idle. The basis of the moral law was the belief that "idleness leads to unchastity" (*Ketubot* 59b).

The rabbis never underestimated the power of temptation. They cautioned even the most virtuous against overconfidence in their ability to remain chaste in the face of provocation. "One should never bring himself to test, since David, the king of Israel, did so and failed" (*Sanhedrin* 107a).

In further recognition of the need for being alert against temptation, the rabbis suggested daily prayers for divine assistance in combating lust. Several such prayers are recorded in the Talmud.

"Rabbi on concluding his worship added the following prayer: 'May it be thy will, O Lord our God . . . to deliver us from the impudent and impudence, from an evil man, evil happenings, from the evil impulse . . .' " (*Berachot* 16b).

A rabbinic bedtime prayer included the following: ". . . bring me not unto sin, or into iniquity, or into temptation . . . and let not the evil impulse have sway over me" (*Berachot* 60b).

Rabbi Tanchuma used to pray: "May it be thy will, Lord our God, that you break and remove the mastery of our evil impulses . . . so that we may do your will with heart entire" (Jer. *Berachot* 4).

Manners

When thou sittest among many [at the dinner table], reach not thy hand out first of all.

—Ecclesiasticus 31:18

GOOD MANNERS, like beauty, are in the eyes of the beholder. Tastes and judgments of beholders may vary from place to place. This accounts for the lack of a universal standard of etiquette. Eating a meal with one's fingers is a repulsive sight in Western society. Not so in some Asiatic and African countries, where such manners are normal and proper. Amorous gestures in public are frowned upon in the Orient but not in the West.

Despite the disparity of standards, there is a common criterion by which mankind determines what constitutes good manners. Whatever behavior is offensive to society at any given time is deemed ill-mannered.

Social perceptions of proper manners are rooted in several factors. Religious influences play a dominant role. The same is true of ancient taboos and mores whose vestiges linger in folk-traditions. The interaction of conservative forces with modern educational trends results in the emergence of a modified moral and aesthetic outlook. The more tolerant the social environment, the more likely it is to breed and accept behavioral changes.

Jews have generally adopted the social manners of their host countries. However, in the event that such manners were in conflict with ancient Judaic perceptions, traditional Jews have resisted alien ideological encroachments. A case in point was the recent progressive trend toward egalitarianism, which sought to narrow the generational gap between parent and

207

child or teacher and student. Parents were advised to treat their child as a pal, and teachers were told to grant their students the rights of an adult. This practice resulted in an erosion of the deferential attitude expected of a child. Children who acted disrespectfully toward their parents were no longer considered ill-mannered. Jewish tradition, rooted in the biblical command to honor one's father and mother, could not accommodate to an educational theory which tended to undermine the commandment.

The subject of etiquette received scant attention in ancient Hebrew literature prior to the talmudic era. The Bible focused primarily on the instruction of laws and morality. However, inasmuch as immoral and illegal conduct is ipso facto ill-mannered behavior, this subject is germane to biblical concerns.

The apocryphal Ecclesiasticus (2nd cent. B.C.E.) is the earliest Jewish source to discuss the subject of manners from a social rather than moral point of view. He dwells mainly on table manners because this is the place where some of the worst manners appear. The powerful hunger drive has the potential for bringing out man's animal instincts. If not for the restraints imposed by civilized society, a hungry person would grab the food off the table, devour it before he sits down, and ignore the needs of his table companions.

Every human drive which generates compulsive behavior is potentially a breeder of bad manners. The hunger drive is the most powerful and persistent force which shapes man's conduct. Ethicists have had ample reason for devoting much of their attention to table manners. The following are some of the admonitions addressed to this subject in the Book of Ecclesiasticus.

"Stretch not thine hand wheresoever it looks, and thrust it not into the dish. . . . Eat as it becomes a man those things which are set before thee, and devour not, lest thou be hated. Leave off first, for manners' sake, and be not unsatiable, lest thou offend" (Ecclus. 31:14–17). The last phrase of this quotation underlines the universal criterion of bad manners, behavior offensive to the public.

Ecclesiasticus also admonishes hosts to join their guests at the table. They may take whatever time is required for the preparation of the meal. As soon as the preparations have been completed, they must join their guests (Ecclus. 32).

This admonition is not inconsistent with the biblical account of Abraham's behavior when he served a meal to his guests while "he stood by them under the tree, and they ate" (Gen. 18:8). The strangers passed Abraham's tent "in the heat of the day," not the normal dinner hour when he would have joined them.

Abraham's good manners were manifested in his eagerness to extend gracious hospitality to his guests. In the words of the Bible, "And Abraham ran unto the herd and fetched a calf, tender and good, and gave it to the servant . . . and he took curd and milk and set it before them" (ibid.). Hebrew moralists considered this conduct instructive. A host should personally involve himself in some aspect of the preparation or serving of a meal to his guests.

Ancient dinner guests were occasionally treated to dinner music. Some may prefer chatter to chamber music. Impolite guests may exhibit their rudeness by disturbing the musicians and preventing their friends from enjoying the music. Ecclesiasticus warned: "Pour not out words when there is a musician, and show not forth wisdom out of time" (Ecclus. 32:4).

Conversation at the dinner table promotes sociability and is highly desirable. However, this practice has its limitations. Conversation by definition should be a dialogue and not a monologue. A guest who monopolizes the floor quickly becomes a bore. The subject of table conversation must be carefully chosen to fit the occasion. Comments on one's practices of limitation of diet are highly inappropriate in the presence of those who indulge their appetites.

The talmudic term for good manners is *derech eretz* ("the way of the world," *Avot* 3:2). In addition to "polite usage," *derech eretz* also means a "worldly occupation" (trade, skill, profession; *Avot* 2:2) and a "prudent course of action" (*Sotah* 44a).

The rabbinic literature of good manners deals with the following four categories: table manners, attire, human relationships, and dignity.

TABLE MANNERS

A guest should not suggest to his host that it is time to serve some food. He must await the host's invitation (*Derech Eretz Rabbah* 8).

A minor should not take a seat at a dinner table without obtaining the permission of his elders (Jer. *Ketubot* 1:1).

One should not join the company at a table if some of the guests are of questionable character (*Sanhedrin* 23a).

A young guest should defer to older guests to let them get their portions first (*Derech Eretz Rabbah* 7).

A respectable person should not eat when standing nor lick his fingers (*Derech Eretz Zuta* 5).

One should not dunk his bread into the communal bowl, nor take a bite of a slice of bread and put the rest into the bowl or give it to his friend. It is improper to eat crumbs which one removes from the table (*Derech Eretz Rabbah* 9).

He who drinks his cup of wine in one gulp is a glutton (*Pesachim* 86b).

It is improper to place raw meat on top of bread (*Berachot* 50b).

One should not eat with his fingers in the manner of the gluttons (Nedarim 49b).

One should not drink from a cup and then hand it to his friend (*Tamid* 27b).

A host who takes his portion ahead of his guests acts in an abominable manner (*Derech Eretz Zuta* 8).

If three have eaten at a table and have spoken there no words of Torah, it is as if they had eaten of sacrifices to the dead (a pagan orgy; *Avot* 3:4). The moral significance of the Temple altar, upon which one brought sacrificial offerings to God, was assumed by the dinner table after the destruction of the Temple. In rabbinic thought the physical importance of the meal in satisfying bodily hunger is matched by the need for satisfying the spiritual hunger of man. The physical and spiritual cravings are thus joined and harmonized at the dinner table. The ultimate aim of the rabbis was to prevent mealtime from degenerating into an orgy of gluttony and droll hilarity.

ATTIRE

The need for circumspection in one's manner of dressing is inherent in the Bible. A preliminary period before the giving of the law on Mount Sinai was set aside to allow the people to launder their clothes so that they would be properly dressed for the occasion (Exod. 19:10). Ecclesiasticus admonished: "Let thy garments be always white, and let thy head lack no oil" (Ecclus. 9:8). Warnings against the wearing of improper clothes abound in the Talmud (see "Appearance and Attire"). This includes provocative clothes (*Yevamot* 63b) and soiled garments (*Shabbat* 114a).

HUMAN RELATIONSHIPS

One should not interrupt an inquirer with an answer before the question has been fully articulated (*Baba Batra* 98b).

It is improper to expectorate in front of another person (*Derech Eretz Rabbah* 10).

One should allow a scholar or an older person to precede him in entering a building (*Shemot Rabbah* 9).

No one may enter a home without giving prior notice (*Pesachim* 112a).

One should not turn down a request of an older person (*Baba Metzia* 87a).

One should be first to greet a person in the street (*Berachot* 17a).

One should not unduly raise his voice in a normal conversation (*Yoma* 86a).

No one may take abrupt leave of his friend without requesting permission (*Derech Eretz Rabbah* 5).

A student who takes leave of his teacher may not turn his back to him until he has removed himself from the teacher's immediate presence (*Yoma* 53a). For the same reason one takes a few steps backward upon leaving the Torah ark in a synagogue.

It is proper to wish good health to a person who sneezes (*Berachot* 53a). This practice derived from an old tradition that sneezes were warnings of imminent death due to a fatal disease. Jacob prayed to God that the dire prognosis of a sneeze be transformed into a sign of recovery from the disease (*Yalkut, Job* 41). In view of the legendary origin of the tradition associated with sneezing, one may be inclined to ignore the custom connected with it. Nevertheless, good manners dictate compliance with a usage which is widely practiced and respected.

DIGNITY

It is undignified to eat in the street (*Kiddushin* 40b). This restriction does not apply to open-air restaurants or areas set aside for public eating.

It is undignified to scratch one's back against a wall in a public area (*Baba Kama* 30a).

It is undignified for a respectable male to wear aromatic perfume (to avoid suspicion of homosexuality; Jer. *Berachot* 8:5).

Good manners must be instilled before one reaches the age of educational instruction (*Avot* 3:21).

The need for ethical instruction in good manners is an unending obligation of the religious leadership for the sake of improving man's manners (*Berachot* 32b). The most effective suggestion was the succinct rabbinical advice: "Let no one deviate in his conduct from the prevailing custom of most people of his locality" (*Tanchuma, Vayera* 11).

Matrimony

And he shall cling unto his wife, and they shall become one.
—Genesis 2:24

PROCREATION IS essential to the continuity of life. In the animal world the perpetuation of the species is generally achieved without the benefit of a familial relationship resembling matrimony. The character and behavior of animal herds are mostly predetermined by fixed laws of nature, with the role of parents limited to the physical preservation of their offspring. A young animal does not need a "home" in the moral sense which this term has assumed in human society.

IMPORTANCE OF A GOOD BACKGROUND

Man, endowed with a free will, does not develop his character by a predetermined pattern of evolution. The influences of the home are essential to the transmission of moral values and perceptions. The spiritual dimension of a human being, and to a large extent of society as a whole, is based on parental guidance and instruction provided in the home. Hence the Judaic stress on the importance of background as a determining factor in an individual's qualification as a good mate.

The importance of background is emphasized in the biblical account of the choice of Rebecca as a wife for Isaac. Abraham entrusted his loyal servant Eliezer with the task of finding a proper wife for his son. He ruled out any choice of a local Canaanite girl because of the immoral environment of Canaanite homes. Abraham was convinced of the lingering effects of the undesirable influences of one's youth. He therefore in-

213

structed Eliezer to go to his native land to find a suitable girl of a Semitic family (Gen. 24:3–4).

GUIDELINES FOR CHOOSING A MATE

Eliezer's choice of a bride is highly illuminating. The decisive consideration was not her wealth or the prominence of her family but her character. Standing at the well, he prayed: "So let it come to pass that the damsel to whom I shall say: 'Let down thy pitcher, I beg of thee, that I may drink,' and she shall say: 'Drink and I will give thy camels drink also,' let the same be she that thou hast appointed for thy servant Isaac" (Gen. 24:14). Such a response, he felt, would qualify her to marry Isaac and would also be a token of God's approval.

The fine character of the wife must be matched by the equally fine character of her husband if the couple is to create the wholesome home environment essential to the upbringing of children. Yet the early Judaic literature on this subject appears to give greater emphasis to the moral stature of the wife. Eliezer informed Rebecca's family of Isaac's great wealth (Gen. 24:36) but did not touch on the question of Isaac's character. The lyrical description of an admirable wife by the author of Proverbs, "A woman of virtue who can find?" (Prov. 31:10), has no parallel passage along the lines of "A man of virtue who can find?" Warnings against the influence of immoral wives (Eccles. 7:26, Prov. 9:13) are not coupled with similar censures of the damaging influence of roguish husbands. Hagiographical admonitions to young men are mostly centered on their obligations to honor their parents. On the other hand, admonitions to young women mainly relate to their roles as wives and their obligations to their husbands.

Any conclusion that the stress on a wife's qualifications and duties is an indication of the prejudicial attitudes of a male-oriented society is fallacious. On the contrary, the Pentateuch lists a husband's obligations to his wife (Exod. 21:10) but has no similar text mandating a wife's duties to her husband. Indeed, according to rabbinic rules, a wife who has the means to hire servants is exempt from performing domestic duties. Surely such a liberal law reflects no antifeminist prejudice. Similarly, the fact that father and mother were placed on an equal level in the Decalogue with regard to filial obligations of parental honor dispels any notion of sexual discrimination.

The biblical emphasis on the woman's qualifications for marriage was primarily due to her vital position as the first teacher in the life of her young children and her ability to influence their ethical perceptions at a most formative age. The Book of Proverbs distinguishes between the role of the father and the role of the mother in the raising of children. The father disciplines but the mother instructs (Prov. 1:8).

The moralist authors of the Hagiographa felt the need for giving prominence to the traits of a good wife because a man's objective judgment of the character of a prospective bride may be clouded by the magnetism of her beauty and the force of his sexual drive. Samson's entrapment by charming Philistine girls was a warning to all moralists. The author of the "Woman of Valor" might have been reacting to the escapades of Samson. The feminine asset of beauty, generally extolled in the Bible and Talmud, was pointedly omitted by him.

Ancient moralists decried the formidable weapon of sexual enticement with which corrupt women can beguile men of weak character. The Book of Proverbs warns against a woman who "makes smooth her words" (Prov. 2:16), or whose lips "drop honey" (Prov. 15:3), or who "with the blandishment of her lips she entices him away" (Prov. 7:21), or persuades men that "stolen waters are sweet" (Prov. 9:13). Ecclesiastes exclaims: "I find more bitter than death the woman whose heart is snares and nets " (Eccles. 7:26).

Ecclesiasticus (2nd cent. B.C.E.) added more invectives against wily women. "Hast thou a wife after thy mind? Forsake her not; but give not thyself over to a light woman" (7:26). "Wine and women will cause men of understanding to fade away" (19:2). "I had rather dwell with a lion and a dragon than to keep house with a wicked woman" (25:16). A virtuous woman rejoices her husband. . . . An evil wife is a yoke shaken to and fro; he that has hold of her is as though he held a scorpion" (26:2, 7). Numerous other admonitions were uttered by moralists of all ages to warn men against sexual pitfalls.

In contrast to men, women are immune to overpowering lust and are able to form objective opinions of the character and personality of prospective husbands. There was obviously little need for warning women against the allure of wicked men.

Marriages entered into hastily are surely vulnerable to divorce. Young people contemplating marriage should carefully examine each other's background and character. The desirable traits of a good man are alluded to in the Book of Proverbs. An ideal man should be God-fearing, educated, industrious, honest, humble, kind, charitable, slow to anger, amenable to correction, and have a joyous disposition. He must be free of addictions, not vindictive, and eschew strife. We must add that there is no claim that all these superb qualities can be found in any one man.

The following traits of a good wife are referred to in the Book of Proverbs: She is her husband's helpmate and confidante. She is willing to assist him in his enterprises. She is a good homemaker and does not complain that her chores are too burdensome. She plans in advance and is never caught short. She is wise and kind and helps people who are in need. She advances her husband's career and does not begrudge the time he must devote to public affairs (Proverbs, chap. 31).

The rabbis were aware of the importance of a girl's physical charm and its role in cementing marital bonds. The ancient practice of arranged matches offered little opportunity for premarital dating. The rabbis insisted, however, that the couple meet at least once prior to the marriage to make sure that each was pleased with the other's appearance (*Kiddushin* 41b).

Several recommendations were offered to girls to keep them from making a wrong choice. A man who intends to use matrimony as a stepping-stone in his pursuit of wealth will not make a good husband. "He who marries a woman for the sake of her money will produce children who are misfits" (*Kid-*

dushin 70a). A money-oriented husband is not interested in the happiness of his wife or in the proper upbringing of his children. The rabbis expressed a similar objection to men who marry women because of the social prominence of their families. "He who marries a woman for the sake of attaining a prominent position will in the end be removed from his exalted status" (*Derech Eretz Zuta* 10). The Talmud commends individuals who marry a scholar's daughter (*Pesachim* 49a). A wife who was raised in a scholarly environment will instill in her children a love for learning.

Rabbi Judah Chasid, the twelfth-century moralist, took a pragmatic stand in his advice to young men. In comparing the advantages of a daughter of a scholar with a girl of an ordinary family who has a fine personality and the ability to be of help to her husband, he prefers the latter (*Sefer Chasidim* 381).

Jews have traditionally attached great importance to the merit of a distinctive family background, commonly known as *yichus* ("genealogy"). Genealogical background is an element which may properly be taken into consideration. However, one should not attach undue importance to it in the absence of other desirable qualifications.

For the sake of domestic peace, the rabbis cautioned against marrying individuals who have been raised in an atmosphere of discord. "One should distance himself from a contentious family beset by strife" (*Tur, Even HaEzer* 2). Most people have a similar objection to the marrying of a child whose parent has a criminal record. While caution is advised, it is unfair to visit the sins of parents upon their children. Every person is entitled to be judged on his or her personal merit.

A number of other useful guidelines are recorded in the Talmud. A young man should not marry an old woman, and a young woman should not marry an old man (*Yevamot* 44a). A man should not marry a woman whom he plans to divorce eventually (*Yevamot* 37b). He who marries off his daughter to an ignoramus is as guilty as if he had tied and placed her before a lion (*Pesachim* 49b). A poor man without prospects of improving his financial position need not desist from marriage. Marital happiness based on love is not destroyed by poverty

(*Yevamot* 118a). Men should not marry into an epileptic or leprous family (*Yevamot* 64b).

THE DESIRABILITY OF MARRIAGE

Despite the misgivings of moralists about the possible misuse of feminine pulchritude, Judaism was not distracted from its goal of promoting the institution of matrimony as the cornerstone of civilized society. Matrimony offers many rewards, chief among them physical comfort, companionship, and gratification of the sex drive and the craving for children. Of course, some of these advantages can be obtained outside of matrimony. Furthermore, matrimonial benefits are offset by heavy responsibilities. Support of family, the onus of child-raising, and domestic friction are serious deterrent considerations.

For the hesitant, Judaism painted a bright picture of the bliss of matrimony. At the same time it branded extramarital sex as grossly immoral. It also condemned celibacy as contrary to God's design. The Bible is quite emphatic in its advocacy of matrimony. "It is not good for man to be alone" (Gen. 2:18). This divine pronouncement proclaims the desirability of marriage. Entering into matrimony is an ethical imperative and a practical act which fulfills God's intent.

The Bible makes matrimony attractive by publicizing its many blessings. "Enjoy life with the wife whom thou lovest . . . for that is thy portion in life" (Eccles. 9:9). "Whoso findeth a wife findeth a great good, and obtains favor of the Lord" (Prov. 18:22). "A woman of virtue who can find? For her price is far above rubies" (Prov. 31:10). "Blessed is the man that has a virtuous wife, for the number of his days shall be double. A virtuous woman rejoices her husband, and he shall fulfill the days of his life in peace" (Ecclus. 26:1–2). "He that gets a wife begins a possession, a help unto himself, and a pillar of rest" (Ecclus. 36:24).

The bliss of matrimony was contrasted with the sad state of bachelorhood. "He that has no wife will wander up and down mourning" (Ecclus. 36:25). "A man who is not married lives without joy" (*Yevamot* 62b). Divine blessings bestowed by God are due to the merit of the wife (*Baba Metzia* 59a). Bachelors were warned of the grievous sin of neglecting procreation, an early biblical injunction (Gen. 1:28). Man is not permitted to live alone without a wife (Tosefta, *Yevamot* 5). A man who has no wife is anathema to God (*Pesachim* 113b). "A man without a wife is not a whole man" (*Yevamot* 63a).

The importance of marriage is reflected in several ordinances enacted by the rabbis. According to rabbinical law, he who possesses a sacred scroll of the Torah may never sell it. However, the law was amended by two exceptions. A Torah may be sold to realize money for the purpose of entering into matrimony or to enable one to pursue the study of the law (*Megillah* 27a). The two goals were thus equated. Matrimony is essential to physical survival, and scholarship is just as essential to spiritual survival. Another example is the law pertaining to the use of charity funds. The superintendent of public charity was given leeway to divert some funds for the purpose of dowering poor brides. "There is no greater charity than this" (*Yoreh Deah* 249:15).

Some ritual restrictions were relaxed for girls to make them more attractive to eligible bachelors. Thus girls in a state of mourning were permitted to use cosmetics (*Yoreh Deah* 381:6). Single girls were not required to cover their hair (*Ketubot* 15b).

The ultimate virtue attached to marriage was the theological doctrine according to which a bridal couple is forgiven all their sins on their wedding day (Jer. *Bikkurim* 3). From a religious point of view, marriage marks the beginning of a new life.

The fervent advocacy of matrimony did not blind the religious leadership to the realities of life. Matrimony can achieve its mission only if it is based on mutual love and respect. To lessen the gambling element of marriage and to enhance the prospects of the couple's compatibility, the rabbis offered a number of guidelines.

Physical development and a mature sense of responsibility are basic prerequisites of a successful marriage. At what age does the average person reach that stage? The answer must of necessity vary, depending on national traditions, economic conditions, and climatic zones of a given society. Solon, the Athenian lawgiver, considered thirty-five years a proper age for man to wed. The Dead Sea Scrolls prohibited sexual activity by men under twenty (*Manual of Discipline*). They regarded the age of twenty as the time "when they reach the age of discretion." The rabbis favored earlier marriages in order to discourage immorality. They viewed the age of eighteen as the most suitable for man to marry (*Avot* 5:26). At age eighteen, a young man is at the peak of his physical fitness and sufficiently mature to assume marital responsibilities. He is also flexible enough to make the necessary adjustments to marital compatibility.

No age limit was set for females entering matrimony. The need to protect young girls was paramount in the eyes of society. The early mortality of fathers dictated the need for early marriages of their daughters. The rabbis objected to marriages of female minors (*Kiddushin* 41a) but did not object to their marriage upon reaching puberty. The marriage of female minors was common in the post-talmudic era due to the dangerous conditions then in existence and the uncertainties of life. This practice was discontinued with the onset of emancipation and the promise of greater security.

The practice of early marriage created a problem of support, which young grooms were unable to provide. The rabbis recommended that a young man should own a home and farm before contemplating marriage (*Sotah* 44a). This advice was practical when agriculture was the main occupation. Medieval Jews, living in the urban setting of a ghetto, devised another solution. They provided board and lodging for the young couple for several years after their marriage. Another solution, adopted by some modern couples, is the assumption by the young wife of the role of breadwinner until such time as the husband completes his studies.

The progress of equality of economic and professional opportunities for both sexes has induced many women to seek a career prior to marriage. This trend, resulting in delayed marriages, has been concurrent with a gradual relaxation of sexual restraints. Such a development is, of course, contrary to Judaic morality. The Talmud insists that a higher education, including the pursuit of Torah scholarship, should be acquired after one is married (*Kiddushin* 29b). Modern sociologists question the assumption that early marriages are more durable. That may be so. However, the overriding concern of the rabbis was the prevention of immorality at an age when young people first become sexually active.

THE WEDDING FEAST

Judaism encourages joyous wedding celebrations. In addition to the couple and their parents, who have every reason to rejoice, all of society shares in this happy event because it strengthens the communal base.

Wedding celebrations are universal. The earliest wedding feast mentioned in the Bible was given in celebration of Jacob's marriage to Leah. "And Laban gathered together all the people of the place and made a feast" (Gen. 29:22). It was the bride's father who arranged the celebration. On the other hand, the earliest-mentioned Jewish wedding feast was prepared by the groom: ". . . and Samson made there a feast, for so used the young men to do" (Jud. 15:10). In the talmudic era there were two nuptial celebrations. A betrothal banquet was served in the home of the bride's father. The wedding feast was served in the home of the groom's father.

Due to the importance of marriage, the rabbis did not discourage expensive wedding feasts, although they did take steps against expensive funerals to prevent the embarrassment of poor families (*Moed Katan* 27a). Some luxurious items of wedding celebrations were temporarily eliminated after the destruction of Jerusalem. That elimination was not based on a public policy against excessive wedding expenses but on the perceived need for symbolizing the mourning for Zion (*Sotah* 49a). Local medieval sumptuary laws, limiting the wedding menu and the number of guests in attendance, were enacted to avoid exciting the jealousy of hostile neighbors. Under normal circumstances, however, people went to great expense to provide a sumptuous feast.

Despite the absence of traditional regulation of wedding

celebrations, the bounds of good taste dictate some ethical restraints. Wasteful lavishness, motivated by ostentation and a desire to outdo one's neighbor, borders on the unethical and even the obscene. Rabbi Judah Chasid (12th cent.) criticized parents who invite many out-of-town guests and then impose on their neighbors to provide free food and lodging for them during the week-long celebration (*Sefer Chasidim* 1121).

Wedding affairs are happy occasions, and it is the duty of all guests to enter into the spirit and mood of the event. Mourning and sadness are out of place at a wedding party (*Derech Eretz Rabbah* 7). The ancient practice of amusing the bride with songs and dancing was praised by the rabbis of the first century. The songs generally extolled the charms and beauty of the bride (*Ketubot* 17a). Rabbi Judah (2nd cent.) used to dance in front of the bride with an aromatic myrtle branch in his hand, chanting "beautiful and gracious bride" (ibid.). The practice of entertaining the bridal couple with skillful acrobatic dances is still popular at traditional weddings.

God is described as "making the groom and his bride rejoice" (seventh nuptial benediction). Yet the rabbinical directive to wedding guests singles out the bride as the one to be amused (*Ketubot* 16b). This may possibly reflect the realization that the bride of that period was in greater need of encouragement because the marital status placed her in a subordinate position to her husband. The major burden of child-raising falls upon the mother. Her financial independence and security were sadly inadequate. The right of divorce was exclusive to the husband, and in the event of his disappearance or desertion, she could not look to remarriage.

MARITAL RIGHTS AND OBLIGATIONS

Despite these disadvantages, ancient women were not necessarily unhappy with their lot. Women needed physical protection, and marriage filled that need. Feminine charm generally turned husbands into pliant and loving companions. In her role of mother, the Bible assigned to her a place of dignity on an equal level with the father. Most of the disadvantages of married women were gradually eliminated by rabbinic enactments.

A husband's marital obligations to his wife are listed in the Pentateuch: "Her food, her raiments, and her conjugal rights, he shall not diminish" (Exod. 21:10). "Food" is the comprehensive term for board and lodging. The standard of living which a husband must provide depends upon his income. It is unethical to demand of a wife that she be content with a living standard below that which is maintained by the average person within her husband's income bracket. It is equally unethical for a husband with a potential for a higher income to deny it to his wife on the ground that he prefers greater leisure than most people of his age enjoy. On the other hand, it is unethical of a wife to demand a higher standard of living which is beyond her husband's ability to attain.

Men who are married to wealthy women may tend to slacken their efforts to make an adequate living. The rabbis were generally critical of husbands who prefer to depend on their wives' income (*Pesachim* 50b). They issued a dire warning to him who secretly entertained hopes of inheriting his wife's estate. "In the end she will bury him" (*Avot deRabbi Natan* 3:3).

Many modern families have two breadwinners. Women seek employment to increase the family income or out of a preference for the stimulation and challenge of a job. A wife's gainful work is perfectly proper, provided it does not preclude the primary function of bringing children into the world or deprive young children of a parent's company and supervision. In the talmudic era, a distinction was drawn between work which women had to do outside of the home, to which there was an objection, and work done at home, which was acceptable (*Pesachim* 50b). Modern women are as secure in public as men, and the ancient objection to women's work outside the home is no longer valid today.

A husband's obligation to provide his wife with proper clothes was stressed in the Bible and Talmud. This emphasis is due to the fact that women are more sensitive than men to styles and fashions. The biblical injunction to husbands to make their wives rejoice on the occasion of a holiday is fulfilled, according to the rabbis, by buying attractive dresses for them (*Pesachim* 109a). Traditional Jews strongly felt the need for having their wives properly attired. In the words of the rabbis, a good husband is willing to do without new clothes for himself so long as he has sufficient means to buy a pretty dress for his wife (Jer. *Ketubot* 6:5). No wife, however, may demand expensive clothes or other luxuries beyond the reach of her husband's income.

A wife who receives a spending allowance from her husband must be given full discretion in the management of the household and the manner in which she spends her allowance. It is unethical to demand a detailed accounting of the money entrusted to her.

SEXUAL RELATIONS

Conjugal sex is the third of the biblical obligations imposed on a husband. In ancient Judaic society, when polygamy was tolerated, though seldom practiced, the right of each wife to the love of her husband had to be guaranteed. The biblical injunction of conjugal sex was addressed to the husband and not to the wife. The rabbis explained this distinction by the different natural inclinations of each sex. Women, unlike men, do not actively pursue sexual intercourse. "It is the practice of men to woo a woman, and it is not the practice of a woman to woo a man" (*Kiddushin* 2b). However, a woman who enters into matrimony assumes a legal obligation to engage in sexual relations with her husband. The refusal of either party to have sex is grounds for divorce (*Even HaEzer* 77:1).

It is unethical of a husband to insist that his wife submit to sexual relations despite her disinclination due to health or emotional state (*Eruvin* 100b; Maimonides, *Hilchot Deot* 5:4). To make coitus a satisfactory experience for both parties, the rabbis advised husbands to get their wives in a proper mood with loving words and tender acts (*Baba Batra* 10b). Husbands who are conscious of the need of gratifying their wives' sexual urges were promised the reward of fine offspring (*Niddah* 71a). Happy wives make happy mothers. On the other hand, he who forces his wife to engage in sex against her wishes will be punished with defective children (*Eruvin* 100b).

Procreation is a primary aim of sexual relations. The biblical command of procreation (Gen. 1:28) is fulfilled with the birth of a boy and a girl (Yevamot 61b). However, a husband's sexual obligation continues in force even after the requirement of procreation has been met. Judaism does not sanction birth control by means of interrupted coitus (Gen. 38:9–10). The use of contraceptives, tampons, or oral sterilizing drugs by pregnant or lactating women is permissible, if it is needed to prevent conception which may endanger the life of the mother or her offspring (Yevamot 12b). Men may not use contraceptives. Continence is the only permissible birth-control method, providing it is practiced with the consent of the wife and that the minimal requirement of procreation has been fulfilled.

Childlessness is a painful problem which confronts some couples. Modern science has achieved remarkable progress in alleviating that condition. Prevailing rabbinical opinion sanctions artificial insemination, using the husband's semen but not the semen of another donor.

Test-tube fertilization with the husband's sperm of a human egg taken from the woman's ovary is permissible. The embryo may be reimplanted in the mother's womb. Some rabbis object to this procedure on moral grounds.

The implantation of a fertilized egg into the womb of a host mother raises a problem of maternal identity. According to one opinion, if the embryo is forty days and older, the child is the offspring of the biological mother. According to another opinion, the woman who experiences the labor and travail of childbirth is regarded as the mother. There is as yet no consensus on the moral aspect of surrogate mothers.

A similar problem regarding parental identity is raised in connection with the transplant of an ovary or testicles. Except for this problem, there seems to be no objection on moral or ethical grounds.

Abortion of a fetus, soon after conception, is an act of aggression prohibited in the Bible (Exod. 21:22–23). According to the Talmud, the killing of a fetus does not constitute murder and is not a capital offense (Sanhedrin 57b). A fetus may be aborted if the mother's life is endangered by the pregnancy (*Ohalot* 7:6). Abortion for the sake of destroying a defective child is not permissible, unless it is essential to the preservation of the physical and emotional health of the mother.

Judaism treats sexual practices as the private domain of each couple. While opposed to any manner of sexual perversion, most rabbis hesitated to interfere in a delicate area which is best left to the discretion of the people involved (*Nedarim* 20b). This, of course, does not include practices expressly prohibited in the Bible.

The natural reserve of women in matters of sex casts a special duty on the husband to be sensitive to his wife's romantic mood. "A woman does not articulate her sexual desires" (*Bereshit Rabbah* 17:8). "A woman solicits [sex] with her heart, a man solicits with his mouth" (*Eruvin* 100b). Men were apprised of some special occasions when women are likely to be desirous of sexual relations. One such occasion is the evening prior to a husband's departure on a long journey (*Yevamot* 62b) and again when he returns from the journey (*Berachot* 55b). Women also yearn for love in the period immediately preceding the onset of the menstrual cycle (*Pesachim* 72b). The same is true of the day of the completion of the postmenstrual purification (*Berachot* 24a).

Marital sex produces a therapeutic emotional sensation of intimacy which transcends the immediate but transitory physical gratification. To enhance this benign process, it is important to perform the sex act under propitious circumstances and at a time which is most conducive to the promotion of mutual love. The rabbis opposed daytime sex (*Niddah* 16b). A sexual act interposed between various daily chores loses its spiritual significance. The rabbis also opposed coitus performed when the couple is fully dressed (*Ketubot* 48a). Without the intimacy of bodily contact, the act is reduced to a pleasurable experience bereft of love.

A late midrashic text lists four categories of objectionable sexual relationships: (1) forcible sex opposed by the wife; (2) coitus at a time when the husband and wife are engaged in a quarrel; (3) coitus with an intoxicated wife; (4) sexual relations between a couple who have previously agreed to a dissolution of their marriage. In all of these circumstances the desirable effects of the sex act are negated.

ADJUSTMENTS AND COMPROMISE

The Talmud stresses the importance of domestic peace and harmony in the establishment of a happy marriage. "He who maintains peace in his household, Scriptures regard it as if he has brought peace to every person in Israel" (*Avot deRabbi Natan* 28:3). A peace-loving family enhances the peace of the entire community of which it is a component. "He who loves his wife as himself, and honors her more than himself, [of him the verse reads] 'You shall know peace' " (*Yevamot* 62b). The rabbis admonished men that women are susceptible to tears (*Baba Metzia* 59a). Husbands must take care not to provoke their wives because they are more sensitive to a hurt. No man may intimidate his wife and children (*Gittin* 6b). Mutual respect between husband and wife is conducive to domestic peace (*Baba Metzia* 59a).

The goal of attaining domestic harmony and compatibility does not dictate that the couple streamline their personalities into unisex human species. The partners are not expected to give up their individual traits. Due recognition should be given to such traits and special skills for the common good. A wise husband consults his wife before making an important decision (*Baba Metzia* 59a). A wise wife seeks to please her husband (*Yalkut, Kum Barak*). However, the claim to individuality must not be asserted to great length if it is detrimental to the happiness of the spouse. A wife must not dominate her husband to the point where he loses his independence of judgment (*Bezah* 32b). A husband may not act unilaterally to force his wife to move to a new location if he deprives her thereby of conveniences available in the old location.

Contentiousness is ruinous of family life. When strife is chronic, only death or divorce can put an end to it. Yet one must exercise great restraint in the effort to establish a satisfactory modus vivendi. Rabbi Judah Chasid, the twelfth-century moralist, wrote: "A man married to a contentious wife should not pray to God for another wife, but that his wife's heart be ennobled and that her hate turn into love" (*Sefer Chasidim* 748).

In the event of domestic conflict, husband and wife have an obligation to reach an amicable understanding. Couples have a need of each other's companionship. The need for temporary separations produced much friction in ancient times. The rabbis prohibited husbands from leaving on extended journeys without first obtaining the wife's consent. They also deemed it improper for a disciple to join his master for a holiday, leaving his wife and children alone at home (Jer. *Sukkah* 2:5). By the same token, it is improper for a wife to travel with her parents out of town to celebrate a family affair if the husband is reluctant to be left alone. This rabbinical objection was valid in ancient times, when a journey by wagon consumed much time, even to destinations which were not distant. Under modern conditions of speedy travel, a husband's objection to his wife's joining a family celebration would hardly be justifiable.

The intent of all parties entering matrimony is to form a lifelong union. This is undoubtedly true even of couples who set up housekeeping without the formality of a religious or civil marriage ceremony. The modern judiciary has increasingly offered these couples the financial security which previously was the privilege of marital status. At the same time the durability of such quasi-marital arrangements is at the sufferance of either party. The right to terminate such an arrangement at will may attract some young people. In reality, however, this freedom is a destabilizing factor conducive to capricious dissolution. It is also destructive of the emotional stability essential to the creation of a proper environment for the raising of children. Judaism is opposed to free love on ethical, moral, and social grounds.

DIVORCE AND ITS AFTERMATH

Needless to say, a marriage ceremony is no guarantee against failure. The popular belief that marriages are made in heaven does not prevent human beings from unmaking them. Indeed, it would be contrary to the interests of the couple, their children, and society to preserve a union which generates unceasing discord and antisocial attitudes. To quote a talmudic maxim: "No individual can live permanently in the same den with a snake" (*Yevamot* 112b). Under some circumstances, the dissolution of a marriage by divorce is not only desirable but meritorious (*Eruvin* 41b).

In the absence of compelling reasons, the termination of a marriage by divorce is regarded in Judaism as a great tragedy. "When a divorce ends a first marriage, the altar sheds tears" (*Gittin* 91b). The altar, a symbol of reconciliation between man and God, sheds tears when two individuals in conflict cannot reconcile to one another.

The Pentateuch seems to be deliberately vague in its description of a legitimate cause for divorce. A man divorces his wife "because he has found an unseemly thing in her" (Deut. 24:1). What is the definition of an "unseemly thing"? Is it in her moral conduct or in her general inadequacy as a wife? Rabbinic interpretations differ. However, the vagueness of the text might indicate that the definition of an "unseemly thing" should be left to the social and moral perceptions of each generation.

A divorce signifies the failure of a marriage. It is the ultimate step in the quest for a change in one's condition. An early discovery that the divorce has not produced the anticipated happy state may hasten a reconciliation. The Talmud considers it proper for a divorced couple to remarry each other, provided the divorced wife has not been married to someone else in the interim. Under such circumstances, remarriage to the first husband is interdicted in the Bible (Deut. 24:4) for moral reasons.

The rabbinical approval of the taking back of one's divorced wife is limited to one remarriage. In the event that the first remarriage also ends in divorce, a second remarriage is strongly discouraged (*Pesachim* 113b). A presumption of failure has been fully established.

Does a divorce sever all links between the couple? Legally yes, morally no. Rabbi Jose the Galilean (2nd cent.) was informed that his former wife was resorting to begging for subsistence. Having previously paid her, at the time of the divorce, the amount required by law, he had no further legal obligations for her support. Nevertheless, he felt morally bound to provide for her future needs (Jer. *Ketubot* 11).

Rabbi Jose based his novel moral doctrine on a verse in Isaiah: "Thou hide not thyself from thine own flesh" (58:7). The term "flesh" is a biblical synonym for "wife" (Gen 2:23). Isaiah bracketed the moral duty of feeding the poor and clothing the naked with a similar obligation to be mindful of the needs of one's "flesh." Surely he was not referring to a wife to whom one is married and to whose care one is legally committed (Exod. 21:10). Rabbi Jose apparently concluded that Isaiah had in mind a former wife who is still referred to as his "flesh."

The union of two people in marriage is legally different from the association of two individuals in a partnership. When a partnership is dissolved, the relationship between the partners comes to a complete end. On the other hand, a divorced mate is like a limb severed from a body. The limb remains forever part of the body and must be treated with respect.

Rabbi Jose's perception has practical implications and gives a new dimension to the moral links which survive a divorce. This is particularly significant when the divorced couple have children who form a permanent bond between their parents. Due to the lingering moral relationship, a divorce must not be permitted to generate a state of festering animosity. The divorced partners must still treat each other with respect. A divorced parent who has custody of the couple's children must not prejudice their minds against the other parent. Grown-up children occasionally reject a parent for whatever they consider justifiable grounds. That decision must be their own and not the result of prejudicial influences to which they were subjected in their childhood.

Divorced parents have an inherent right to participate in their children's celebrations of important events. It is in this area where breaches of the surviving moral relationships between divorced people are most common. A parent who pays for a daughter's wedding affair may, in a spirit of vindictiveness, bar the former spouse from attending the wedding. Such conduct is cruel and unethical.

The part assigned to parents in a wedding ceremony is another area of potential conflict. Divorced parents have a moral right to escort their child and march together down the aisle. Such an arrangement is warranted by the surviving moral relationship between the parents which dictates consideration for one another's feelings.

The propriety of having divorced parents join together in escorting their child is not affected by the remarriage of one or both of the parents. A remarried parent may bring his or her second spouse to the wedding affair of a child. The second wife or husband is entitled to an invitation as a matter of right. They are well advised, however, to try to be as unobtrusive as possible to spare the feelings of the part of the family which views their presence with distaste. Needless to say, under no circumstances should a second spouse take the place of a living parent in the wedding procession.

Judaic tradition does not attach any stigma to the status of a divorcee. However, the rabbis advised against marrying a divorcee in the lifetime of her previous husband. Their objection was based on social rather than moral grounds. They felt that a divorcee might still retain some affection for her previous husband and as a result be unable to develop a true physical and emotional intimacy with her second husband (*Pesachim* 112a). The rabbis implied a similar objection to the marriage of a divorced man in the lifetime of his former wife. The rabbinic reservation about the wisdom of marrying a divorced person would seem to have little validity in the event where a divorce ended a marriage in an explosion of hostility. A number of medieval rabbis also opposed marrying a twice-divorced woman because her fitness for matrimony has been put in question (*Even HaEzer* 9:1).

WIDOWS AND WIDOWERS

The rate of divorce has grown to alarming proportions in modern times. However, death is still the major cause of the termination of matrimony. The tragic lot of the widow and widower is frequently referred to in ancient Hebrew literature. "A man who lost his wife, his world is plunged in darkness, his steps are shortened" (*Sanhedrin* 22a). "It is as if the holy sanctuary [in Jerusalem] was destroyed in his time" (ibid.). It is the wife who creates the atmosphere which converts a home into a sanctuary. "The full impact of the tragedy of death is only felt by the mate of the deceased" (*Sanhedrin* 22b).

The marital links which survive a separation by death are much stronger than the links which survive a divorce. A widow has the right to insist that she prefers living in her deceased husband's home, and the heirs should respect her wishes (Jer. *Ketubot* 12:3). A widow has a right of burial near her husband's grave. In ancient times, widows who declined remarriage out of respect for their deceased husbands were considered models of marital faithfulness and rectitude (Judith, chap. 16).

REMARRIAGE

For practical reasons, the rabbis strongly favored the remarriage of widowers and widows. There were some limitations. A widow who lost two husbands was deemed a bad risk (*Even HaEzer* 9:1). A pregnant or nursing widow should not remarry before the infant is at least two years old (*Yevamot* 42a). A widower with young children may remarry when thirty days have passed since the death of his wife. If there are no young children he should wait a year. A widower who has children of marriageable age should marry them off first before taking another wife (*Bereshit Rabbah* 60:16).

There was special advice for widowers who are unable to sire children due to their sterility. They were urged to marry women who have children from a previous marriage. Judaism does not recognize the legal effect of adoption. The children of the second wife will continue to trace their lineage from their natural father. However, they will enjoy the protection and support of their stepfather, who is credited with performing an act of particular merit (*Yevamot* 61b).

Mourning and Condolence

And he made a mourning for his father seven days.

—Genesis 50:10

MOURNING IS to grief what rejoicing is to happiness. Both are instinctive reactions to the two extremes of man's emotional gamut.

The primary cause of mourning is the loss of a beloved kin or friend. The manifestation of grief serves a twofold purpose. It reflects the anguished state of mind of the bereaved individual. It also projects a desire to honor the deceased as a person whose death is worthy of mourning.

There are some misguided people who consider a public display of grief a sign of weakness, inconsistent with a manly character. Such vain pretense denies the mourner an opportunity for venting his sorrow. What is worse, it denies the deceased the honor due him. According to the rabbis, he who withholds mourning mocks the dead (*Berachot* 18a).

The Bible records some mourning practices of antiquity in vogue prior to the mandatory Judaic mourning rituals. Abraham mourned Sarah (Gen. 23:2), Jacob mourned Joseph (Gen. 37:34), and was later mourned by his children (Gen. 50:10). Mourning is universal. However, the manner of expressing it varies, depending on the sociological development and religious traditions of each society.

Judaism has established a rigid code of rituals for the guidance of mourners. It prescribes the conduct which tradition regards as proper and respectful in the period of bereavement. These rules are particularly instructive for the maintenance of

233

an atmosphere of dignified solemnity in a house of mourning where there is little grief. A death which terminates a prolonged agonizing sickness is understandably accepted by the surviving kin with a muted sense of relief. The same is true of a death which lifts a crushing physical and financial burden from the family of the deceased. Yet, even under such circumstances, the observance of mourning rituals is important as an expression of honor for the memory of the decedent.

The duty of the bereaved kin to mourn their loss has as its counterpart the duty of friends to offer condolences. This obligation similarly serves a double purpose. It brings solace to the mourners. It also gives the friends an opportunity for paying tribute to the memory of the departed. The latter aspect of condolence visitations was stressed by Rabbi Judah (3rd cent.). The Talmud relates the story of a man who died without heirs. Hence there were no mourners in need of consolation. Yet Rabbi Judah was disturbed by the fact that the deceased "had no comforters." Why was he concerned about the absence of "comforters"? Rabbi Judah was troubled because the decedent was denied the honor which comforters would have paid to his memory had they had the opportunity to make a condolence visit. He therefore assembled a quorum of men to sit with him in the house of the departed to receive condolence visitations (*Shabbat* 152b).

The practice of offering condolences is as ancient as the custom of mourning. When Jacob mourned Joseph, "all his sons and all his daughters rose up to comfort him" (Gen. 37:35). Ecclesiastes acclaimed the virtue of condolence visits: "It is better to go to the house of mourning than to the house of feasting" (Eccles. 7:2).

How should a visitor behave in a house of mourning? According to the rabbis, a visitor should sit in silence (*Berachot* 6b, *Moed Katan* 28b). The ancient sages apparently felt that a mourner engrossed in his grief is in no mood for conversation. They were also undoubtedly aware of the fact that unsophisticated people might say something which would bruise painfully raw nerves. In their opinion, a visit, even if no words are spoken, is in itself a gesture of sympathy which will bring comfort to the bereaved. The silence was always broken before leaving, when visitors recite the traditional message of condolence.

The maintenance of silence by visitors was an acceptable practice in ancient times because all mourners understood the significance of the silence. Modern people, not familiar with this practice, might misinterpret such silence as a sign of indifference. Visitors therefore feel constrained to express some sentiments that will ease the pain of the mourners. Unfortunately, the wisdom for choosing the right words at such a delicate moment eludes many people.

The injection of humor in a house of mourning is highly improper. In the words of the rabbis: "Let no one smile in the company of mourners, nor grieve in the company of celebrators" (*Derech Eretz Rabbah* 7). The practice of serving refreshments and drinks to visitors is also objectionable because it turns the atmosphere of solemnity into conviviality. Such a disregard of propriety is a mockery of the dead.

There are visitors who try to distract the mourner by taking his mind off his loss. That is a misguided strategy. Mourners need sympathy, not distraction. It is also a disservice to the memory of the dead. Comments on the merits of the deceased and an expression of a sense of personal loss are always proper and comforting to the bereaved.

Parental Obligations

And thou shalt teach them [the laws] diligently unto thy children.

—Deuteronomy 6:7

PARENTAL CARE of children is motivated by love and instinctive inclination. Yet if love is the sole force shaping parental attitudes, it may destroy the goal which most parents seek to achieve. Loving parents frequently shrink from taking disciplinary measures to enforce their instructions. The erring child of a doting father and mother is even spared stern admonitions. Innate love must be balanced by a mature sense of responsibility if the child's moral development is not to suffer.

In addition to parents who love foolishly, there are, at the other end, parents who are bereft of affection for their children and do not have the true interests of their offspring at heart. To protect children against parents who love too much or too little, religious and civil laws have been promulgated, detailing specific parental duties.

The Bible stresses parental responsibility for the education of children. Religious principles which are fundamental to the national psyche must be implanted into the child's consciousness. Thus the message of the festival of Passover, eternal opposition to oppression and enslavement, is a mandatory subject of parental instruction (Exod. 13:9). In addition to the transmission of ideals which are central to the faith, it is a parent's duty to acquaint his children with all the rules and regulations of the Torah (Deut. 6:7).

The importance attached to education was reiterated by Ecclesiasticus (2nd cent. B.C.E.): "Hast thou children? Instruct them, and bow down their neck from the youth" (7:23).

236

Education of children is so basic to Judaism that Josephus wrote in the first century: "Our principal duty of all is thus to educate our children well" (*Apion*, bk. I, 12).

Education is a gradual process which must be in tune with the child's capacity to absorb the knowledge offered to him. The biblical injunction commonly rendered "Train a child in the way he should go" (Prov. 22:6) is more properly translated: "Train a child in accordance with his ability" (*al pi darko*). Rav (3rd cent.) declared the age of six to be the proper time for beginning formal education (*Baba Batra* 21a). A network of elementary schools was set up in Judea as far back as the first century (ibid.).

Parents are enjoined to supervise the moral and ethical conduct of their children. Discipline is an essential tool in the shaping of character. A stern reprimand is a helpful correctional measure. If administered in time, it may obviate the need of punishment. "Chasten thy son, for there is hope, but set not thy heart on his destruction" (Prov. 19:18). However, corporal punishment was not ruled out. "He that spares the rod hates his son, but he that loves him chastens him betimes" (Prov. 13:24).

Parental educational duties extend beyond the narrow limits of religious instruction. Parents of the biblical era were expected to continue the supervision of their children for the duration of their lives in the parental home. Parents were charged with the duty of marrying off their children and seeing to it that they took proper mates. The Bible warned against the giving of a child in marriage to a heathen (Deut. 7:3). When Samson sought parental consent for his marriage to a Philistine girl, he was administered a stern rebuke: "Is there never a woman among the daughters of thy brethren, or among all my people, that thou goest to take a wife of the uncircumcised Philistines?" (Jud. 14:3). The fact that Samson's parents eventually surrendered to his persistence illustrates a common parental weakness in permitting love to overcome their sense of responsibility.

Parental control over the marriage of their children had as its primary aim the safeguarding of religious continuity. However, it was also intended to be used as a restraint on hasty marriages to individuals of improper character. Ecclesiasticus declared: "Marry thy daughter, and so shalt thou have performed a weighty matter, but give her to a man of understanding" (7:25).

The Talmud lists the following parental duties: "A father is obligated to circumcise his son, to redeem him [a religious ceremony performed when the infant is thirty-one days old], to teach him Torah, to marry him off, and to teach him a trade. Some say, even to give him swimming instruction" (Kiddushin 29a). The rabbis cautioned against excessive discipline which may give a child an erroneous impression that the parent hates him. Rabbi Simon b. Elazar (2nd–3rd cent.) said: "A child should be pushed away with the left hand and drawn near with the right hand" (Sotah 47a).

Parents must not favor one child over the others (Shabbat 10b). Favoritism incites discord among siblings. The biblical Joseph became a victim of his brothers' jealousy because their father had singled him out for special favorable treatment (Gen. 37:3–4).

Ethical instruction is most effective when the parents set a personal example. Rabbi Zera (3rd cent.) said: "One should not promise a gift to a child and later withhold it, because he will thereby teach him lying" (Sukkah 46b). It is unethical to teach a child to lie, even if it is only a white lie, the kind that most people condone. A young child will not analyze the distinction between various degrees of lies. The most common example is the practice of parents who instruct a child to lie about his age so that they may take advantage of cheaper fares charged for younger children.

A child's happiness is essential to his sense of security and development of character. Parental love expressed by the giving of gifts is an important contributor to a child's stability. The biblical injunction "And thou shalt rejoice in thy feast, thou, and thy son, and thy daughter" (Deut. 16:14) mandates, according to rabbinic interpretation, the giving of gifts to children on festive occasions (Pesachim 109a).

In selecting a trade or profession for one's child, the rabbis ruled out financial remuneration as an incentive. They noted that in every craft there is both poverty and wealth, and that much depends upon the honesty and skill of the craftsman. They objected to any trade which is susceptible to corruption and listed a number of them which, in their view, are most likely to induce dishonesty (*Kiddushin* 82a). The medical profession was particularly denigrated because of the primitive state of the medical science of that period. Rashi's (11th cent.) explanation of the talmudic objection to medical practitioners strikes a high moral tone. Many doctors, he noted, are guilty of refusing to treat indigent patients because they are unable to pay them for their services (ibid., *tov she-barofim*).

The responsibility for choosing children's careers has been shifted in modern times from the parents to the children themselves. However, parents still play a crucial role in influencing a child's ultimate choice. They must still weigh the moral implications of any career which they would like their children to pursue.

Parental relations to grown children take on an added nuance. Parents must realize that their instructions no longer command absolute obedience. The respect of grown children for their parents depends on a reciprocal parental respect for their grown children. Striking an adult son is strictly prohibited in the Talmud (*Moed Katan* 17a). An aroused son may strike back and thus be guilty of a violation of a strict biblical injunction (Exod. 21:15).

A widowed father should not take a second wife if his grown children still make their home with him. His remarriage should be postponed until such time as the children are out of the house (*Bereshit Rabbah* 60). This restriction does not apply when the children are young and in need of a mother. In another practical suggestion, the rabbis urged parents not to transfer title to their property to grown children. "He who transfers his property to his children in his lifetime acquires a master over himself" (*Baba Metzia* 75b).

Parents have a legal right to disinherit their children. However, the rabbis looked with strong disfavor upon such actions, unless warranted by serious misconduct (*Baba Batra* 133b).

Parenthood imposes obligations toward children, but at the same time it also renders a beneficial service to the parents by deepening their understanding of human behavior. In the course of raising their children, parents face an unending cycle of confrontations which teach the need for compromise and conciliation. These qualities arc essential to good parenthood and equally important to people in a position of leadership, particularly those who hold judicial office. Indeed, only a parent could qualify for a seat on the supreme court of ancient Judea (*Sanhedrin* 36b).

Preservation of Life and Property

Therefore choose life, that thou mayest live, thou and thy seed.
—Deuteronomy 30:19

IT IS the religious duty of every individual to keep fit and to refrain from practices which endanger health and shorten life. This obligation is a corollary of the general prohibition of waste and needless destruction of living creatures or inanimate useful articles.

The instruction to safeguard one's health and life is additionally based on several theological rationales. In view of the biblical declaration that man was created in the image of God, any injury to one's body constitutes an assault upon its divine aspect and hence an affront to the Almighty.

The belief that parents create the body of their offspring but that it is God who implants the soul (*Berachot* 60b) further contributed to the tenet that life must be preserved and that suicide is a crime against God. Man owns his body, but he is merely the custodian of the soul which resides within him. Only God may decide when the soul is to depart the body.

This rationale was well known to ancient Jewry, including its nonrabbinic elements. In his discussion with survivors of the Roman assault upon Jotapata, Josephus (1st cent.) offered several reasons why they should not consider suicide a permissible alternative. "And do you not think that God is very angry when a man does injury to what he has bestowed on him? For from him it is that we have received our being, and we ought to leave it to his disposal to take that being away from us. . . . The soul is ever immortal, and is a portion of the divinity that

241

inhabits our bodies. . . . if anyone cast out of his body this divine essence, can we imagine that he who is thereby affronted does not know it!" (*Wars*, bk. 3, chap. 8:5).

The philosophic explanation of the interaction between the soul and the body provided another basis for the principle of the preservation of life. The soul which is implanted in a human body is pure, without any blemish. That is the gist of the morning prayer recited upon waking: "My God, the soul which thou hast planted in me is pure. . . . thou preservest it in me, and thou shalt someday take it from me" (*Berachot* 60b). According to the teachings of Kabbalah, the soul is tainted by the corruption of the body. Biblical references to sin and impurity are frequently addressed to the soul: "If a soul sin through error" (Lev. 4:2), "If a soul sin and commit a trespass against the Lord" (Lev. 5:21). When the body atones for its sins, the purity of the soul is restored. The willful destruction of one's body precludes an eventual purging of the soul of its acquired flaws, forcing it to return to heaven in a state of impurity.

Josephus touched on this theme too in his discourse against suicide. "Do you not know that those who depart out of this life, according to the law of nature . . . that their souls are pure and obedient and obtain a most holy place in heaven . . . while the souls of those who have acted madly against themselves are received in the darkest place in hell" (*Wars*, bk. 8, chap. 3:5).

Aside from doctrinaire considerations, there is a universal consensus that life is man's most precious gift. Every effort must therefore be made to preserve and prolong it.

The rabbis cited several biblical injunctions as the source of the obligation to safeguard one's health. The commands "Only take heed to thyself, and watch thy soul carefully" (Deut. 4:9) and "You should be very careful of your souls" (Deut. 4:15) were regarded as warnings against endangering one's life (*Berachot* 32b). Another source is a verse in Genesis (2:7): "And man became a living soul." "The Bible thereby implies, 'Keep alive the soul which I gave you' " (*Taanit* 22b).

Maimonides (12th cent.) addressed a warning to those who

allege that their state of health should be of no concern to other people. "There are many things which the rabbis have prohibited because they endanger human life. He who says: 'I am only endangering myself, and no others have a right to interfere,' the rabbis may administer to them disciplinary flogging" (*Hilchot Rotzeach* 11:5).

Man has a right to put himself to shame, if he is indifferent to public opinion, but no one may lawfully injure himself (*Baba Kama* 91b). It is also prohibited to curse oneself (curses may be self-fulfilling) (*Shavuot* 35a). No man may degrade himself by eating things which are universally deemed nauseating and repugnant. The biblical source of this prohibition is a verse in Leviticus (11:43): "You shall not make yourself detestable with swarming things that swarm." The rabbis interpreted this prohibition to include the eating of food contaminated with dirt, the eating of food with slimy hands, and the drinking of fluids from vessels which were used previously as urinals (Maimonides, *Maachalot Asurot* 17:29). Self-degradation insults the body, which was made in the image of God

Suicide is a transgression which by its very nature can never be atoned for. The biblical verse "But for your own life-blood I will require [an accounting]" (Gen. 9:5) was interpreted by Rabbi Elazar (2nd cent.) as meaning: "I will require your blood if shed by your own hands" (*Baba Kama* 91b).

Judaism denies all religious burial rites to people who commit suicide. There is no doubt that these stringent sanctions kept the number of suicides low, despite the tragic conditions under which Jews were forced to live in the diaspora. When forcible apostasies became common occurrences during and after the era of the Crusades, many Jews sought an escape in martyrdom. Those who committed suicide were accorded full honors by the medieval rabbis, and their deaths were regarded as a "sanctification of the name of God" (Tosafot, *veal, Avodah Zarah* 18a).

One may violate most religious injunctions in order to save his life. Even an infant who is one day old, legally not considered viable, is entitled to the same consideration (*Shabbat* 151b). There are three cardinal prohibitions which may not be violated even at the cost of one's life: idolatry, adultery, and murder (*Sanhedrin* 74a). Any commission of suicide for the sake of avoiding a transgression of other religious injunctions is a serious offense (Maimonides, *Yesodei haTorah* 5:4).

The moral question whether religious laws may be transgressed in order to preserve a life was in issue for a long time. Some sectarian groups, such as the Qumran sect, apparently believed that the primacy of the law should never be compromised (see Bloch, *The Biblical and Historical Background of Jewish Customs and Ceremonies*, p. 117). On the other hand, a Hasmonean court (2nd cent. B.C.E.) ruled that one may desecrate the Sabbath to defend his life (I Macc. 2:41). It seems that no such dispensation was ever granted prior to the Hasmonean era.

The Talmud accepted the principle of the primacy of life. Rabbi Ishmael (2nd cent.) voiced a minority opinion that even the law forbidding idolatry may be transgressed (not in public) when one is ordered to do so at the risk of his life. He based his view on a verse in Leviticus (18:5): "You shall therefore keep my statutes and my judgments, which if a man do he shall live in them." Rabbi Ishmael commented on the last phrase of the verse: " 'he shall live in them' but not die by them" (*Sanhedrin* 74a).

The primacy of life was apparently paramount in the moral code of the Semitic patriarchs. Abraham requested Sarah to tell Pharaoh that she was his sister, not his wife, so that the king would have no need of killing him (Gen. 12:13). This request can only be rationalized by a prevailing ethical principle that all virtues, including marital fidelity, may be waived in the interest of saving a life.

The rabbinical majority opinion was crystallized after a long debate in the upper chamber of the house of Nitzah in Lydda (ca. 135). It was during the Hadrianic persecution, when the practice of Judaism was forbidden, that the issue was finally resolved. "In every law of the Torah, if a man is commanded: 'Transgress and suffer not death,' he may transgress and not suffer death, excepting idolatry, adultery, and murder" (*Sanhedrin* 74a).

One may not save his life by causing the death of another

person. Thus if a company of people is approached by bandits who issue an ultimatum, "Deliver one of you to us so we may kill him; if you do not, we will kill all of you," all of them should submit to death rather than surrender any individual. The same is true when bandits accost a company of women and demand that one woman be delivered to them so that they may violate her (Maimonides, *Yesodei HaTorah* 5:5).

One need not sacrifice his life in order to save the life of another person. The following classic illustration is cited in the Talmud: "If two are traveling on a journey [in a desert], and one has a pitcher of water, if both drink they will die [i.e., there is not enough water to sustain two lives], but if one only drinks he can reach civilization. The Son of Patura taught: 'It is better that both should drink and die, rather than that one should behold his companion's death.' Until Rabbi Akiva [2nd cent.] came and taught: ' "That thy brother may live with thee" [Lev. 25:36], "thy life takes precedence over his'" (*Baba Metzia* 62a).

The Son of Patura expressed a highly ethical view. The owner of the pitcher, who witnesses the death of his companion, cannot but feel morally guilty as an accomplice to his death, considering that it was within his power to save him. Yet such a lofty ethical concept is impractical and a disservice to society. It is better that one survive than that both perish. One life is as good as the other and need not be sacrificed to save the other.

There are, however, exceptional occasions when self-sacrifice for the sake of saving another life is called for, transcending normal ethical standards. Most parents would instinctively forfeit their lives to save their children. In the case of the two men traveling in the desert, if the companion is a man of great stature because of his scholarship, and his survival would be beneficial to society, the owner of the water should carefully weigh the consequences of his decision. Rabbi Judah Chasid (13th cent.) expressed his opinion in unequivocal terms: "When two people, one a scholar and the other uneducated, are attacked, the latter should sacrifice his life, if he can thereby save his companion" (*Sefer Chasidim* 698).

The injunction against the impairment of one's health has its parallel in the prohibition of wasting food and destroying useful objects. This prohibition is based on sociological grounds. Privation and abundance have coexisted for as long as man has inhabited this earth. Charity is mandatory in Judaism as a means of narrowing the gap between the affluent and the indigent. Waste of food and wanton destruction of serviceable articles is an outrageous disregard of the plight of the poor.

One cannot but decry the common practice of large food producers who destroy their crops when low prices make sales unprofitable. Wholesale destruction of food may raise the price of a commodity. Yet the same result could be obtained by withholding the food from the market but permitting relief agencies to distribute it to the poor.

The prohibition of the destruction of food is based on a verse in Deuteronomy (20:19): "When thou shalt besiege a city . . . thou shalt not destroy the trees thereof . . . for thou mayest eat them, but thou shalt not cut them down." The rabbis interpreted this injunction as a comprehensive prohibition of the destruction of food or anything useful (*Baba Kama* 91b). Thus Rabbi Ishmael (2nd cent.) said that not only the tree, which is a producer of food, must be spared but the fruit, which is no longer on the tree, also may not be wasted (*Sifre*, Deut. 127).

Maimonides listed several destructive acts which are in violation of the biblical negative injunction "Thou shalt not destroy." "Whoever breaks dishes, rips clothes, demolishes a structure [for no reason], clogs a spring, and does away with food by destroying it, transgresses the injunction 'thou shalt not destroy'" (*Hilchot Melachim* 6:10). This prohibition equally applies to the killing of animals for no gainful purpose (*Chulin* 7b).

The injunction against destruction does not apply to destructive acts which serve a useful purpose. It is permissible to demolish a building to replace it with a new structure. However, destruction of useful articles merely to satisfy one's yen for extravagance and luxury is improper. It is immoral to kill animals for their fur when synthetic furs, albeit less attractive, are available. It is similarly improper to cut down fruit-bearing trees when lumber of unproductive trees is available, even if less ostentatious.

The rabbis pointed out that the boards used in the construction of the biblical tabernacle came from acacia trees. "The Almighty wished to teach the generations of posterity a lesson in ethics." Should anyone building a home ever wish to use lumber of a fruit tree, let him ponder. If God was satisfied with acacia wood, surely a mortal should be content with it (*Shemot Rabbah* 35).

Those who destroy property in the heat of anger are in violation of the injunction against destruction. Rabbi Yochanan b. Nuri (2nd cent.) said: "He who rends his garment in anger, he who breaks his vessels in anger, he who scatters his money in anger, regard him as an idolater" (who destroys property to propitiate a deity; *Shabbat* 105b).

Implied in the injunction against the destruction of food is an obligation to handle it respectfully. It should be handed to people, not thrown to them (*Berachot* 50b). Thus food was accorded a degree of sanctity given to religious articles (*Eruvin* 98a). It is disrespectful to step on food. Passers-by who see food lying on the ground must pick it up so that it may not be trodden under the feet of pedestrians.

It is demeaning to serve food fit for human consumption to animals (*Taanit* 20b). Additionally, people in need of nutrition have a prior claim on this food. The nutritional needs of animals can properly be met by feeding them the food which is unfit for humans.

Promises

That which is gone out of thy lips thou shalt observe diligently to do.

—Deuteronomy 23:24

AN INSPIRATIONAL folktale quotes a dialogue between a mother bird and her fledglings who lived contentedly in a nest at the bottom of the thick underbrush on a farmer's lawn. "Are you happy this morning?" mama chirped to her little ones. "No, mama. We are very much afraid. We overheard the farmer tell his wife: 'The neighbors promised to come this afternoon to mow our lawn.' Please get us out of here." "Have no fear," said mama. "It is only a promise." The next morning the little birds were even more agitated. "We overheard the farmer tell his wife: 'Our sons promised to come in the afternoon to mow our lawn.'" "No reason to get alarmed. It is only a promise," said mama. On the third day, mama found her offspring shaking with fear. "We overheard the farmer tell his wife: 'This afternoon we will set aside all our chores and mow the lawn.'" Deeply scared, mama agreed. "I had better move you right away."

What the wise old bird knew is equally known to everyone. Few people take their promises seriously. An individual who scrupulously keeps a promise is singled out for special praise as a man whose "word is as good as his bond."

With some minor exceptions, promises are not enforceable. The law reflects the common cynical appraisal of promises. They are hollow words spoken by someone eager to make a good impression. There are several reasons for the failure of the law to give promises a binding force. A promise may be a declaration of intent rather than a formulation of an irrevocable

248

decision. Promises flow from sudden impulses and do not represent a reasoned conclusion. The extemporaneous phraseology of a promise lacks careful framing. Promises are frequently made in jest.

From a legal point of view, promises may be broken with impunity. What about the moral point of view? Does a person who has no regard for his word brand himself as untrustworthy? Does a breach of promise constitute a breach of faith and trust?

Most biblical passages and injunctions dealing with promises relate to oaths and vows, which are legally binding. Jacob made Joseph swear that he would transport his body for burial at the Cave of Machpelah (Gen. 47:31). Jacob realized that Joseph's responsibilities might make it difficult for him to get a leave of absence. This might force him to break a promise, but he would never violate an oath. Prior to Joseph's death, he too made his kinsmen swear that his skeleton would be removed from Egypt when all the Hebrew slaves departed the land (Gen. 50:25). A later generation might not feel bound by a mere promise made several centuries earlier, especially if circumstances rendered such a time-consuming task a most difficult assignment. He therefore demanded an oath.

To preclude the possibility of retraction, all promises made to God were put in the form of a vow. "And Jacob vowed a vow, saying: 'If God will be with me . . . of all that thou shalt give me, I will give a tenth unto thee' " (Gen. 28:20–22). "And Israel vowed a vow unto the Lord, and said . . ." (Num. 21:2). Ecclesiastes warned people against breaking a vow on the excuse that it was unintentional and "made in error" (Eccles. 5:5). Apparently there was no significant opprobrium attached to a breach of a verbal promise to a fellowman.

The Talmud takes up the question of the morality of a breach of a verbal promise. It bases its conclusion on a verse in Leviticus: "Just balances, just weights, a just ephah [a dry measure], and a just hin [a liquid measure] shall you have" (Lev. 19:36). Why did the text mention the measure called "hin" in addition to the measure called "ephah"? Hin, according to Rabbi Judah, is a double-entendre. It is the name of a measure, and it also means "yes" in Aramaic. "It is to teach you that your yes should be just, and your no should be just" (*Baba Metzia* 49a). Man's words must be as honest as his scales.

The moral imperative of keeping one's promise was stated as follows: "He who keeps his promise, the sages are pleased with him" (Jer. *Shevi'it* 10:9). "Individuals whose yes, is yes and whose no is no are righteous" (*Ruth Rabbah* 7). In the case of unilateral promises of a gift, Rabbi Yochanan (3rd cent.) differentiates between a promise of a large sum, which belies a serious intent, and a promise of a reasonable sum, which must be honored by the promisor. If he is delinquent, he is guilty of a breach of faith and trust (*Baba Metzia* 49a).

There are dissenting opinions regarding the morality of a breach of a verbal business transaction, which is not legally binding. If the initial promise was made in good faith but subsequent developments, such as a rise in the price of the merchandise to be delivered, render the deal unprofitable, a seller may, according to Rav (3rd cent.), disregard his promise. Rabbi Yochanan dissents. According to him, a refusal to implement the deal constitutes a breach of faith (*Baba Metzia* 49a).

As an incentive to people to keep their promises, the Talmud recorded the names of some individuals whose reputation for keeping promises gave them great distinction. It was said of Rabbi Samuel b. Zutra (4th cent.), "if he were given all the underground treasures of the world he would not break his word" (*Baba Metzia* 49a).

A pledge to charity is binding and enforceable. The term "charity" enbraces contributions to religious and philanthropic institutions and also to indigent individuals. A promise of money to a poor person is a charitable pledge which cannot be retracted (*Yoreh Deah* 258:12). In the view of some medieval rabbis, even a mental decision to give charity is a binding obligation which must be morally fulfilled, though it cannot be enforced (Rema, *Yoreh Deah* 258:13).

Respect for the Dead

The memory of the righteous shall be for a blessing.
—Proverbs 10:7

THE HUMAN body, created in the image of God, commands respect even in death. One manifests respect by performing deeds and expressing sentiments which honor the deceased. Additionally, one must refrain from physical desecration of the body and from demeaning it by speaking ill of the deceased. The affirmative and the negative aspects of respect for the dead are based on biblical sources.

The account of the death of Sarah illustrates the tradition of *kavod hamet* ("honor of the dead"). "And Abraham came to mourn for Sarah and to weep for her" (Gen. 23:2). Mourning and lamenting are important aspects of *kavod hamet.* The prohibition of degrading the dead is inherent in the law which provides for the removal of the body of a criminal who died on the gallows before the day is over (Deut. 21:23). A deteriorating body is offensive to the sight. "For he that is hanged is a reproach unto God" (ibid.). According to Rashi's interpretation (ad loc.), the desecration of a body created in the image of God is an insult to the Almighty. The Bible's opposition to the desecration of a body extends even to the corpse of a criminal. How much more should one be careful to avoid degrading the body of a law-abiding person.

Tradition prescribes the proper conduct which constitutes honor of the dead. A corpse must not be left unattended. It should be watched up to the time of burial to prevent its desecration by rodents (*Berachot* 18a; Rema, *Yoreh Deah* 373:5). The body should be washed and cleansed (*Shabbat*

151a). It should be swaddled in shrouds (ibid.). The virtues of a deceased should be lauded by eulogizers (*Moed Katan* 8a).

It is the obligation of all people living in the community of the deceased to attend the funeral service (*Berachot* 18a). Josephus (1st cent.) attests to the prevalence of this custom. "All who pass by when one is buried must accompany the funeral procession and join in the lamentation" (*Against Apion* II, 27). Rav (3rd cent.) ordained that even people engaged in labor or commerce should take time out to attend the funeral service (*Moed Katan* 27b).

The religious code lists many rituals which the next of kin of a deceased must observe prior to and after the burial. Most of these rituals were enacted in response to the obligation of honoring the dead (see "Mourning and Condolence").

The prohibition of demeaning the dead engendered many regulations. It is prohibited to speak ill of the deceased (*Bet Yosef, Tur, Orach Chaim* 606). It is disrespectful to eat in a room where a corpse reposes (*Yoreh Deah* 341:1). Eating over graves was deemed a heathen practice (Jubilees, chap. 22). It is disrespectful to display a corpse, with face uncovered, for family and friends to gaze at (*Horayot* 13b). Observing the change in appearance is demeaning to the dead. The prohibition of postponing the burial beyond the day of death was relaxed in the event that the postponement was needed for the completion of proper funeral arrangements, such as the procurement of shrouds and coffin (*Sanhedrin* 46a).

Respect for the dead is common to the traditions of all races. However, in some cultures an exaggerated respect degenerated into worship of ancestors and invocation of their spirits. This practice was strongly denounced by Isaiah (65:3–4).

The Judaic concern for the dignity of the dead gave rise to the unique law of *met mitzvah* (*Eruvin* 17a). The Talmud defines a *met mitzvah* (literally a "command body") as the body of an individual who has no relatives to attend to his funeral. The duty of burying the body devolves on any person who discovers it. The right of the corpse to a decent burial takes precedence over conflicting laws and restrictions. Thus even a high priest, who is normally under stringent biblical prohibition of defilement by contact with the dead, must personally attend to the burial of a *met mitzvah* (*Berachot* 20a). The body may be buried on the spot where it was discovered, disregarding the proprietary rights of the owner of the land (*Eruvin* 17a).

Incising or puncturing a corpse is considered a desecration. Embalming a corpse, involving removal of organs or perforations, is prohibited. In the event that burial has to be postponed beyond the day of death, the body may be preserved by freezing.

Autopsies are generally disapproved because of the prohibition of desecration of the body. According to some religious authorities, there are several exeptions to this rule. Autopsies performed for the purpose of discovering whether death was due to a criminal act of violence are permissible. The same is true when an autopsy is essential to obtaining information which may save the life of a sick person. An autopsy may also be performed when prior consent was given by an individual while in full possession of his mental faculties.

Dissection of bodies for anatomical research is not approved except in the event that such research is needed for the saving of another life. The removed human organs must be handled respectfully and properly buried when no longer needed.

Judaism objects to cremation on two grounds. It is deemed a desecration of the body. It also contravenes the belief in resurrection (Jer. *Ketubot* 11:5).

The donation of organs for transplantation is approved by some rabbinic authorities on the ground that it saves the life of another human being. Furthermore, the transplanted organ is kept alive when grafted to a living body.

Respect for Man

Love thy neighbor as thyself.

—Leviticus 19:18

MAN'S MORAL obligations to his fellowman derive from religious perceptions of human rights and from practical considerations of the needs of society. The Judaic doctrine of the equality of all men, inherent in the biblical account of Creation, grants every individual equal rights and privileges. Man's freedom of action is consequently circumscribed by the rights of other people. One may do or say whatever he desires so long as he does not infringe upon the prerogatives and sensitivities of his neighbors. These bounds are expressed in Hillel's (1st cent.) paraphrase of the Golden Rule: "What is hateful unto thee, do not do unto others" (*Shabbat* 31a).

The principle of equality, which bars men from assuming dominion over other people, is linked in the Bible to the creation of human beings in the image of God. "And God said: 'Let us make man in our image, after our likeness; and let them have dominion over the fish of the sea, and over the fowl in the air and over the cattle'" (Gen. 1:26). This verse pointedly excludes the dominion of men over other men, who are equally endowed with divine qualities. Any act which disregards the rights of other people constitutes an unlawful exercise of dominion.

The restatement of this basic principle by Ecclesiasticus (2nd cent. B.C.E.) is also based on the aforementioned sequence of the biblical text. "The Lord created man of the earth . . . and made him according to his image . . . and gave him dominion over beasts and fowl" (Ecclus. 17:1–4).

Malachi (6th cent. B.C.E.) used the theme of man's equality

before God as the basis of his appeal for respect for man. "Have we not all one father? Has not one God created us? Why do we deal treacherously everyman against his brother, profaning the covenant of our fathers?" (Mal. 2:10).

In addition to curbing man's offensive acts, respect for man dictates affirmative measures in support of those who need help. Every individual is a beneficiary of society's companionship and protection. This is the sense of the text in Genesis: "And the Lord God said: 'It is not good that the man should be alone. I will make him a helpmate' " (Gen. 2:18). Mutual interdependence, essential to man's happiness, imposes an obligation to balance the benefit derived from human intercourse with a reciprocal contribution to the welfare of others.

Isaiah (8th cent. B.C.E.) surveyed the public scene of his day and reacted with a caustic remark. He had found a desirable degree of cooperation among some people, but unfortunately they put it to use for wrong ends. "They [the evildoers] helped everyone his neighbor; and everyone said to his brother: 'Be of good courage' " (Isa. 41:6).

The Talmud devotes much space to the various practices entering into a proper social relationship. Greeting strangers whom one meets in the street is an important manifestation of respect. The rabbis pointed out that he who is aloof to strangers will in the end develop indifference to those who are close to him (*Bamidbar Rabbah* 8:4). It was related of Rabban Yochanan b. Zakkai (1st cent.), the most revered scholar of his generation, that "no man ever gave him greetings first, even a heathen in the street" (*Berachot* 17a).

All visitors should be received with a cheerful countenance (*Avot* 1:15). Shammai, the author of this dictum, was topped by Rabbi Ishmael (2nd cent.), who urged: "Receive all men with joy" (*Avot* 3:16). Meiri (13th cent.) commented that even when one resents the intrusion of a visitor he must make believe that he is happy to receive him (on *Avot* 1:15). Such a posture is not to be regarded as hypocritical but as a show of courtesy.

Respect for man promotes peace and friendship. Hillel (1st cent.) said: "Love peace, pursue peace, love thy fellowman and draw him close to the Torah" (*Avot* 1:12). Rabbi Mattithyah b. Charash (2nd cent.) said: "Be the first in the salutation of peace to all men" (*Avot* 4:20). "Peace" (*shalom*) is the universal salutation among Jews.

The importance of a friendly disposition was stressed in the following statement: "When a man gives his friend the finest gift in the world but shows an angry [or stern] face, the Scriptures regard it as if he had not given anything. On the other hand, if he receives his friend with a cheerful countenance, Scriptures regard it as if he had given the finest gift in the world" (*Avot deRabbi Natan* 13).

The various nuances of respect are discussed in the Talmud. According to one rabbi, respect is synonymous with endearment (*Derech Eretz Zuta* 2). Another rabbi equated respect with honor. "Let the honor of your friend be as dear to you as your own" (*Avot* 2:13). Rabbi Yonah Gerondi (13th cent.) interpreted this statement as follows: "One's desire to see another man honored should be as strong as his desire to be honored by others."

One demonstrates respect for man by manifesting a deferential regard for man's dignity and a consideration for his rights. In the event of a conflict between one's own rights and the rights of other people, an ethical person will defer to his neighbors. This principle is in keeping with a rabbinic dictum: "Yield your will to the will of your friend" (*Derech Eretz Zuta* 1).

Rabbi Judah Chasid (12th cent.) offered the following illustration of a conflict of rights: "A man walking on a narrow road comes across another man carrying a heavy load, walking in the opposite direction. Let the man [without the load] step onto the shoulder of the road, even if it is muddy, so that the man with the load can pass by" (*Sefer Chasidim* 551). A delay is more onerous to a man carrying a heavy burden. The person who is told to step aside may muddy his clothes, and they will have to be laundered. That is a small price to pay compared to the great exertion of the carrier of the load. One wonders, however, what Rabbi Judah's decision would have been if all things were equal. Obviously an ordinary sense of ethics would offer little guidance. In the end, it is the man who puts the rights of others ahead of his own who will step aside.

The Talmud defines the distinction between respect and love. Respect is expressed through good deeds, love is reflected in one's emotional attitude (*Ketubot* 103b).

Respect for man also imposes a respect for his faith and religious practices. The rabbis asserted that "the righteous people of all nations have a share in the hereafter" (Tosefta, *Sanhedrin* 13). Judaism was tolerant of all religions except paganism, with which it was incompatible. At the time when ancient Judea was a sovereign state and the nation had the jurisdiction to enforce its laws within the borders of its country, the practice of idolatry was proscribed. However, Jews never entertained a desire to forcibly root out heathenism in other countries.

There were some occasions when, for humane reasons, the practice of idolatry was tolerated even in Israel. A captive pagan woman, brought home by a Jewish soldier, was permitted to continue her heathen worship for thirty days, (Deut. 21:13, *Yevamot* 48b). According to Maimonides (*Moreh Nevuchim* 3:41), this dispensation was motivated by consideration for the plight of the captive woman and a desire to provide her with the solace that she might derive from practicing her ancestral faith. At the end of the thirty days, if the soldier had a change of heart, the woman was free to return to her home, without having been forced to renounce her faith (Nachmanides, Deut. 21:13).

Josephus interpreted the biblical injunction against the blasphemy of God to include the blasphemy of idols sacred to other nations (*Antiq.*, bk. 4, chap. 8:10). This view, which is not in accord with traditional Judaic doctrine, was probably expressed for the benefit of the Romans. It is a fact, however, that the ancient Jewish postbiblical literature is free of denigration or ridicule of any specific pagan deity.

To respect man is to respect his practices and habits. A person who is never late for an appointment should not be kept waiting. A hostess who is fastidious about the cleanliness of her home should not be given any offense by people with sloppy habits. Guests who bring their children along should not permit conversation or entertainment to distract them from their duty to supervise the conduct of the children. A guest in the home of a nonsmoker should refrain from smoking, unless the presence of ashtrays signals an invitation to smoke. Nonreligious guests in the home of observant hosts must refrain from acts or words offensive to religious people. Heated partisan discussions are out of place at social gatherings. The rabbis summed up these and similar situations with the dictum: "Let no one deviate from the prevailing practice" (*Baba Metzia* 86b).

There are many occasions when affirmative action is called for. An individual in financial straits should be offered assistance (Lev. 25:35). The finder of a lost article must make every effort to restore it to its rightful owner (Deut. 23:3). The rabbis listed several affirmative social obligations. One should provide shelter for the homeless, dower a poor bride, visit the sick, attend a funeral service, and make peace between contending parties (*Shabbat* 127a). One should extend his arm to an elderly person walking in the street if he needs support (*Yoreh Deah* 244:7). One who has knowledge of information needed by a plaintiff in a civil action must come forward and testify, if so requested. However, in criminal cases involving a capital offense, one must volunteer his testimony even if not requested (*Chinuch* 122).

Doing favors for people accomplishes two goals. It renders a useful service by filling an avowed need. It also lifts the morale and builds up the ego of the recipient of the favor. A benefactor should not minimize the value of his service by saying: "It is only a small matter." On the contrary, by agreeing that the service was valuable and that it took some effort to render it, one raises the esteem of the beneficiary by the implication that he was worthy of it (*Sifre*, Deut. 3:25).

Over and above the ethical duty of doing all sorts of favors is the moral imperative of coming to the aid of people who are under attack or otherwise in danger of death. This affirmative duty is inherent in the biblical text: "Neither shalt thou stand idly by the blood of thy neighbor" (Lev. 19:16). Based on this injunction, the rabbis amplified: "How do we know that if you see someone drowning in a river, or attacked by bandits or a wild beast, you are obligated to come to his rescue, even at the cost of the life of the attacker? Because it is written: 'Neither shalt thou stand idly by the blood of thy neighbor' " (*Sifra*, Lev. 19:16).

Obviously, the duty of rescuing people in danger entails some risk to the rescuer. Nevertheless, that does not relieve one of his obligation, unless his own life would thereby be placed in jeopardy. A nonswimmer need not attempt life-saving because he would sacrifice his life in vain (*Sefer Chasidim* 674). Furthermore, there is no moral imperative to give one's life in order to save the life of another (see "Preservation of Life and Property").

The Talmud ridicules individuals who may be reluctant to save a life due to a distorted sense of religious values. A pious person who believes that he must remove the tefillin from his head and arm before jumping into the river to save a drowning person is a "pious fool." The same is true of one who holds back from saving a drowning woman because of her nudity (*Sotah* 21b, *Tosafot Heichi Domi*).

The right of a rescuer to kill an attacker is one of last resort. If it is possible to stop him by any means short of death, killing is an unwarranted defensive action, tantamount to murder (*Sanhedrin* 49a).

In addition to the obligation to save another person's life there is also a duty to preserve his reputation. Everyone is entitled to the benefit of a doubt. Joshua b. Perachyah (1st cent.) said: "Judge all men in the scale of merit" (*Avot* 1:6). This rule is the ancient forerunner of the modern democratic doctrine which places the burden of proof on the accuser rather than the accused.

It is immoral to entertain ungrounded suspicions. Resh Lakish (3rd cent.) said: "He who entertains a suspicion of innocent men is bodily afflicted" (i.e., heaven will punish him; *Shabbat* 97a). According to Rabbi Elazar (3rd–4th cent.), one who wrongfully suspects another person of a sin or a crime must beg his forgiveness and appease him (*Berachot* 31b).

The degree of respect one owes a fellowman has a broad range, depending upon the latter's kinship, age, position, and stature in society. Respect for parents is the most demanding obligation (see "Filial Obligations"). The same is true of the elderly, teachers, scholars, and heads of state.

A student visiting a teacher must remain standing until he is invited to sit. A student must never occupy a seat normally used by the teacher (*Yoreh Deah* 24:15). When saluting a teacher, a student should say: "Shalom, my rabbi and teacher" (*Sanhedrin* 100a). When a legal question is submitted to a master, his disciple may not express an opinion in his presence (*Yoreh Deah* 242:1). One should never speak disrespectfully of his teacher or any other scholar (*Shabbat* 119b). A teacher who is an expert in one branch of the law should not be queried in public in an area with which he is less familiar, lest he be embarrassed (*Shabbat* 3b). When a teacher or scholar passes a public place where people are seated, or when he enters an academy or synagogue, all must rise in his honor (*Kiddushin* 32b).

Spiritual leaders and public officials have occasion to meet thousands of people in the course of their careers. Some of them establish intimate relationships and are well known to the leaders. The acquaintances with other people are the result of casual introductions which leave no lasting impression. Their faces and their names are soon forgotten. Yet some of these individuals, eager to make an impression, challenge the leader with the question, "Do you remember me, what is my name?" Such questions are potentially embarrassing and highly improper.

Widows and orphans are entitled to special consideration because of their unfortunate lot. Strangers, frequent objects of discrimination, are similarly classed as individuals deserving of kind treatment. "And a stranger shalt thou not wrong, neither shalt thou oppress him. . . . You shall not afflict any widow or orphan" (Exod. 22:20–21). Indeed, a widow was granted some preferential legal protection. If she defaults on a payment of a loan, her garment may not be taken as a pledge (Deut.

24:17). All transactions with widows as also with orphans and strangers, must be free of rancor and animated by compassion (*Chinuch* 63, 65).

Modern social laws have done much to improve the financial security of widows. However, these laws do not lessen the trauma of widowhood nor ameliorate the sense of loneliness and sensitivity to society's indifference. The ancient biblical concern for the psychological deprivation of defenseless people is as vital today as it was in a more primitive era.

Sick people have a special claim upon the attention and consideration of their fellowmen. Judaism emphasizes the moral obligation of visiting the sick. The term "visiting" is used in the broad connotation of rendering a service and providing care. Rabbi Akiva (2nd cent.) said: "He who does not visit the sick may be regarded as if he sheds blood" (*Nedarim* 40a).

It is physically impossible to visit all the people who are sick. One should therefore be selective in his visitations. Rabbi Judah Chasid (12th cent.) said: "When there are two sick people in a community, one rich and one poor, and you have time to visit only one of them, attend to the poor patient. The rich patient will receive many visitors, even if you cannot pay your respects" (*Sefer Chasidim* 361).

Even a condemned criminal who has been sentenced to death is entitled to humane treatment. Rabbi Nachman (3rd cent.) said that the Golden Rule also covers criminals. The court must therefore "choose an easy death for him" (*Pesachim* 75a).

A condemned criminal who was hanged must be removed and buried by the end of the day so as not to bring undue indignity to his body (Deut. 21:23). Furthermore, the pole from which he was hung is also buried so that it should not serve as reminder to people that "so-and-so was hanged on this tree" (*Sanhedrin* 46b, *Chinuch* 535). The injunction to bury the criminal's body on the day of his death is in keeping with the law applicable to all burials (*Yoreh Deah* 357:1).

Personal dislikes and animosities do not affect one's social obligations to his fellowman. This rule is expressed forcefully in the Book of Proverbs: "If thy enemy is hungry give him bread to eat, and if he is thirsty give him water to drink" (Prov. 25:21).

All biblical social commands are applicable to friend and foe alike. "If thou meet thine enemy's ox or his ass going astray, thou shalt surely bring it back to him again. If thou see the ass of him that hates you lying under its burden, thou shalt forbear to pass by him, thou shalt surely release it with him" (Exod. 23:4–5).

The temptation to disregard an enemy in need is very intense. Indeed it requires much character training to ignore one's normal inclination to look the other way. To emphasize the urgency of such character training, the rabbis promulgated an amendment to an established law: "If a friend requires unloading [of an animal which has fallen because the burden was too heavy for it—normally such an obligation has priority], and an enemy requires loading, one's [prior] obligation is toward his enemy, in order to subdue his evil inclination" [to offer no help to an enemy] (*Baba Metzia* 32b).

Saving a human life is the most meritorious deed. By the same token, taking a human life is the most heinous crime (Exod. 20:12). Even a nation at war must take all possible steps to avoid the shedding of blood. According to a biblical injunction, the Jewish army must offer peace before launching an attack (Deut. 20:10). In the words of Maimonides (12th cent.), one may not wage war against a nation without first offering peace, regardless of whether it is a permissive war or a war of obligation (i.e., in self-defense; *Melachim* 6:1).

Josephus (1st cent.), a military commander in the early stages of the Jewish rebellion against Rome, wrote as follows: "When you are about to go to war . . . it is a right thing to make use of words to them before you come to use your weapons of war. . . . assure them that you do not wish to wage war, nor take from them what they have . . . and if they hearken, it would be proper for you to keep peace with them" (*Antiq.*, bk. 4, chap. 8:41).

Josephus also reasserted the regard which Judaism has for the enemy who is killed in battle. "Let our enemies that fall in battle be also buried; nor let any dead body lie above ground, or suffer a punishment beyond what justice requires" (*Antiq.*, bk. 4, chap. 24).

The moral repugnance against taking another person's life, even an enemy's, was expressed by Rabbi Yitzchak (4th–5th cent.): "Just as David was praying to God that he should not fall into the hands of Saul, he also prayed that Saul should not fall into his hands" (*Shochar Tov*, Ps. 7:1).

A defeated enemy, who no longer poses any danger, should be accorded humane treatment. Rabbi Chamam b. Chanina (3rd cent.) struck a highly moral tone in the following statement: "Even though your enemy has 'risen up early' to kill you [Exod. 22:12], and [after being disarmed] he comes hungry and thirsty to your house, give him food and drink" (*Midrash Prov.* 25:21).

There are several exceptions, some previously mentioned, to the stringent prohibition of killing. One may kill in self-defense. One may also kill an individual who attacks another person. Another exception was the ancient right granted to the kin of one who was accidentally killed to pursue the person responsible for the accident. The avenger was called a "redeemer of the blood" (Deut. 19:6).

"Avenging of blood" was a deeply rooted practice in ancient societies, which could not be abruptly outlawed. By providing "cities of refuge," the incidence of revenge killings was greatly reduced, if not totally eliminated. According to the Talmud, signs pointing to the cities of refuge were prominently displayed on highways to facilitate the killer's escape (Jer. *Makkot* 6:6).

A willful murder was punished by the courts. An accidental killer, however, was not deemed legally guilty of any crime. Yet there was a common perception of a moral guilt attached to a person who causes another man's death, even if he was not negligent in the legal sense of the word. This view was supported by the biblical law of the goring ox. An ox which killed a human being must be destroyed (Exod. 21:28). The destruction of the ox is justified by the need to prevent future mishaps. However, the law has an additional proviso. The meat of the ox is unfit for human consumption, even if the animal was ritually slaughtered. Rabbi Aaron of Barcelona (13th cent.) explained the prohibition on moral grounds. It is a pointed lesson, he alleged, that an animal which caused a human death is an odious creature, repugnant to all men. This will teach us to be extremely careful not to be the cause of the loss of a life, even in the absence of negligence (*Chinuch* 52).

The attachment of moral guilt even to an unintentional killer is also evident in the law which prohibits a priest who has caused an accidental death from blessing a congregation by reciting the Priestly Benediction (*Berachot* 32b). Although he is innocent, there is a moral stigma which stains his record. This consideration should weigh heavily for those who commit suicide and involve others in their death. The person who jumps in front of a moving train gives little thought to the impact of his act upon the innocent motorman, who may carry the burden of guilt on his conscience for the rest of his life.

Euthanasia, or mercy-killing, may be another exception to the prohibition of murder. Is it permissible to ease a dying person's agony by expediting his death? It is an accepted tenet that every individual is entitled to die in peace and with dignity. This is the sense of the verse in Ecclesiastes: "A time to be born and a time to die" (3:2). It is obviously improper to create a condition which interferes with the right to die in peace. There was no life-sustaining equipment available in the talmudic era. However, there was a common belief that a loud noise, which distracts a dying person's attention, extends life for a short period. The rabbis ruled that the noise may be stopped to permit death to take its natural course (*Sefer Chasidim* 234). It is also morally right to pray to God that a terminally ill patient who suffers pain may die (*Nedarim* 40a; Ran, *Ein Mevakesh*).

No overt act that may hasten death, such as jolting the body of a dying person is permitted. On the other hand, there is a disagreement as to whether there is a moral obligation to attach life-supporting instruments to a person who suffers pain if his death is irreversible. There is a consensus that such instruments, once attached, may not be removed to hasten death.

Respect for man inhibits any physical assault on a human being, even if it does not result in injury. An assailant who raises his hand to strike someone is called a *rasha* ("wicked"; *Tanchuma, Korach* 8). Statements or actions which provoke people to anger are prohibited (*Yoma* 87a). It is similarly prohibited to aggrieve people by embarrassing them in public (*Baba Metzia* 59a). It is improper to request a favor of a friend if one is aware that the friend is in no position to grant it. His inevitable refusal may embarrass him.

A sinner or a criminal who has reformed should not be embarrassed by a reminder of his past record (*Baba Metzia* 58b). It is improper to utter curses. An individual who is cursed, even when he does not believe in the efficacy of curses, is slighted and embarrassed (*Chinuch* 231).

Every person has a right to speak his mind and is entitled to a respectful hearing. One should not interrupt him before he has completed his statement (*Sifre, Beha-alotcha* 102; Dead Sea Scrolls, *Manual of Discipline* VI).

No person may be disturbed by unnecessary noise (*Choshen Mishpat* 156:2, Rema). The hopes of a merchant should not be falsely raised by an inquiry about the price if one has no intention of buying the item (*Baba Metzia* 58b).

One should not impose on the generosity of neighbors by asking for help in the performance of a task which he can accomplish on his own. If help is essential, one must limit his request to the barest minimum. When calling for a favor, it is improper, if the friend is not at home, to leave a message: "Let him call me when he gets home." It is the place of the one asking for help to call again until his friend is reached.

Most people shrink from knowingly offending or inconveniencing their neighbors. Too many, however, fail to perceive the undesirable consequences of some of their acts. One who double-parks his car is guilty of a lack of foresight. One who leaves a shopping cart across a narrow aisle in a supermarket while he marches off to examine prices is equally blind to the consequences of his act. It is to such thoughtless people that the rabbis addressed themselves: "Who is wise [and ethical] who can foresee results" (*Taanit* 32a). It is similarly a measure of wisdom not to harbor objects or animals which pose a danger to others (see "Endangerment").

He who respects other people will in turn be respected by them. The civilized tone of society is thus greatly enhanced.

Respect for Nature

And the earth brought forth grass, herb yielding seed after its kind, and tree bearing fruit, wherein is the seed thereof, after its kind, and God saw that it was good.

—Genesis 1:12

THE BIBLICAL account of the Creation lists two categories of agricultural products, vegetation and trees. After the emergence of these distinct species, God surveyed them and declared them "good." Religious ethicists have assumed that the phrase "after its kind" expresses a divine design to preserve each of the distinct species in its natural state. Does man have a moral right to tamper with the laws of nature, divinely ordained, to create products superior to that which God proclaimed to be "good"?

This ethical question is predicated on a theological principle. If we put the religious issue aside, it is hard to perceive any ethical breach in the cross-fertilization of different species. However, modern genetic engineering, which promises to yield the secret of "creation" to man, enabling him to predetermine the gender, traits, and character of a newborn, surely projects the moral issue inherent in the altering of the laws of nature. Will a future dictator have it within his power to decree the birth of a generation of fanatical fighting men?

The Bible is opposed to indiscriminate intermingling of different species. "Thou shalt not let thy cattle gender with a different species; thou shalt not sow thy field with two kinds of seed; neither shalt thou put upon thee a garment of two kinds of stuff" (Lev. 19:19). If there is any significance to the sequence of this verse, which follows the Golden Rule, there seems to be an implication that love or respect for nature demands the preservation of the species in their natural state.

A Deuteronomic passage is more explicit in its details. "Thou shalt not sow thy vineyard with two kinds of seed [cereal and grapes]. . . . Thou shalt not plow with an ox and ass together. Thou shalt not wear mingled cloth, wool and linen together" (Deut. 22: 9–11).

Various rationales have been offered in explanation of the biblical prohibition of the mixing of species. The reason for the prohibition of the yoking together of different species of animals of burden is a humane consideration for the welfare of animals, each of which works at a different pace (Ibn Ezra on Deut. 22:10). The mixing of seeds was a pagan practice (*Moreh Nevuchim* 3:37). It exhausts the fertility of the soil (Philo, *Species* 4:21). Garments made of wool and linen are prohibited because they are reserved exclusively for the uniforms of priests (Josephus, *Antiq.*, 4:11).

The aforementioned rationales do not present a common denominator applicable to all the prohibitions of mixed species. Furthermore, the passage in Leviticus (19:19) categorizes the prohibitions as *chukim*, religious statutes without a revealed or known reason.

Despite the lack of a clearly understood rationale, there is an evident trend against the obliteration of hereditary traits of all species. This emerges in the laws prohibiting the grafting of different species of trees to each other and the grafting of vegetables to trees (*Kiddushin* 39a). The same trend is also reflected in the prohibitions of mating between creatures of different species and of altering the normal functions of each gender. Homosexuality and bestiality are forbidden (Lev. 20:13, 15). Man may not shave his beard (and thus erase his masculine distinctiveness; Lev. 19:27). A man may not wear a woman's garments, nor a woman, the garments of a man (Deut. 22:5). The rabbis extended this prohibition to the performance of tasks normally the function of the opposite sex. Thus they barred women from bearing arms in a combat of war (*Nazir* 59a).

The modern trend toward the equality of the sexes has

blurred to some extent the distinct outward appearance of each gender. The preference for unisex styles, widely accepted, no longer offends one's sense of morality. Yet the basic ethical perception reflected in the biblical prohibition of altering the hereditary traits of nature continues to pose a challenge. To what extent may science be permitted to alter the laws of nature in disregard of the potential dangers which may ensue?

It is the function of nature to provide a healthful environment to sustain life. Is the manipulation of natural laws, with the intent of creating catastrophic destructive forces, an attack upon the established order of the universe? The existence of nuclear weapons, posing the greatest menace ever faced by mankind, brings to mind several questions.

Is the atomic bomb a legitimate defensive implement of war or a criminal and immoral weapon? The moral question of the legitimacy of weapons capable of total destruction is resolved in the biblical account of the Flood. God used the Flood, the ancient equivalent of the atomic bomb, to eradicate mankind, which had degenerated into a state of utter corruption. Yet in the aftermath of the frightful devastation of the Flood, God resolved never to use such a weapon again. He formalized this resolution in a covenant with Noah and his sons "and with every living soul that is with you, the fowl, the cattle, and every beast of the earth with you. . . . no more will all the flesh be cut off by the waters of a deluge, neither shall there any more be a flood to destroy the earth" (Gen. 9:10–11). The condemnation of the atomic bomb is clearly implicit.

The next question is, was the initial American production of the atomic bomb immoral? The answer is definitely no. In view of reliable reports of the imminent acquisition of a nuclear missile by a ruthless enemy, the preemptive production of that weapon by a nation at war was legitimate under the universally accepted principle of self-defense.

Was the use of the bomb against Japan immoral? There were no nuclear weapons in the enemy's arsenal. Nevertheless, the principle of self-defense lends a degree of legitimacy to the dropping of the bomb. It had been estimated that about 100,000 American lives would be lost in the invasion of Japan in an attack with conventional weapons. Despite the knowledge of inevitable defeat, the enemy refused to sue for peace. To the end of terminating the needless carnage, it was proper to use every means at one's disposal, provided that adequate warning was given to the enemy to evacuate the civilian population.

Is the possession of nuclear weapons by nations at peace morally justifiable? The answer is no. Nevertheless, the principle of self-defense precludes any unilateral nuclear disarmament. The only way out of this dilemma is to follow the biblical precedent. God made a covenant outlawing his weapon of wholesale destruction. Nuclear weapons must be outlawed by an international covenant to which all nations must be signatories. The morality of every nation will be judged by its active pursuit of such a covenant.

Is the use of atomic energy for peaceful purposes justifiable, in view of the potential risk of accidents? Energy is essential to the survival of mankind. Considering the rapid depletion of natural sources of energy, the exploitation of atomic energy is legitimate, until such time as alternate sources are available. All precautions must be taken to minimize the risks. Financial considerations must not influence the relaxation of safeguards. To prevent the element of profit from entering into judgments of safety, power plants should be owned by the government.

Suffering and Pain

For my life is spent in sorrow and my years in sighing; my strength fails because of my iniquity.

—Psalm 31:11

PAIN IS a major contributor to human unhappiness (see "Contentment and Discontent"). In addition to the physical discomfort, pain exacerbates the sufferer's mental anguish by its implication of his guilt. The Pentateuch emphasizes the link between sin and sickness. "But it shall come to pass, if thou wilt not hearken of the Lord thy God, to observe to do all his commandments . . . and he will bring back upon thee all the diseases of Egypt . . . also every sickness which is not written in the book of this law" (Deut. 28:15, 60–61).

The dire prediction of the punishment of sin was preceded by a comforting reassurance: "And it shall come to pass, if thou shalt hearken diligently unto the voice of the Lord thy God . . . all these blessings shall come upon thee" (Deut. 28:1–2).

The confidence inspired by the promise of reward for the righteous was frequently put to the test in the face of seemingly contradictory events in real life. The author of Ecclesiastes was perturbed by the fact that "there is a righteous man that perishes in his righteousness, and there is a wicked man that prolongs his life in his evil-doings" (Eccles. 7:15). He voiced his misgivings in another sentence: "All things come alike to all; there is one event to the righteous and to the wicked" (Eccles. 9:2). The rabbis portrayed the angels as being similarly puzzled by recorded history, which at times appears to be inconsistent with the doctrine of reward and punishment (*Shabbat* 55a).

The average observant man justifiably ponders several ques-

271

tions. Does suffering serve a higher moral purpose? Is pain due to divine punishment? Is it proper to cry out against pain if it is divinely ordained? Is it proper to berate a person who persistently complains of pain? Is it proper to seek remedial help to ease one's pain?

The rabbis provided answers to these questions. In many instances pain is indeed inflicted in punishment for sin. "He who can engage in the study of Torah and he does not do so, the Almighty brings upon him severe suffering." (*Berachot* 5a). "Man's sins bring upon him divine retribution" (*Tanchuma, Tazria* 8).

Judaism also ascribes some pain to a divine design to open the sufferer's heart to penitence (*Menachot* 53b). Rabbi, the saintly editor of the Mishnah (2nd–3rd cent.), was said to have suffered excruciating pain for thirteen years because he had neglected to show humane compassion for a calf which sought his protection against a butcher who was taking it to a slaughterhouse. The pain disappeared when Rabbi, in an obvious mood of contrition, demonstrated compassion for a brood of weasels which were discovered by a maid in his home (*Baba Metzia* 85a). This incident supports the view that pain ennobles man's character.

It is axiomatic that every individual who goes through life inevitably commits some indiscretion or a transgression of law. In the words of Ecclesiastes: "For there is not a righteous man upon earth, that does [only] good, and sinneth not" (Eccles. 7:20). However, one is not necessarily aware of his wrongdoing. Suffering in the here and now is an atonement which spares the sinner punishment in the hereafter (*Berachot* 5a). Under such circumstances, the suffering is evidence of God's love and is regarded as a "suffering of love" (ibid.). It brings reward in the hereafter by purging one's sins on this earth (*Yoma* 86a). Rabbi commented that such suffering is "precious" (*Baba Metzia* 85a).

The true rationale of one's pain is never revealed to man. The rabbis therefore advised sufferers to examine their past deeds. If they discover some faults they should repent. If they fail to find any personal guilt, they may assume that the suffering does not reflect divine anger but divine love (*Berachot* 5a).

Despite theological rationalizations of pain, most people cannot make peace with suffering and surely do not welcome it. Those who are confident of their virtue and merit plaintively echo the biblical outcry: "To punish also the righteous is not good, nor to strike the noble for their uprightness" (Prov. 17:26). Even a religious leader of the stature of Rabbi Yochanan (3rd cent.) exclaimed: "I want neither the pain nor its reward" (*Berachot* 5b).

The Talmud concludes that not all pain serves a high moral purpose. "There is death without sin and suffering without iniquity" (*Shabbat* 55b). Man is mortal, and he is subject to a process of aging in which pain is endemic. An individual who cries out in the agony of his pain is not unethical. It is wrong to preach to him that he deserves his fate. It is absolutely proper to try to ease one's pain. Those who are induced by pain to reexamine their daily conduct provide a useful redeeming feature to a period which is otherwise bleak and dismal.

Trade

For the merchandise of it [wisdom] is better than the merchandise of silver.

—Proverbs 3:14

THERE WAS little commerce in Judea in the biblical era. Most financial transactions were confined to the sale of agricultural products or real estate and the hiring of labor. There were also craftsmen who sold their wares to the public. Poor people borrowed money from neighbors and left pawns as security. All of these transactions came under biblical regulation.

The basic rule of business ethics is expressed in Leviticus: "And if thou sell aught to thy neighbor, or if you buy of thy neighbor's hand, you shall not defraud one another" (25:14). The rights and obligations of buyers and sellers were thus placed on an equal footing.

Supplementing the general law against fraud is the injunction pertaining to honest scales and measures. "You shall do no unrighteousness in judgments, in meteyard, in weight, or in measure. Just scales, just weights . . . shall you have" (Lev. 19:35–36).

It was left to the rabbis of the talmudic era to spell out the conditions which constitute fraud and its legal consequences. The emergence of a substantial merchant class, the middlemen between producers and consumers, created a need for discussion and codification of business laws.

Despite the rise in commerce and its importance to the economy of the nation, Jewish merchants had little influence upon the shaping of commercial law. Unlike developments in most commercial countries, whose governments enacted laws slanted in favor of mercantile interests, the rabbis insisted on

274

fair practices and were zealous in protecting the welfare of the public. The widely accepted principle of caveat emptor ("let the buyer beware"), which offered a wide latitude for fraud, was anathema to the rabbinic authors of business laws. Whereas some societies regarded a cheating merchant as a shrewd businessman, to the rabbis he was a crook and a thief. Nonetheless they were strong believers in free enterprise, and the regulations they enacted were intended to encourage individual initiative and the promotional skill of merchants, so long as it was not done at the expense of buyers.

Every shopkeeper enjoyed a legal presumption of honesty. For example, a wine dealer was entitled to the assumption that he did not dilute his wines for the sake of profit. However, the rabbis were aware, and even understanding, of the irresistible temptation to which merchants are subjected. To protect the integrity of merchants, the rabbis ruled that one may not put a merchant's honesty to the test by offering him the opportunity for fraud. Thus producers were forbidden to sell adulterated wine, at a cheaper rate, to a merchant who sold exclusively unadulterated wine (*Baba Metzia* 16a). Such a sale would practically have amounted to entrapment, which is prohibited.

The same motivation that is behind modern antitrust laws was very much in the minds of the rabbis. The majority opinion favored competitive practices which work to the advantage of consumers. Thus they approved of the practice of some enterprising merchants to reduce prices, even if this might force other merchants out of business (*Baba Metzia* 60a). They also approved of the promotional tactics of some merchants of giving a bonus of sweets to young children who were sent on shopping errands by their mothers (ibid.).

Opposing the majority opinion was a dissenting view which favored strict regulation of the free enterprise system, for the sake of merchants of lesser skill. Rabbi Judah (2nd cent.) regarded promotional practices which might force some merchants out of business as injurious to the trade and to the general public. He also considered it unfair to use young children to pressure their mothers to patronize a specific merchant when they might prefer to shop elsewhere. The ethics of modern business practices that direct television advertisements for juvenile foods and toys at young viewers is currently the subject of serious debate.

The majority opinion, which favored unfettered free enterprise, prevailed. That, however, did not include a license to practice deception or to take advantage of ignorant customers by charging them excessive prices.

The Talmud lists guidelines controlling overcharges. If the overcharge amounts to more than one-sixth of the market value of the merchandise, the buyer has the option of voiding the sale. An overcharge of one-sixth of the fair value of the sold item does not invalidate the sale. However, the buyer is entitled to restitution of the overcharge. If the overcharge is less than one-sixth of the market value, the sale is valid and the buyer has no legal claim for restitution (*Baba Metzia* 50b). The underlying basis of these guidelines is a policy of evenhanded fairness for the merchant and consumer. An unconscionable overcharge is not tolerated. A variable in price, which is deemed acceptable, is overlooked on the ground that enforced price-fixing is not desirable. Some leeway must be given to merchants to set their prices, and customers are forewarned to do some comparison shopping.

By general consensus, all deceptive promotional practices are prohibited. Painting old articles to make them appear new, bloating lean animals to make them appear fat, and similar subterfuges are illegal (*Baba Metzia* 60a).

Students interested in other aspects of Jewish business ethics will find a reading of *Free Enterprise and Jewish Law* by Aaron Levine highly enlightening and richly rewarding.

It is needless to point out that ethical considerations are as important in the practice of other professions as they are in trade. If one is unsure as to what constitutes a breach of ethics, he need merely recall the dictum of Hillel: "What is hateful unto thee, do not do unto others" (*Shabbat* 31a).

Glossary

Apocrypha. Fourteen books included in the Greek and Latin Bibles but not in the canonical Hebrew Bible.

Bible. Twenty-four sacred Hebrew books, comprising the Pentateuch, Prophets, and Scriptures. Christians call it the Old Testament.

Day of Atonement. Solemn penitential fast-day falling on the tenth of the Hebrew month of Tishri; its biblical name is Yom Kippur (Lev. 23:27).

Essenes. Jewish sect of zealots living mostly in the neighborhood of the Dead Sea; their sacred writings are called the Dead Sea Scriptures.

Haggadah. Liturgical book used for the home service on Passover eve.

Hagiographa. Greek name of the third division of the Bible, the Scriptures.

Kabbalah. Jewish philosophic speculations on the mysteries of God and the universe.

Kaddish. Hebrew traditional prayer for the dead.

Kashrut. Hebrew religious dietary laws.

Kiddush. Prayer of sanctification recited over wine or two loaves of bread prior to the evening meal on the Sabbath or festivals.

Lex talionis. Legal principle calling for a punishment commensurate with the crime, such as "an eye for an eye" (Exod. 21:24).

Midrash. Homiletical and exegetical books written by the sages of the talmudic era.

Mishnah. Collection of rabbinic laws edited by Rabbi Judah HaNasi (d. after 200 C.E.).

Mitzvah. Religious command; in common parlance, a meritorious deed.

Nazirite. Individual who takes a vow to abstain from liquor, not cut his hair, and not defile himself by contact with a dead body (Num. 6:1–21).

Patriarchate. Office of the religious head of Palestinian Jewry after the destruction of the Temple in 70 C.E.

Pentateuch. Greek name of the Five Books of Moses.

Qumran sect. Members of the Essenic movement. *See* Essenes.

Sanhedrin. Supreme Hebrew theological and legal tribunal.

Seder. Religious home celebration on Passover eve.

Shechitah. Slaughtering of an animal in accordance with dietary laws.

Sukkah. Outdoor booth where meals are eaten on Sukkot (Lev. 23:42).

Talit. Prayer shawl worn at morning service.

Talmud. Complete collection of rabbinic legal and theological dissertations produced in the period from about 200 B.C.E. to 500 C.E. It consists of the Mishnah (see above) and the Gemara, commentaries on the Mishnah. There are two editions of Gemara, the Babylonian and the Palestinian.

Tannaim. Sages of the period of the Mishnah, whose opinions appear in the Mishnah, Beraita (laws not included in the Mishnah), and Tosefta (addenda to the Mishnah).

Tefillin. Two leather cases containing parchments on which four biblical selections are inscribed. They are worn on the arm and head, secured with leather straps, at weekday morning services.

Temple. The sanctuary in Jerusalem; the First Temple was destroyed in 586 B.C.E., the Second Temple was destroyed in 70 C.E.

Torah. Hebrew name of the Five Books of Moses. In its broader connotation, the term Torah ("instruction") is synonymous with Judaism.

Abbreviations

Antiq.	*Antiquities of the Jews*
ca.	circa (about)
Deut.	Deuteronomy (Devarim)
Eccles.	Ecclesiastes (Kohelet)
Ecclus.	Ecclesiasticus (Ben Sira)
Exod.	Exodus (Shemot)
Gen.	Genesis (Bereshit)
Isa.	Isaiah
Jer.	Jeremiah; Jerusalem Talmud
Josh.	Joshua
Jud.	Judges
Lev.	Leviticus (Vayikra)
Macc.	Maccabees
Mal.	Malachi
Matt.	Matthew
Num.	Numbers (Bamidbar)
Prov.	Proverbs (Mishlei)
Ps.	Psalms
Sam.	Samuel
Zech.	Zechariah

Bibliography

Abudrahim, by David b. Joseph. Jerusalem, 1973.

Against Apion, by Flavius Josephus. Translated by Haver-camp.

Al Chazari, by Judah Halevi. Israel, 1959.

Antiquities of the Jews, by Flavius Josephus. Translated by Havercamp.

Apocrypha. Edited by Manuel Komroff. New York, 1936.
>   Ecclesiasticus
>   Esdras
>   Judith
>   Maccabees
>   Tobit
>   The Wisdom of Solomon.
>   The Book of Jubilees. Tel Aviv: HeSeforim HaChitzonim, 1936.
>   The Vision of Shealtiel. Translated by Nicholas de Lange. New York, 1978.

Bet HaBechirah on *Avot*, by Menachem Meiri. New York 1944.

Bet Yosef, by Joseph Caro. Commentary on *Tur* Code. Warsaw, 1867.

Bible
>   Pentateuch. Vilna: Mikraot Gedolot, 1930.
>   The Former Prophets. Warsaw: Kitvei Kodesh.
>   Joshua
>   Judges
>   Samuel
>   The Later Prophets. Warsaw: Kitvei Kodesh.
>   Habakkuk

Haggai
Ezekiel
Isaiah
Jeremiah
Jonah
Malachi
Micah
Zechariah
Hagiographa. Warsaw: Kitvei Kodesh.
Chronicles
Ecclesiastes
Job
Nehemiah
Proverbs
Psalms
Ruth
Song of Songs
Chafetz Chaim on *Avot.* New York, 1966.
Chovat HaLevavot, by Bachya Ibn Pekuda. Warsaw, 1954.
Dead Sea Scriptures. Edited by Theodor H. Gaster. Garden
City, N.Y., 1956.
Book of Hymns
Manual of Discipline.
Hasidic Anthology, by Louis I. Newman. New York, 1944.
Iggeret HaRamban, by Moses Nachmanides. Appended to
Mesilat Yesharim.
Mesilat Yesharim, by Moses Luzzatto. New York.
Midrashim
Avot deRabbi Natan. Berlin, 1935.
Masechet Derech Eretz
Masechet Derech Eretz Zuta
Masechet Kallah
Masechet Soferim
Masechet Semachot
Mechilta. Vilna: *Chamishah Chumshei Torah,* 1891.
Mechilta deRabbi Simon b. Yochai. Berlin, 1955.
Midrash Aseret HaDibrot. Otzer HaMidrashim, edited by
J. D. Eisenstein. New York, 1928.

Midrash Rabbah. New York, 1925. Pentateuch, Kohelet, Shir HaShirim.

Midrash Shochar Tov. Jerusalem, 1960.

Pesikta Rabbah. Vienna, 1880.

Pirkei deRabbi Eliezer. Edited by D. Luria. Warsaw, 1852.

Seder Eliyahu Rabbah veSeder Eliyahu Zuta. Jerusalem, 1959.

Sifra, VaYikra. Warsaw: Chamisha Chumshei Torah, 1879.

Sifre, Bamidbar, Devarim. Warsaw: Chamisha Chumshei Torah, 1879.

Tanchuma. New York, 1925.

Tanna devei Eliyahu. Spring Valley, N.Y., 1960.

Yalkut Shimoni. New York, 1944.

Mishneh Torah, by Moses Maimonides. Berlin, 1926.

Nachmanides, Commentary on Pentateuch. Vilna: Mikraot Gedolot, 1930.

New Testament. Luke, Matthew. Brooklyn, N.Y.: New World Translation, 1970.

Onkelos, Aramaic translation of the Pentateuch. All editions.

Philo the Alexandrian. *Works of Philo Judaeus.* Translated by C. D. Younue. London, 1854.

Ran (Nissim Gerondi). Commentary on *Nedarim.* Vilna, 1880.

Rashi (Shlomo Yitzchaki). Commentary on the Talmud and Pentateuch.

Rema. Annotations to *Shulchan Aruch* by Moses Isserles. Berlin, 1918.

Sefer Chasidim, by Judah Chasid. New York, 1953.

Sefer HaChinuch, by Aaron Halevi of Barcelona. Brooklyn, N.Y., 1965.

Shemonah Perakim, by Moses Maimonides. Introduction to *Avot.* Vilna, 1880.

Shulchan Aruch, by Joseph Caro. Berlin, 1918.

Talmud (Babylonian). Vilna, 1880.

Arachin	*Berachot*
Avot	*Eruvin*
Baba Kamma	*Gittin*
Baba Metzia	*Horayot*
Baba Batra	*Ketubot*

Kiddushin
Menachot
Moed Katan
Nazir
Nedarim
Niddah
Ohalot
Pesachim
Rosh HaShanah
Sanhedrin
Shabbat
Shekalim
Sotah
Sukkah
Taanit
Tamid
Yevamot
Yoma

Talmud (Jerusalem). Vilna, 1926.
Baba Kama
Berachot
Bikkurim
Demai
Ketubot
Kiddushin
Makkot
Nedarim
Peah
Yevamot

Tosefta. Appended to Jerusalem Talmud. Vilna, 1926.
Tur Code, by Jacob b. Asher. Warsaw, 1863.
Wars of the Jews, by Flavius Josephus. Translated by Haver-camp. New York.
Zohar. Vilna, 1894.

Index

I. Biblical Passages

II. Postbiblical Sources

III. Names And Subjects